D1269669

Hazlitt on Theatre

Hazlitt on Theatre

᪂ EDITED BY WILLIAM ARCHER
AND ROBERT LOWE ᪂ INTRO-
DUCTION BY WILLIAM ARCHER

HYPERION PRESS, INC.
Westport, Connecticut

Quotations from Shakespeare have been changed in this edition to conform to the text edited by W. J. Craig for the Oxford University Press, except where the editors, Archer and Lowe, have deliberately left an incorrect quotation by Hazlitt and made note of the error.

Hazlitt on Theatre was originally published in 1895 by Walter Scott, Ltd., London, as the second of a three volume collection of *Dramatic Essays* edited by William Archer and Robert W. Lowe. The first volume contains the criticism of Leigh Hunt and the third contains the criticism of John Forster and George Henry Lewes.

Published in 1957 by Hill and Wang, New York
Hyperion reprint edition 1979
Library of Congress Catalog Number 78-20469
ISBN 0-88355-847-5
Printed in the United States of America

Library of Congress Cataloging in Publication Data
Hazlitt, William, 1778-1830.
  Hazlitt on theatre.
  "Originally published in 1895 . . . as the second of a three volume collection of Dramatic essays."
  Reprint of the 1957 ed. published by Hill and Wang, New York, issued as a A Dramabook, D7.
  Includes index.
  1. Theater—England—London. 2. English drama—History and criticism. 3. Actors—England—London.
I. Archer, William, 1856-1924. II. Lowe, Robert William, 1853-1902. III. Title.
[PN2596.L6H3 1979]   792'.0941   78-20469
ISBN 0-88355-847-5

CONTENTS

CONTENTS

INTRODUCTION

WILLIAM HAZLITT, born on April 10, 1778, was thirty-five years of age, when, in 1813, he became the theatrical critic of the *Morning Chronicle.* Up to this time he had published nothing about the stage; but he had been for several years a constant playgoer. His first recorded visit to the theatre took place in 1790; and even then, at the age of eleven, we find him taking a quite intelligent interest in what he saw. On March 18 of that year he wrote to his father from Liverpool:—

"On Friday I went to the play with Mr. Corbett, at whose house I dined and drank tea. The play was *Love in Many Masks,*[1] and the farce, *No Song No Supper.* It was very entertaining, and was performed by some of the best players in London, as, for instance, Kemble, Suett, Dignum, the famous singer, Mrs. Williams, Miss Hagley, Miss Romanzini, and others. Suett, who acted in the character of 'Ned Blunt,' was enough to make any one laugh, though he stood still; and Kemble acted admirably as an officer. Mr. Dignum sang beautifully, and Miss Hagley acted the country girl with much exactness."

"With much exactness" is delightful, and proves that the boy had already read or listened to the theatrical criticism of the day; for this was one of its favorite stereotypes. In his boyhood, however, and indeed up to his twenty-fifth year, his opportunities for playgoing were probably scanty. He has told us how strolling companies would occasionally visit Wem in Shropshire (see p. 157), where for the most part he lived with his father; and as Wem was only some

[1] An alteration of Mrs. Aphra Behn's *Rover,* produced at Drury Lane only a few days before, March 8, 1790.

vii

twelve miles from Shrewsbury to the south and
Whitchurch to the north, he may now and then have
"resorted to the theatre" at these intellectual centres.
His critical acquaintance with the stage probably
dated from about 1803, when, at the house of William
Godwin, he made the acquaintance of his life-long
friend, Charles Lamb. He had spent the winter of
1802-3 in Paris, studying painting; but I find no evidence that he took any interest in the French stage.
From 1803 until his marriage in 1808 his headquarters
were still at Wem, and from 1808 to 1812, at Winters-
low, in Wiltshire. During these nine years, however,
he paid frequent visits to London, and must have done
a good deal of theatre-going, often, we may be sure,
in the incomparable society of Lamb. On July 4,[2] 1806,

[2] Mr. W. C. Hazlitt, in his life of his grandfather, dates this
letter "July 2," but in his *Poems, Letters, and Remains of
Charles and Mary Lamb*, he prints the same letter and puts
the date in brackets, as though to show that it is conjectural.
It is evident from the letter itself that it was begun on a
Friday, whereas July 2, 1806, was a Wednesday. The year
1806 is certainly correct; and assuming that Mr. Hazlitt had
some evidence (postmark, endorsement, or something of the
sort) for placing the date early in July, I think it most probable that he made a mistake of two days only, and that the
letter was begun on July 4. On that date the programme at
Sadler's Wells was as follows—and if this was not the very
entertainment which Lamb and Hazlitt witnessed, it was certainly something of exactly the same nature:—

"In consequence of the great demand for Places to see
HARLEQUIN and the WATER KELPE, it will be performed a few
nights longer only.

"AQUATIC THEATRE, Sadler's Wells, under the
Patronage of his Royal Highness the DUKE of CLARENCE. This
present THURSDAY, June 3, and following Evenings will be
presented a new Dance composed by Mr. Hartland, the Music
by Mr. Reeve, jun., called GRIST and PUFF, or the HIGHLAND
FLING.—Principal dancers, Mr. Hartland, Mr. Norman, Mr.
Lewis, and Miss Taylor.—After which, in consequence of
the very great demand for places, the admired Comic Pantomime called HARLEQUIN and the WATER KELPE, for a
few nights longer only. The Entertainment to conclude with

Mary Lamb writes to Sarah Stoddart, who ultimately became Mrs. Hazlitt—"Charles and Hazlitt are going to Sadler's Wells, and I am amusing myself in their absence with reading a manuscript of Hazlitt's"; adding on the following day: "They [Charles and Hazlitt] came home from Sadler's Wells so dismal and dreary dull on Friday that I gave them both a good scolding—quite a *setting to rights;* and I think it has done some good, for Charles has been very cheerful ever since." Mr. W. C. Hazlitt remarks that at this date his grandfather "could almost count upon his fingers the times he had seen the inside of a playhouse"; but I cannot find that he had evidence for the statement. It is much more probable that this was one of many visits. Had Lamb had to deal with a neophyte, he would scarcely have haled him off to Sadler's Wells. The two winter theatres, it is true, were then closed, but his favorite Liston was to be seen that night at the Haymarket[3] as Lord Grizzle in Fielding's *Tom Thumb.* On the 10th of the following December, Hazlitt sat by the side of Lamb, his sister, and H. Crabb Robinson, in the front row of the pit at Drury Lane—"next the tweedledees," as Lamb says— to witness the production of *Mr. H——,* with Elliston

a new Grand Melo-Dramatic Romance, with new Music, Scenery, Dresses, and Decorations, called The INVISIBLE RING; or The WATER MONSTER and FIRE SPECTRE. Principal Characters by Messrs. Hartland, Smith, Slader, Norman and Grimaldi; Mrs. C. Dibdin, Misses Bloomgreen, Taylor, and Madame Louis. In the last scene will be presented a Combat with the Water Monster and a Fiery Dragon, the Ascension of a good Spirit, the Appearance and Fate of the Fire Spectre, with the Liberation of a good Genius from the Volcano. The whole of this scene performed on Real Water. The Harlequinade and Melo-Drama both written by Mr. C. Dibdin, jun. The Music composed by Reeve, and the scenery by Mr. Andrews; the Decorations by the most eminent Professors of that art in the Kingdom."

*It is curious to note that Edmund Kean was at this time playing "utility" parts at the Haymarket.

and Miss Mellon in the leading parts. This is how
Hazlitt wrote of the occasion many years afterwards,
in his *Table Talk* (Essay "On Great and Little
Things"):—

"We often make life unhappy in wishing things to have
turned out otherwise than they did, merely because that is
possible to the imagination which is impossible in fact.
I remember, when Lamb's farce was damned (for damned
it was, that's certain), I used to dream every night for a
month after (and then I vowed I would plague myself no
more about it) that it was revived at one of the Minor or
provincial theatres with great success, that such and such
retrenchments and alterations had been made in it, and
that it was thought *it might do at the other House.* I had
heard, indeed (this was told in confidence to Lamb), that
Gentleman Lewis was present on the night of its performance, and said, that if he had had it, he would have made
it, by a few judicious curtailments, 'the most popular little
thing that had been brought out for some time.' How
often did I conjure up in recollection the full diapason of
applause at the end of the *Prologue,* and hear my ingenious friend in the first row of the pit roar with laughter at
his own wit! Then I dwelt with forced complacency on
some part in which it had been doing well: then we would
consider (in concert) whether the long, tedious opera of
The Travellers, which preceded it, had not tired people
beforehand, so that they had not spirits left for the quaint
and sparkling 'wit skirmishes' of the dialogue; and we all
agreed it might have gone down after a Tragedy, except
Lamb himself, who swore he had no hopes of it from the
beginning, and that he knew the name of the hero, when
it came to be discovered, could not be got over. *Mr.
H——,* thou wert damned! Bright shone the morning on
the playbills that announced thy appearance, and the
streets were filled with the buzz of persons asking one
another if they would go to see *Mr. H——,* and answer-
ing that they would certainly: but before the night the
gaiety, not of the author, but of his friends and the town,
was eclipsed, for thou wert damned! Hadst thou been
anonymous, thou haply mightst have lived. But thou didst

come to an untimely end for thy tricks, and for want of
a better name to pass them off! In this manner we go back
to the critical minutes on which the turn of our fate, or
that of any one else in whom we are interested, depended;
try them over again with new knowledge and sharpened
sensibility; and thus think to alter what is irrevocable, and
ease for a moment the pang of lasting regret."

We may take it, then, that probably from 1803—
certainly from 1806—onwards, Hazlitt was a pretty
frequent playgoer. He was brought up, as he says
(p. 110), in the Kemble religion. For Mrs. Siddons his
reverence was absolute; and though he admired her
brother more soberly, he was not, like Leigh Hunt,
disposed to let the actor's mannerisms outweigh his
merits. This is how, in after years, he spoke of Mrs.
Siddons. The passage occurs in an essay entitled,
"Whether Actors ought to Sit in the Boxes" (*Table
Talk*), the argument being that, though players on the
active list ought not to let themselves be seen in the
front of the house, there is no reason why retired actors should not revisit the scenes of their triumphs:—

"Mrs. Siddons seldom if ever goes [to the boxes], and
yet she is almost the only thing left worth seeing there.
She need not stay away on account of any theory that I
can form. She is out of the pale of all theories, and an-
nihilates all rules. Wherever she sits there is grace and
grandeur, there is tragedy personified. Her seat is the un-
divided throne of the Tragic Muse. She had no need of
the robes, the sweeping train, the ornaments of the stage;
in herself she is as great as any being she ever represented
in the ripeness and plenitude of her power!"

This is indeed an uncompromising utterance of "the
Kemble religion"; but Hazlitt was at no time a bigot.
He did not share Leigh Hunt's contempt for the
Young Roscius, Master William Henry West Betty,
whose splendour and decline fell between the years
1804 and 1808. In his essay "On Patronage and

Puffing" (*Table Talk*), he speaks thus of the boy-rival of the Kembles.—

"Master Betty's acting was a singular phenomenon, but it was also as beautiful as it was singular. I saw him in the part of Douglas, and he seemed almost like 'some gay creature of the element,' moving about gracefully, with all the flexibility of youth, and murmuring Æolian sounds with plaintive tenderness. I shall never forget the way in which he repeated the line in which Young Norval says, speaking of the fate of two brothers—

"'And in my mind happy was he that died!'

The tones fell and seemed to linger prophetic on my ear. Perhaps the wonder was made greater than it was. Boys at that age can often read remarkably well, and certainly are not without natural grace and sweetness of voice. The Westminster schoolboys are a better company of comedians than we find at most of our theatres. As to the understanding a part like Douglas, at least, I see no difficulty on that score. I myself used to recite the speech in Enfield's *Speaker*, with good emphasis and discretion, when at school, and entered, about the same age, into the wild sweetness of the sentiments in Mrs. Radcliffe's *Romance of the Forest*, I am sure, quite as much as I should do now; yet the same experiment has been often tried since, and has uniformly failed."

To this passage Hazlitt appends the following footnote:—

"I (not very long ago) had the pleasure of spending an evening with Mr. Betty, when we had some 'good talk' about the good old times of acting. I wanted to insinuate that I had been a sneaking admirer, but could not bring it in. As, however, we were putting on our great-coats downstairs, I ventured to break the ice by saying, 'There is one actor of that period of whom we have not made honourable mention—I mean Master Betty.' 'Oh!' he said, 'I have forgot all that.' I replied that he might, but that I could not forget the pleasure I had had in seeing him. On which he turned off, and shaking his sides heartily,

and with no measured demand upon his lungs, called out,
'Oh, memory! memory!' in a way that showed he felt the
full force of the allusion. I found afterwards that the
subject did not offend, and we were to have drunk some
Burton ale together the following evening, but were prevented. I hope he will consider that the engagement still
stands good."

It is curious to reflect that the Young Roscius sur-
vived his admirer nearly half a century, dying in 1874.

The reader will find a sketch of theatrical history
during the first thirteen years of the century in the Introduction to Leigh Hunt's *Dramatic Essays* (pp. xvi
to xxxi). While Hunt was carrying on his campaign
against fanatical Kemble-worship, critical corruption,
and literary imbecility, Hazlitt, as we have seen, was
silently and no doubt unconsciously qualifying himself to step into the breach, when Hunt was compelled, by circumstances over which he had no control, to lay down his arms. Hazlitt's entrance on the
field of theatrical criticism was not, however, a direct consequence of Hunt's withdrawal from it.
Hazlitt settled in London in 1812 (the year of Mrs.
Siddons's retirement from the stage), and became a
parliamentary reporter and writer of political articles
on the staff of the *Morning Chronicle*. Hunt was sent
to prison in February, 1813; it was not until about nine
months later that Hazlitt undertook the theatrical
criticism of the *Morning Chronicle*;[4] and it was after

[4] Hazlitt's first theatrical article in the *Morning Chronicle*
(the first, at any rate, that is included in his *View of the
English Stage*), appeared on October 18, 1813. It is misdated
September 24, in the book. Miss Stephens did, indeed, make
her first appearance on September 23, but the criticism published on September 24 is not by Hazlitt—at least he does not
reprint it. He wrote two notices of Miss Stephen's Polly in
The Beggar's Opera, which appeared on October 23 and 30,
and a criticism by him of *Antony and Cleopatra* at Covent
Garden appeared on November 16 (misdated December 1, in
the book). These are all the 1813 articles which he reprints.

another interval of nine months (July, 1814), that his first theatrical article appeared in the *Examiner*.

Of his relations with Perry, the editor of the *Morning Chronicle*, Hazlitt himself gives an amusing account, in the already-quoted essay "On Patronage and Puffing":

"When I formerly had to do with these sort of critical verdicts, I was generally sent out of the way when any *débutant* had a friend at court, and was to be tenderly handled. For the rest, or those of robust constitutions, I had *carte blanche* given me. Sometimes I ran out of the course, to be sure. Poor Perry! what bitter complaints he used to make, that by *running-a-muck* at lords and Scotchmen I should not leave him a place to dine out at! The expression of his face at these moments, as if he should shortly be without a friend in the world, was truly pitiable. What squabbles we used to have about Kean and Miss Stephens, the only theatrical favourites I ever had! Mrs. Billington had got some notion that Miss Stephens would never make a singer, and it was the torment of Perry's life (as he told me in confidence) that he could not get any two people to be of the same opinion on any one point. I shall not easily forget bringing him my account of her first appearance in *The Beggar's Opera*. I have reason to remember that article: it was almost the last I ever wrote with any pleasure to myself. I had been

---

It is perhaps worth noting that a four-column letter "On Modern Comedy," signed "H." appeared in the *Morning Chronical* of October 15—that is to say, three days before Hazlitt's first acknowledged theatrical article. It was the longest and weightiest contribution to a discussion on the decline of comedy which had been going on intermittently for some weeks. Does it not seem probable that this letter may have suggested to Perry Hazlitt's fitness for the post of dramatic critic? The criticisms which appeared in the early days of October were evidently by an inferior hand. Hazlitt would scarcely have said of Conway's Othello (October 8) that "his personal appearance was extremely grand," or that "he had evidently studied the part with care, and though he threw no new lights on any of the passages, he certainly made no lapses."

down on a visit to my friends near Chertsey, and on my
return had stopped at an inn near Kingston-upon-Thames,
where I had got *The Beggar's Opera*, and had read it
overnight. The next day I walked cheerfully to town. It
was a fine sunny morning, in the end of autumn, and as I
repeated the beautiful song, 'Life knows no return of
Spring,' I meditated my next day's criticism, trying to
do all the justice I could to so inviting a subject. I was not
a little proud of it by anticipation. I had just then begun
to stammer out my sentiments on paper, and was in a
kind of honeymoon of authorship. But soon after, my
final hopes of happiness and of human liberty, were
blighted nearly at the same time; and since then I have
had no pleasure in anything:—

" 'And Love himself can flatter me no more.'

. . . I deposited my account of the play at the *Morning
Chronicle* office in the afternoon, and went to see Miss
Stephens as Polly. Those were happy times, in which she
first came out in this character, in Mandane, where she
sang the delicious air, 'If o'er the cruel tyrant, Love' (so
as it can never be sung again), in *Love in a Village*, where
the scene opened with her and Miss Matthews in a painted
garden of roses and honeysuckles, and 'Hope, thou nurse
of young Desire,' thrilled from two sweet voices in turn.
Oh! may my ears sometimes still drink the same sweet
sounds, embalmed with the spirit of youth, of health, and
joy, but in the thoughts of an instant, but in a dream of
fancy, and I shall hardly need to complain! When I got
back, after the play, Perry called out, with his cordial,
grating voice, 'Well, how did she do?' and on my speaking in high terms, answered, that 'he had been to dine with
his friend the Duke, that some conversation had passed on
the subject, he was afraid it was not the thing, it was not
the true *sostenuto* style; but as I had written the article'
(holding my peroration on *The Beggar's Opera* carelessly
in his hand) 'it might pass!' I could perceive that the
rogue licked his lips at it, and had already in imagination
'bought golden opinions of all sorts of people' by this
very criticism, and I had the satisfaction the next day to
meet Miss Stephens coming out of the Editor's room, who

had been to thank him for his very flattering account of her."

We may pretty safely guess that Napoleon's defeat at Leipzig (October 16-18) and the advance of the Allies were the events that "blighted" Hazlitt's "hopes of human liberty," but one suspects a touch of Byronism in the assertion that this article was "almost the last he ever wrote with any pleasure to himself." It was certainly hard, however, that his editor, after pooh-poohing it, should take to himself the gratitude of the fascinating Polly. Talfourd calls it an "exquisite morsel of criticism," and says: "What a surprise it was to read it for the first time, amidst the tempered patriotism and measured praise of Mr. Perry's columns." Here is the article in question, which appeared on October 23, 1813:—

"*The Beggar's Opera* was acted at Covent Garden last night, for the purpose of introducing Miss Stephens in the character of Polly. The play itself is among the most popular of our dramas, and one which the public are always glad to have some new excuse for seeing acted again. Its merits are peculiarly its own. It not only delights, but instructs us, without our knowing how, and though it is at first view equally offensive to good taste and common decency. The materials, indeed, of which it is composed, the scenes, characters, and incidents, are in general of the lowest and most disgusting kind; but the author, by the sentiments and reflections which he has put into the mouths of highwaymen, turnkeys, their wives and daughters, has converted the motley groupe into a set of fine gentlemen and ladies, satirists, and philosophers. What is still more extraordinary, he has effected this transformation without once violating probability, or 'o'erstepping the modesty of nature.' In fact, Gay has in this instance turned the tables on the critics; and by the assumed license of the mock-heroic style, has enabled himself to *do justice to nature*, that is, to give all the force, truth, and locality of real feeling to the thoughts and expressions, without being called to the bar of false taste and affected delicacy. We might particularly refer to Polly's description of the death of her lover, and to the song, 'Woman is like the fair flower in its lustre,' the extreme beauty and feeling of which are only equalled by their characteristic propriety and *naïveté*. Every line of this sterling Comedy sparkles with wit, and is fraught with the keenest and bitterest invective.

"It has been said by a great moralist, 'There is some soul of goodness in things evil'; and *The Beggar's Opera* is a good-natured, but severe comment on this text. The poet has thrown all the gaiety and sunshine of the imagination, the intoxication of pleasure, and the vanity of despair, round the short-lived existence of his heroes, while Peachum and Lockitt are seen in the background, parcelling out their months and weeks between them. The general view of human life is of the most refined and abstracted kind. With the happiest art, the author has brought out the good qualities and interesting emotions almost inseparable from humanity in the lowest situations, and with the same penetrating glance, has detected the disguises which rank and circumstance lend to exalted vice. It may be said that the moral of the piece (which some respectable critics have been at a loss to discover), *is to show the vulgarity of vice;* or that the sophisms with which the great and powerful palliate their violations of integrity and decorum, are, in fact, common to them with the vilest, most abandoned and contemptible of the species. What can be more galling than the arguments used by these would-be politicians, to prove that in hypocrisy, selfishness, and treachery, they are far behind some of their betters? The exclamation of Mrs. Peachum, when her daughter marries Macheath, 'Hussey, hussey, you will be as ill used and as much neglected as if you had married a Lord,' is worth all Miss Hannah More's laboured invectives on the laxity of the manners of high life!

"The innocent and amiable Polly found a most interesting representative in Miss Stephens. Her acting throughout was simple, unaffected, graceful, and full of tenderness. Her tones in speaking, though low, and suited to the gentleness of the character, were distinct, and varied with great flexibility. She will lose by her performance of this part none of the reputation she has gained in Mandane. The manner in which she gave the song in the first act, 'But he so teased me,' &c., was sweetness itself the notes undulated through the house, amidst murmurs of rapturous applause. She gave equal animation and feeling to the favourite air, 'Cease your funning.' To this, however, as well as to some other of the songs, a more dramatic effect might perhaps be given. There is a severity of feeling, and a plaintive sadness, both in the words and music of the songs in this Opera, on which too much stress cannot be laid."

We should scarcely regard this as an epoch-making criticism nowadays, but it was no doubt an important and original utterance in its time. Talfourd declares that it "restored *The Beggar's Opera*, which had long been treated as a burlesque appendage to the Newgate Calendar, to its proper station."

It was a pure coincidence, and a happy one, that Hazlitt should have taken to dramatic criticism just in time to chronicle and celebrate the advent of Edmund Kean. Drury Lane Theatre, burnt down in 1809, had been rebuilt, and opened in October, 1812, Elliston speaking Byron's prologue. The company was not a strong one, Rae being its leading tragedian, while comedy was represented by Dowton, Bannister, Miss Mellon and Mrs. Glover. It could make no head against the opposition of Covent Garden, where, though Kemble did not appear, tragedy was represented by Charles Kemble and Charles Mayne Young, comedy by Liston, Emery, Mathews, Mrs. Charles Kemble and Mrs. Jordan. The season of 1813-14 opened still more disastrously, though Munden had meanwhile joined the company; and the theatre was on the verge of bankruptcy when, on the 26th of January, 1814, "Mr. Kean, from the Theatre Royal, Exeter," was announced to make his first appearance in Shylock. Only two newspapers, says Kean's biographer, were represented; but fortunately one of them was the *Morning Chronicle*, the editor of which had specially commended the new actor to the notice of his new critic. This is how Hazlitt spoke of the occasion many years after. (*Table Talk:* "On Patronage and Puffery"):—

"I was sent to see Kean the first night of his performance in Shylock, when there were about a hundred people in the pit, but from his masterly and spirited delivery of the first striking speech—

> " 'You spurn'd me such a day; another time
> You call'd me dog;'

&c., I perceived it was a hollow thing. So it was given out in the *Chronicle;* but Perry was continually at me as other people were at him, and was afraid it would not last. It was to no purpose I said *it would last:* yet I am in the right hitherto. It has been said, ridiculously, that Mr. Kean was written up in the *Chronicle.* I beg leave to state my opinion that no actor can be written up or down by a paper. An author may be puffed into notice, or damned by criticism, because his book may not have been read. An artist may be over-rated, or undeservedly decried, because the public is not much accustomed to see or judge of pictures. But an actor is judged by his peers, the play-going public, and must stand or fall by his own merits or defects. The critic may give the tone or have a casting voice where popular opinion is divided; but he can no more *force* that opinion either way, or wrest it from its base in common sense and feeling, than he can move Stonehenge. Mr. Kean had, however, physical disadvantages and strong prejudices to encounter, and so far the *liberal* and *independent* part of the press might have been of service in helping him to his seat in the public favour. May he long keep it with dignity and firmness!"

To this passage, again, a curious foot-note is appended, whence we learn that, even in those early days, the brethren of the critical craft did not always dwell together in unity:—

"I cannot say how in this respect it might have fared if

a Mr. Mudford, a fat gentleman, who might not have
'liked yon lean and hungry Roscius,' had continued in the
theatrical department of Mr. Perry's paper at the time of
this actor's first appearance; but I had been put upon this
duty just before, and afterwards Mr. Mudford's *spare*
talents were not in much request. This, I believe, is the
reason why he takes pains every now and then to inform
the readers of the *Courier* that it is impossible for any one
to understand a word that I write."

It was, of course, a piece of almost fabulous good-
fortune for Kean that Hazlitt happened to be on the
spot just at the critical moment. "The belief of the
time was," we are told,[5] "that Hazlitt received
£1,500 from the management of Drury Lane for
those articles. They made Kean's reputation and saved
the theatre." The money payment is doubtless a mere
romance; but the fact that such a myth should have
arisen and found any credence shows what influence
was commonly attributed to the articles. Even after
his great first-night success, some of the Drury Lane
Committee were for shelving Kean, and had he not
found powerful support in the press, he might quite
possibly have sunk back again into obscurity. But if
Hazlitt was a godsend to Kean, Kean was scarcely less
of a godsend to Hazlitt. The critic made the actor's
reputation, but the actor made the critic's immortality
as a theatrical critic. If Hazlitt had not had Kean to
write about, he would certainly have written much
less, with far inferior life and gusto, and would probably never have collected his articles. We should nowadays scarcely remember that he ever tried his hand
at theatrical criticism. He himself thought highly of
his *Morning Chronicle* articles, and it is certain that
if we struck out of his theatrical writings the passages
devoted to Kean, either in himself or in comparison
with other actors, we should deprive them of three-
fourths of their interest and value.

[5] L'Estrange's "Life of Mary Russell Mitford," vol. ii. p. 47.

Hazlitt's connection with the *Morning Chronicle* seems to have terminated rather unpleasantly. This is his own account of it:—

"A writer whom I very well knew . . . having written upwards of sixty columns or original matter on politics, criticism, *belles-lettres*, and *virtù* in a respectable morning paper, in a single half-year, was, at the end of that period, on applying for a renewal of his engagement, told by the editor 'he might give in a specimen of what he could do.' One would think sixty columns of the *Morning Chronicle* were a sufficient specimen of what a man could do. But while this person was thinking of his next answer to Vetus, or his account of Mr. Kean's performance of Hamlet, he had neglected 'to point the toe,' to hold up his head higher than usual (having acquired a habit of poring over books when young), and to get a new velvet collar to an old-fashioned great-coat. These are 'the graceful ornaments to the columns of a newspaper—the Corinthian capitals of a polished style.' This unprofitable servant of the press found no difference in himself before or after he became known to the readers of the *Morning Chronicle*, and it accordingly made no difference in his appearance or pretensions."

His last *Morning Chronicle* article appeared on May 27, 1814—a notice of the opera of *Richard Cœur de Lion*. It is worth remarking, by the way, that on the previous day there had appeared a notice of Kean as Luke in *Riches*, which is not included in the *View of the English Stage*. In the summer of 1814 (July 24 and August 7) he contributed to the *Examiner* two articles on Kean's Iago (see pp. 36 and 41), to which the regular critic of the paper replied on September 4, eliciting a rejoinder from Hazlitt in the following weeks, to which the critic put in a sur-rejoinder on September 18. These contributions to the *Examiner*, however, were merely occasional. During the autumn of 1814, Hazlitt was the regular critic of the *Champion*, a weekly paper edited by John Scott, who was afterwards editor of the *London Magazine*. Hazlitt's first theatrical contribution to the *Champion* was a criticism of the opera *Didone Abbandonnata*, August 14, 1814, and his last a notice of Kean's Romeo, January 8, 1815 (see p. 30). He became the regular critic of the *Examiner* in the spring of 1815, opening his campaign with a notice of Kean's Richard II., March 19 (see p. 49); and that post he retained until June, 1817. Thus more than three-fourths of the articles included in his *View of the English Stage* (372 pp. out of a total of 461 pp.) were contributed to the *Examiner*. Some of his articles are initialled, the majority are not. Some half-dozen articles which are certainly, or probably, by him, are not reprinted in the *View of the English Stage*, and one of the reprinted articles, on Meggett's Octavian and a farce entitled *My Wife! What Wife?* (July 30, 1815—not included in this volume) is initialled "T.M."! On November 3, 1816, Leigh Hunt contributed a criticism of Kean's Timon of Athens, and from that date onwards Hunt's mark (☞) is appended to a good many theatrical papers. Hazlitt's last article in the *Examiner* was a notice of Mrs. Siddons' Lady Macbeth (see p. 121), which appeared on June 8, 1817,[6] and on June 25, he contributed to the *Times* the article on Kemble's retirement (see p. 122), which closes the *View of the English Stage*. One other article from the *Times* is included in that volume—a notice of Mr. Maywood's Shylock (September 26) not here reprinted. I cannot guess why Hazlitt should have included no more of

[6] In all probability: the pages are missing from the British Museum copy of the *Examiner*. After Hazlitt's complete withdrawal, Leigh Hunt continued for some years to write all, or almost all, the "Theatrical Examiners," devoting a great deal of attention and space to the theatres. In the Introduction to *Dramatic Essays*, vol. i. (p. xvi.) I stated that Leigh Hunt wrote very little theatrical criticism in the *Examiner* after his release from prison. That was a mistake which I beg hereby to correct.

his *Times* work. During the autumn and winter of 1817 there appeared many important criticisms, almost certainly from his pen, all of which he omits, to include a trivial paragraph (for it is no more) on "Mr. Maywood from the Theatre Royal, Glasgow"! It might be thought that he designed to close his "View" with Kemble's retirement; but Mr. Maywood's appearance did not occur till three months after that event, the article being inserted out of its chronological order. We may, if we please, conjecture that Hazlitt sent his book to press at the end of September, 1817; but as the preface is dated April 24, 1818, this seems improbable; and even if the bulk of the matter went to the printer at the earlier date, one sees no reason why he should not have supplemented it while it was passing through the press. It is true that before April 1818, he had been, as he tells us in his preface, "forced to quit the *Times* by want of health and leisure"; but we can scarcely suppose that he resigned his post after writing only two articles, with an interval of three months between them. It is much to be regretted that Hazlitt did not omit some of the trivialities of his *View of the English Stage*,[7] and include a few of his more important *Times* criticisms of 1817-18; but one cannot, of course, venture to reprint any of these articles as his, however strong the external or internal probabilities of the case.

It appears, then, that sometime before April, 1818, Hazlitt had ceased to write criticisms for the daily or weekly press. For eighteen months or so, he probably wrote nothing about the theatre; but when the *London Magazine* was started in January, 1820, under the editorship of John Scott, formerly of the *Champion*, Hazlitt undertook to contribute a monthly article on the drama, and did so throughout the year, with the exception of one month (November). At the begin-

[7] Announced in the *Times* of July 20, 1818, as "This day published, in 8vo, price 12 shillings."

ning of 1821 he handed over this monthly task to another, and no longer wrote, save incidentally, about the stage. These *London Magazine* articles were reprinted by his son in 1851, along with large selections from the *View of the English Stage*, under the general title of *Criticisms and Dramatic Essays of the English Stage*.

We are afforded some curious glimpses of Hazlitt's habits as a playgoer. His own account, quoted above, of his rupture with the *Morning Chronicle* seems to indicate that he was not considered, in dress and personal appearance, a creditable representative of that organ. Perhaps some of Mr. Perry's ducal friends had been shocked by the shabbiness of his velvet collar, and the general Bohemianism of his exterior; though one is rather surprised to learn that anything else was expected in those days of a "writing fellow." His eccentricities, at any rate, must have made him a well-known figure to the playgoers of the day, and he must often have enjoyed the pleasure (for a pleasure it was to him) of being pointed out to country cousins as one of the literary celebrities of the metropolis. His grandson writes (*Memoirs of William Hazlitt*, ii. 310):—

"A visit to the theatre in Mr. Hazlitt's company was not always the most comfortable thing in the world. He had a slow way of moving on such occasions, which, to less habitual playgoers, was highly trying. He took my mother to the play one evening, when he was in Half-Moon Street—it must have been in 1828: there was a great crowd, but he was totally unmoved by that circumstance. At the head of the staircase he had to sign the Free Admission Book, and perfectly unconscious that he was creating a blockade, he looked up at the attendant in the middle of the operation—a rather lengthy one with him—and said, 'What sort of a house is there to-night, sir?' It was a vast relief to his two companions, my mother and her elder sister, when they had run the gauntlet of all this and were safe in their places."

Hazlitt's friend, P. G. Patmore, known to readers of the *Liber Amoris*, gives a more detailed account of his manner of playgoing, which must refer, however, to his later years. It is certain that in earlier times he did not "invariably" resort to the second tier of boxes, for he has numerous allusions to taking, like Charles X. of France, "his place in the pit." "It is pleasant," he writes,[8] "to have your opinion quoted against yourself, and your own sayings repeated to you as good things. I was once talking to an intelligent man in the pit, and criticising Mr. Knight's performance of Filch. 'Ah!' he said, 'little Simmons was the fellow to play that character.' He added, 'There was a most excellent remark made upon his acting it in the *Examiner* (I think it was), *That he looked as if he had the gallows in one eye, and a pretty girl in the other.*' I said nothing, but was in remarkably good humour the rest of the evening." The saying, of course, was Hazlitt's own, in an article not included in this volume. Again, he tells[9] how, "having got into the middle of the pit, at considerable risk of broken bones, to see Mr. Kean in one of his early parts," he perceived a little behind him two young men attired in the height of fashion, who he thought might be Lord Byron and Mr. Hobhouse, but who turned out to be two clerks in the Victualling Office. It is clear, then, that in his early critical days Hazlitt was not tied to the boxes; but Mr. Patmore's account is doubtless correct enough as regards later years, when the now famous critic was on the free list, and, it must be remembered, was not regularly engaged in criticism. So much premised, we let Mr. Patmore[10] speak for himself:—

"When Hazlitt dined at all—which was often not more

[8] "On the Disadvantages of Intellectual Superiority" (*Table Talk*).
[9] "Whether Actors ought to sit in the Boxes" (*Table Talk*).
[10] *My Friends and Acquaintance*, vol. ii. p. 317.

than two or three times a week—this meal seemed only a sort of preliminary to his everlasting Tea, for which he returned home as soon as he had dined, and usually sat over it for a couple of hours. Afterwards he almost invariably passed two or three hours at one or other of the large theatres, placing himself as invariably in a back corner seat of the second tier of boxes, and, if possible, shrouding himself from view, as if he felt himself 'a weed that had no business there,' in such a scene of light, gaiety, and artificial seeming.

"To the play itself, on these occasions, he paid scarcely any attention, even when he went there in his capacity as a writer for the critical journals; for, notwithstanding the masterly truth and force of most of his decisions on plays and actors, I will venture to say that, in almost every case, except those of his two favourites, Kean and Liston, they might be described as the result of a few hasty glances and a few half-heard phrases. From these he drew instant deductions that it took others hours of observation to reach, and as many more of labour to work out. In this respect his faculty was, I imagine, never before equalled or even approached; and his consciousness of and confidence in it led him into a few ridiculous blunders. Still, upon the whole, he was doubtless right in trusting to these brief oracles and broken revelations, rather than pursuing them to their ultimate sources—as most others must do if they would hope to expound them truly and intelligibly: for his was a mind that would either take its own course or none; it was not to be 'constrained by mastery' of rule or discipline. It was a knowledge of this truth, and his habit of acting on it, which constituted the secret of his success as a writer."

Talfourd, in the following passage from his introduction to *Hazlitt's Literary Remains*,[11] bears out in some measure Mr. Patmore's remarks on the critic's habit of inattention to plays and acting which did not vividly interest him; and no one, indeed, can blame him for "criticising new plays" (such as came in his way) "with a reluctant and indecisive hand."

[11] Vol. i. p. cxx.

Talfourd's comparison between Hazlitt and Leigh
Hunt is particularly interesting, and probably just
enough; but it can scarcely be doubted that Hazlitt's
criticisms, by reason of the greater decision and vigour
of their style, have left, and will always leave, the
deeper impression on the reader's mind:—

"The strong sense of pleasure, both intellectual and
physical, naturally produced in Hazlitt a rooted attachment to the theatre, where the delights of the mind and
the senses are blended; where the grandeur of the poet's
conception is, in some degree, made palpable, and luxury
is raised and refined by wit, sentiment, and fancy. His
dramatic criticisms are more pregnant with fine thoughts
on that bright epitome of human life than any others
which ever were written; yet they are often more successful in making us forget their immediate subjects than in
doing them justice. He began to write with a rich fund
of theatrical recollection; and, except when Kean, or
Miss Stephens, or Liston supplied new and decided impulses, he did little more than draw upon this old treasury.
The theatre to him was redolent of the past: images of
Siddons, of Kemble, of Bannister, or Jordan, thickened
the air; imperfect recognitions of a hundred evenings,
when mirth or sympathy had loosened the pressure at the
heart, and set the springs of life in happier motion,
thronged around him, and 'more than echoes talked along
the walls.' He loved the theatre for these associations, and
for the immediate pleasure which it gave to thousands
about him, and the humanising influences it shed among
them, and attended it with constancy to the very last; and
to those personal feelings and universal sympathies he
gave fit expression; but his habits of mind were unsuited
to the ordinary duties of the critic. The players put him
out. He could not, like Mr. Leigh Hunt, who gave theatrical criticism a place in modern literature, apply his
graphic powers to a detail of a performance, and make it
interesting by the delicacy of his touch; encrystal the cobweb intricacies of a plot with the sparkling dew of his
own fancy—bid the light plume wave in the fluttering
grace of his style—or 'catch ere she fell the Cynthia of

the minute,' and fix the airy charm in lasting words. In
criticism, thus just and picturesque, Mr. Hunt has never
been approached; and the wonder is, that instead of falling off with the art of acting, he even grew richer; for
the articles of the *Tatler*,[12] equalling those of the *Examiner* in niceness of discrimination, are superior to them
in depth and colouring. But Hazlitt required a more powerful impulse; he never wrote willingly, except on what
was great in itself, or, forming a portion of his own past
being, was great to him; and when both these felicities
combined in the subject, he was best of all—as upon
Kemble and Mrs. Siddons. Mr. Kean satisfied the first
requisite only, but in the highest possible degree. His extraordinary vigour struck Hazlitt, who attended the theatre for the *Morning Chronicle*, on the night of his *début*,
in the very first scene, and who, from that night, became
the most devoted and efficient of his supporters. Yet if,
on principle, Hazlitt preferred Kean to Kemble, and sometimes drew parallels between them disparaging to the idol
of his earlier affections, there is nothing half so fine in his
eloquent eulogies on the first, as in his occasional recur-
rences to the last, when the stately form which had realised full many a boyish dream of Roman greatness 'came
back upon his heart again,' and seemed to reproach him
for his late preference of the passionate to the ideal. He
criticised new plays with a reluctant and indecisive hand,
except when strong friendship supplied the place of old
recollection, as in the instances of Barry Cornwall and
Knowles—the first of whom, not exhausting all the sweetness of his nature in scenes of fanciful tenderness and
gentle sorrow, cheered him by unwearied kindness in
hours of the greatest need—and the last, as kind and as
true, had, even from a boy, been the object of his warmest
esteem."

The often-quoted remark, "the players put him
out," is probably to be accepted with a certain reserva-
tion. Hazlitt's critical career really falls into two parts,
represented by the two divisions of this volume. In
the first he is the regular critic of either a daily or a
weekly paper, who is bound to concentrate his

---

[12] See *Dramatic Essays*, vol. i.

thoughts on individual productions and performances, and to report as well as to judge the occurrences of a given evening. At this period, if "the players put him out," he was successful in dissembling the fact. Later, when his prime favourites were past their prime, and the rising talents were of the second order, when he was no longer a daily critic but a monthly essayist (if not a mere unattached playgoer), and when the drama in general, rather than this or that performance in particular, was the subject of his considerations—it may very well be that his early interest in acting declined, and that he resorted to the playhouse rather for its associations than for its realities. The theatre-habit is like the opium-habit: we cannot relinquish it even when its pristine raptures are things of the remote past. It is very likely that in his later years the theatre became to Hazlitt a place of memories and reflections rather than of present enjoyments; but it would be a mistake to suppose that the criticisms in this volume were conceived and written in any such vague and reminiscent frame of mind. In the great majority of them, his perceptions are certainly acute enough, his interest vivid and unforced.

This volume contains, we believe, all of Hazlitt's theatrical essays that have any abiding interest for the general reader. The specialist, of course—the student either of Hazlitt or of the stage—will not be content with a selection; but even he, on referring to the *View of the English Stage* and the *Criticisms and Dramatic Essays*, will probably find that there is not very much matter of moment to be gleaned from the pages we have omitted. Our editorial task has been somewhat laborious, for we very soon found that the dates attached to the articles in the *View of the English Stage* were absolutely untrustworthy, and that not a single quotation could be allowed to pass unverified. It was somewhat bewildering, for instance, to find a criticism of Miss O'Neill's Juliet, dated August 15,

1814, when Miss O'Neill did not make her first appearance until the 6th of the following October. Hazlitt appears, in fact, to have dated the papers almost at random in arranging them for republication. Being compelled by this unaccountable inaccuracy on his part to refer back to the original files, we have prefixed to each article not only the correct date of its appearance, but the name of the paper in which it appeared, a point on which Hazlitt himself is quite silent. We should perhaps apologise for this pedantic research on matters of no importance; but it has always seemed to us that if a fact or date is worth stating at all it is worth stating correctly. On the other hand, we need certainly make no apology for having substituted the words of Shakespeare for the haphazard approximations to them with which Hazlitt was content in the way of quotation. Not a single passage of any length, so far as we can remember, is given with reasonable accuracy. We cannot even conjecture how these errors arose. Our first theory was that Hazlitt habitually quoted from some garbled acting edition; but the acting editions we have consulted are not responsible for these particular corruptions. In some cases he may simply have quoted from memory; but it is scarcely conceivable that he would trust to memory for a long passage like that on p. 46. This looseness of citation, at any rate, seems to have been a standing custom with him, though surely more honoured in the breach than in the observance. Mr. Carew Hazlitt, in the preface to the 1869 edition of the *Characters of Shakespeare's Plays,* says: "All the extracts have been collated with the late Mr. Dyce's revised and final text of 1868. In all the former editions, these quotations were corrupt beyond measure." This habitual impressionism of citation, if we may call it so, scarcely tends to strengthen our faith in Hazlitt's judgments as to the delivery of verse.

WILLIAM ARCHER

PREFACE

THE Stage is one great source of public amusement,
not to say instruction. A good play, well acted, passes
away a whole evening delightfully at a certain period
of life, agreeably at all times; we read the account of it
next morning with pleasure, and it generally furnishes
one leading topic of conversation for the afternoon.
The disputes on the merits or defects of the last new
piece, or of a favourite performer, are as common, as
frequently renewed, and carried on with as much
eagerness and skill, as those on almost any other subject. La Rochefoucauld, I believe, it was, who said that
the reason why lovers were so fond of one another's
company was, that they were always talking about
themselves. The same reason almost might be given
for the interest we feel in talking about plays and
players; they are "the brief chronicles of the time,"
the epitome of human life and manners. While we
are talking about them, we are thinking about ourselves. They "hold the mirror up to Nature;" and
our thoughts are turned to the stage as naturally and
as fondly as a fine lady turns to contemplate her face
in the glass. It is a glass, too, in which the wise may
see themselves; but in which the vain and superficial
see their own virtues, and laugh at the follies of others.
The curiosity which every one has to know how his
voice and manner can be mimicked, must have been
remarked or felt by most of us. It is no wonder, then,
that we should feel the same sort of curiosity and
interest in seeing those whose business it is to "imitate
humanity" in general, and who do it sometimes
"abominably," at other times admirably. Of these
some record is due to the world; but the player's art

is one that perishes with him, and leaves no traces of
itself but in the faint descriptions of the pen or pencil.
Yet how eagerly do we stop to look at the prints from
Zoffany's pictures of Garrick and Weston! How
much we are vexed that so much of Colley Cibber's
life is taken up with the accounts of his own manager-
ship, and so little with those inimitable portraits which
he has occasionally given of the actors of his time!
How fortunate we think ourselves when we can meet
with any person who remembers the principal performers of the last age, and who can give us some
distant idea of Garrick's nature, or of an Abington's
grace! We are always indignant at Smollett, for
having introduced a perverse caricature of the English
Roscius, which staggers our faith in his faultless excellence while reading it. On the contrary, we are pleased
to collect anecdotes of this celebrated actor, which
show his power over the human heart, and enable us
to measure his genius with that of others by its effects.
I have heard, for instance, that once, when Garrick
was acting Lear, the spectators in the front row of the
pit, not being able to see him well in the kneeling
scene, where he utters the curse, rose up, when those
behind them, not willing to interrupt the scene by remonstrating, immediately rose up too, and in this
manner the whole pit rose up without uttering a syllable, and so that you might hear a pin drop. At another time, the crown of straw which he wore in the
same character fell off, or was discomposed, which
would have produced a burst of laughter at any common actor to whom such an accident had happened;
but such was the deep interest in the character, and
such the power of riveting the attention possessed by
this actor, that not the slightest notice was taken of
the circumstance, but the whole audience remained
bathed in silent tears. The knowledge of circumstances
like these serves to keep alive the memory of past excellence, and to stimulate future efforts. It was

thought that a work containing a detailed account
of the stage in our own times—a period not unfruitful
in theatrical genius—might not be wholly without
its use.

The first, and (as I think) the best articles in this
series, appeared originally in the *Morning Chronicle*.
They are those relating to Mr. Kean. I went to see him
the first night of his appearing in Shylock. I remember
it well. The boxes were empty, and the pit not half
full: "some quantity of barren spectators and idle rent-
ers were thinly scattered to make up a show." The
whole presented a dreary, hopeless aspect. I was in
considerable apprehension for the result. From the first
scene in which Mr. Kean came on, my doubts were
at an end. I had been told to give as favourable an account as I could: I gave a true one. I am not one of
those who, when they see the sun breaking from behind a cloud, stop to ask others whether it is the moon.
Mr. Kean's appearance was the first gleam of genius
breaking athwart the gloom of the stage, and the public have since gladly basked in its ray, in spite of actors,
managers, and critics. I cannot say that my opinion
has much changed since that time. Why should it? I
had the same eyes to see with that I have now, the
same ears to hear with, and the same understanding
to judge with. Why, then, should I not form the same
judgment? My opinions have been sometimes called
singular: they are merely sincere. I say what I think:
I think what I feel. I cannot help receiving certain impressions from things; and I have sufficient courage
to declare (somewhat abruptly) what they are. This
is the only singularity I am conscious of. I do not shut
my eyes to extraordinary merit because I hate it, and
refuse to open them till the clamours of others make
me, and then affect to wonder extravagantly at what I
have before affected hypocritically to despise. I do
not make it a common practice to think nothing of

an actor or an author because all the world have not
pronounced in his favour, and after they have, to persist in condemning him, as a proof, not of imbecility
and ill-nature, but of independence of taste and spirit.
Nor do I endeavour to communicate the infection of
my own dulness, cowardice, and spleen to others, by
chilling the coldness of their constitutions by the poi-
sonous slime of vanity or interest, and setting up my
own conscious inability or unwillingness to form an
opinion on any one subject, as the height of candour
and judgment. I did not endeavour to persuade Mr.
Perry[1] that Mr. Kean was an actor that would not last,
merely because he had not lasted; nor that Miss
Stephens[2] knew nothing of singing, because she had
a sweet voice. On the contrary, I did all I could to
counteract the effect of these safe, not very sound, insinuations, and "screw the courage" of one principal
organ of public opinion "to the sticking-place." I do
not repent of having done so.

With respect to the spirit of partisanship in which
the controversy respecting Mr. Kean's merits as an
actor was carried on, there were two or three things
remarkable. One set of persons, out of the excess of
their unbounded admiration, furnished him with all
sorts of excellences which he did not possess or pre-
tend to, and covered his defects from the wardrobe
of their own fancies. With this class of persons,

Pritchard's genteel, and Garrick's six feet high![3]

I never enlisted in this corps of Swiss body-guards; I
was even suspected of disloyalty and *lèse-majesté*, because I did not cry out, *Quand même!* to all Mr.
Kean's stretches of the prerogatives of genius, and was

[1] James Perry (1756-1821) was sole editor and proprietor of
the *Morning Chronicle*.
[2] "Kitty" Stephens (Countess of Essex) was born in 1794,
and died in 1882. She was a very popular singer.
[3] Churchill's *Rosciad*.

placed out of the pale of theatrical orthodoxy, for not
subscribing implicitly to all the articles of belief im-
posed upon my senses and understanding. If you had
not been to see the little man twenty times in Richard,
and did not deny his being hoarse in the last act, or
admire him for being so, you were looked on as a
lukewarm devotee, or half an infidel. On the other
hand, his detractors constantly argued not from what
he was, but from what he was not. "He was not tall.
He had not a fine voice. He did not play at Covent
Garden. He was not John Kemble." This was all you
could get from them, and this they thought quite sufficient to prove that he was not anything, because he
was not something quite different from himself. They
did not consider that an actor might have the eye of
an eagle with the voice of a raven, a "pigmy body,"
and "a fiery soul that o'erinformed its tenement;" that
he might want grace and dignity, and yet have enough
nature and passion in his breast to set up a whole corps
of regular stagers. They did not inquire whether this
was the case with respect to Mr. Kean, but took it for
granted that it was not, for no other reason than because the question had not been settled by the critics
twenty or thirty years ago, and admitted by the town
ever since, that is, before Mr. Kean was born. A royal
infant may be described as "un haut et puissant prince,
âgé d'un jour," [4] but a great and powerful actor cannot be known till he arrives at years of discretion, and
he must be first a candidate for theatrical reputation
before he can be a veteran. This is a truism, but it is
one that our prejudices constantly make us not only
forget, but frequently combat with all the spirit of
martyrdom. I have (as it will be seen in the following
pages) all along spoken freely of Mr. Kean's faults, or
what I considered such, physical as well as intellectual;
but the balance inclines decidedly to the favourable

[4] See *The Fudge Family*, edited by Thomas Brown, jun.
(W. H.) [By Thomas Moore.]

side; though not more, I think, than his merits exceed
his defects. It was also the more necessary to dwell on
the claims of an actor to public support, in proportion
as they were original, and to the illiberal opposition
they unhappily had to encounter. I endeavoured to
prove (and with some success) that he was not "the
very worst actor in the world." His Othello is what
appears to me his masterpiece. To those who have seen
him in this part, and think little of it, I have nothing
further to say. It seems to me, as far as the mind alone
is concerned, and leaving the body out of the question, fully equal to anything of Mrs. Siddons's. But I
hate such comparisons, and only make them on strong
provocation.

Though I do not repent of what I have said in praise
of certain actors, yet I wish I could retract what I have
been obliged to say in reprobation of others. Public
reputation is a lottery, in which there are blanks as
well as prizes. The stage is an arduous profession, requiring so many essential excellences and accidental
advantages, that though it is an honour and a happiness
to succeed in it, it is only a misfortune, and not a
disgrace, to fail in it. Those who put themselves upon
their trial must, however, submit to the verdict; and
the critic in general does little more than prevent a
lingering death, by anticipating, or putting in immediate force, the sentence of the public. The victims of
criticisms, like the victims of the law, bear no good
will to the executioners; and I confess I have often
been heartily tired of so thankless an office. What I
have said of any actor, has never arisen from private
pique of any sort. Indeed, the only person on the stage
with whom I have ever had any personal intercourse
is Mr. Liston, and of him I have not spoken "with the
malice of a friend." To Mr. Conway and Mr. Bartley
my apologies are particularly due: I have accused the
one of being tall, and the other of being fat. I have
also said that Mr. Young plays not only like a scholar,

but like "a master of scholars"; that Miss O'Neill shines more in tragedy than comedy; and that Mr. Mathews is an excellent mimic. I am sorry for these disclosures, which were extorted from me, but I cannot retract them. There is one observation which has been made, and which is true, that public censure hurts actors in a pecuniary point of view; but it has been forgotten that public praise assists them in the same manner. Again, I never understood that the applauded actor thought himself personally obliged to the newspaper critic; the latter was merely supposed to do his duty. Why, then, should the critic be held responsible to the actor whom he *damms* by virtue of his office? Besides, as the mimic caricatures absurdity off the Stage, why should not the critic sometimes caricature it on the Stage? The children of Momus should not hold themselves sacred from ridicule. Though the colours may be a little heightened, the outline may be correct; and truth may be conveyed, and the public taste improved, by an alliteration or a quibble that wounds the self-love of an individual. Authors must live as well as actors; and the *insipid* must at all events be avoided as that which the public abhors most.

April 24, 1818.   W. HAZLITT

❧ Critical Essays

◄§ Critical Essays

MR. KEAN'S SHYLOCK

Morning Chronicle, January 27, 1814
MR. KEAN (of whom report had spoken highly) last
night made his appearance at Drury Lane Theatre in
the character of Shylock. For voice, eye, action, and
expression, no actor has come out for many years at
all equal to him. The applause, from the first scene to
the last, was general, loud, and uninterrupted. Indeed,
the very first scene in which he comes on with Bas-
sanio and Antonio, showed the master in his art, and
at once decided the opinion of the audience. Perhaps
it was the most perfect of any. Notwithstanding the
complete success of Mr. Kean in the part of Shylock,
we question whether he will not become a greater favourite in other parts. There was a lightness and
vigour in his tread, a buoyancy and elasticity of spirit,
a fire and animation, who would accord better with
almost any other character than with the morose, sullen, inward, inveterate, inflexible malignity of Shylock. The character of Shylock is that of a man brooding over one idea, that of its wrongs, and bent on one
unalterable purpose, that of revenge. In conveying a
profound impression of this feeling, or in embodying
the general conception of rigid and uncontrollable
self-will, equally proof against every sentiment of humanity or prejudice of opinion, we have seen actors
more successful than Mr. Kean; but in giving effect to
the conflict of passions arising out of the contrasts of
situation, in varied vehemence of declamation, in keenness of sarcasm, in the rapidity of his transitions from

1

one tone and feeling to another, in propriety and
novelty of action, presenting a succession of striking
pictures, and giving perpetually fresh shocks of delight
and surprise, it would be difficult to single out a com-
petitor. The fault of his acting was (if we may hazard
the objection), an over-display of the resources of the
art, which gave too much relief to the hard, impenetrable, dark groundwork of the character of Shylock.
It would be endless to point out individual beauties,
where almost every passage was received with equal
and deserved applause. We thought, in one or two instances, the pauses in the voice were too long, and too
great a reliance placed on the expression of the countenance, which is a language intelligible only to a part of
the house.

Morning Chronicle, February 2, 1814

MR. KEAN appeared again in Shylock, and by his admirable and expressive manner of giving the part, fully
sustained the reputation he had acquired by his former
representation of it, though he laboured under the disadvantage of a considerable hoarseness. He assumed a
greater appearance of age and feebleness than on the
first night, but the general merit of his playing was the
same. His style of acting is, if we may use the expression, more significant, more pregnant with meaning,
more varied and alive in every part, than any we have
almost ever witnessed. The character never stands still;
there is no vacant pause in the action; the eye is never
silent. For depth and force of conception, we have
seen actors whom we should prefer to Mr. Kean in
Shylock; for brilliant and masterly execution, none. It
is not saying too much of him, though it is saying a
great deal, that he has all that Mr. Kemble *wants* of
perfection.[1] He reminds us of the descriptions of the

[1] Two years later, Hazlitt reprinted in the *Examiner* this criticism of Kean's Shylock, and added the following comment:
—"The accounts in the other papers were not to be sure so

"far-darting eye" of Garrick. We are anxious to see
him in Norval and Richard, and anticipate more complete satisfaction from his performance of the latter
part, than from the one in which he has already
stamped his reputation with the public.

Miss Smith played Portia with much more animation
than the last time we saw her, and in delivering the
fine apostrophe on Mercy, in the trial scene, was highly
impressive.

MR. KEAN'S RICHARD

Morning Chronicle, February 15, 1814
MR. KEAN's manner of acting this part has one peculiar
advantage; it is entirely his own, without any traces of
imitation of any other actor. He stands upon his own
ground, and he stands firm upon it. Almost every scene
had the stamp and freshness of nature. The excellences

---

favourable; and in the above criticism there are several errors.
His voice, which is here praised, is very bad, though it must
be confessed its defects appear less in Shylock than in most of
his other characters. The critic appears also to have formed
an overstrained idea of the gloomy character of Shylock,
probably more from seeing other players perform it than from
the text of Shakespeare. Mr. Kean's manner is much nearer
the mark. Shakespeare could not easily divest his characters of
their entire humanity: his Jew is more than half a Christian.
Certainly, our sympathies are much oftener with him than
with his enemies. He is honest in his vices; they are hypocrites
in their virtues. In all his arguments and replies he has the
advantage over them, by taking them on their own ground.
Shylock (however some persons may suppose him bowed
down by age, or deformed with malignity) never, that we
can find, loses his elasticity and presence of mind. There is
wonderful grace and ease in all the speeches in this play. "I
would not have parted with it [the jewel that he gave to Leah]
for a *wilderness* of monkeys!" What a fine Hebraism! The
character of Shylock is another instance of Shakespeare's power
of identifying himself with the thoughts of men, their prejudices, and almost instincts."

and defects of his performance were in general the same as those which he discovered in Shylock; though, as the character of Richard is the most difficult, so we think he displayed most power in it. It is possible to form a higher conception of this character (we do not mean from seeing other actors, but from reading Shakespeare) than that given by this very admirable tragedian; but we cannot imagine any character represented with greater distinctness and precision, more perfectly *articulated* in every part. Perhaps, indeed, there is too much of this; for we sometimes thought he failed, even from an exuberance of talent, and dissipated the impression of the character by the variety of his resources. To be perfect, it should have a little more solidity, depth, sustained, and impassioned feeling, with somewhat less brilliancy, with fewer glancing lights, pointed transitions, and pantomimic evolutions.

The Richard of Shakespeare is towering and lofty, as well as aspiring; equally impetuous and commanding; haughty, violent, and subtle; bold and treacherous; confident in his strength, as well as in his cunning; raised high by his birth, and higher by his genius and his crimes; a royal usurper, a princely hypocrite, a tyrant and a murderer of the House of Plantagenet.

> . . . but I was born so high,
> Our aery buildeth in the cedar's top,
> And dallies with the wind, and scorns the sun.

The idea conveyed in these lines (which are omitted in the miserable medley acted for *Richard III.*) is never lost sight of by Shakespeare, and should not be out of the actor's mind for a moment. The restless and sanguinary Richard is not a man striving to be great, but to be greater than he is; conscious of his strength of will, his powers of intellect, his daring courage, his elevated station, and making use of these advantages, as giving him both the means and the pretext to commit unheard-of crimes, and to shield himself from remorse and infamy.

If Mr. Kean does not completely succeed in concentrating all the lines of the character, as drawn by Shakespeare, he gives an animation, vigour, and relief to the part, which we have never seen surpassed. He is more refined than Cooke; more bold, varied, and original that Kemble, in the same character. In some parts, however, we thought him deficient in dignity; and particularly in the scenes of state business, there was not a sufficient air of artificial authority. The fine assumption of condescending superiority, after he is made king—"Stand all apart—Cousin of Buckingham," &c., was not given with the effect which it might have received. There was also at times a sort of tip-toe elevation, an enthusiastic rapture in his expectations of obtaining the crown, instead of a gloating expression of sullen delight, as if he already clutched the bauble, and held it within his grasp. This was the precise expression which Mr. Kean gave with so much effect to the part where he says that he already feels

The golden rigol bind his brows.

In one who *dares* so much, there is little indeed to blame. The only two things which appeared to us decidedly objectionable, were the sudden letting down of his voice when he says of Hastings, "Chop off his head," and the action of putting his hands behind him, in listening to Buckingham's account of his reception by the citizens. His courtship scene with Lady Anne was an admirable exhibition of smooth and smiling villainy. The progress of wily adulation, of encroaching humility, was finely marked throughout by the action, voice, and eye. He seemed, like the first tempter, to approach his prey, certain of the event, and as if success had smoothed the way before him. We remember Mr. Cooke's manner of representing this scene was more violent, hurried, and full of anxious uncer-

tainty. This, though more natural in general, was, we
think, less in character. Richard should woo, not as a
lover, but as an actor—to show his mental superiority,
and power to make others the playthings of his will.
Mr. Kean's attitude in leaning against the side of the
stage before he comes forward in this scene, was one
of the most graceful and striking we remember to have
seen. It would have done for Titian to paint. The
opening scene in which Richard descants on his own
deformity, was conceived with perfect truth and character, and delivered in a fine and varied tone of natural
recitation. Mr. Kean did equal justice to the beautiful
description of the camps the night before the battle,[1]
though, in consequence of his hoarseness, he was
obliged to repeat the whole passage in an under-key.[2]
His manner of bidding his friends good-night, and his
pausing with the point of his sword drawn slowly
backward and forward on the ground, before he retires to his tent, received shouts of applause. He gave
to all the busy scenes of the play the greatest animation
and effect. He filled every part of the stage. The concluding scene, in which he is killed by Richmond, was
the most brilliant. He fought like one drunk with
wounds: and the attitude in which he stands with his
hands stretched out, after his sword is taken from him,
had a preternatural and terrific grandeur, as if his will
could not be disarmed, and the very phantoms of his
despair had a withering power.

Morning Chronicle, February 21, 1814
THE house was crowded at an early hour in every
part, to witness Mr. Kean's second representation of
Richard. His admirable acting received that meed of
applause which it so well deserved. His voice had not

[1] Cibber's interpolation from *King Henry V*.
[2] The defects in the upper tones of Mr. Kean's voice were
hardly perceptible in his performance of Shylock, and were
at first attributed to hoarseness. (W. H.)

entirely recovered its tone and strength; and when (after the curtain had dropped, amidst a tumult of approbation) Mr. Rae came forward to announce the play for Monday, cries of "No, no," from every part of the house testified the sense entertained by the audience of the impropriety of requiring the repetition of this extraordinary effort, till every physical disadvantage had been completely removed.

We have little to add to our former remarks, for Mr. Kean went through the part nearly as before, and we saw no reason to alter our opinion. The dying scene was the most varied, and, we think, for the worse. In pronouncing the words in Richard's soliloquy, "I am myself alone," Mr. Kean gave a quick and hurried movement to his voice, as if it was a thought that suddenly struck him, or which he wished to pass over; whereas it is the deep and rooted sentiment of his breast. The reduplication of the words in Shakespeare points out the manner in which the voice should dwell upon, and, as it were, brood over the feeling, loth to part with the bitter consolation. Where he says to Buckingham, "I am not i' the vein," the expression should, we imagine, be that of stifled hatred and cold contempt, instead of sarcastic petulance. The scene tells for itself, without being pointed by the manner. In general, perhaps, if Mr. Kean were to give to the character less of the air of an ostentatious hypocrite, of an intelligible villain, it would be more correct, and would accord better with Shakespeare's idea of the part. The description which he has put into the mouth of Hastings is a perfect study for the actor.

His Grace looks cheerfully and smooth this morning:
There's some conceit or other likes him well,
When that he bids good morrow with such spirit.
I think there's never a man in Christendom
Can lesser hide his hate or love than he;
For by his face straight shall you know his heart.

In the scene with Lady Anne, in the sudden alter-

ation of his manner to the messenger who brings him
the news of Edward's illness, in the interview with
Buckingham, where he desires the death of the children, in his infinitely spirited expostulation with Lord
Stanley, in his triumph at the death of Buckingham,
in the parting scene with his friends before the battle,
in his treatment of the paper sent to Norfolk, and in
all the tumult and glowing interest of the last scenes
of the play, we had fresh cause for admiration. It were
in vain, however, to point out particular beauties; for
the research, the ingenuity, and the invention mani-
fested throughout the character are endless. We have
said before, and we still think so, that there is even
too much effect given, too many significant hints, too
much appearance of study. There is a tone in acting, as
well as in painting, which is the chief and master excellence. Our highest conception of an actor is, that
he shall assume the character once for all, and be it
throughout, and trust to this conscious sympathy for
the effect produced. Mr. Kean's manner of acting is,
on the contrary, rather a perpetual assumption of his
part, always brilliant and successful, almost always true
and natural, but yet always a distinct effort in every
new situation, so that the actor does not seem entirely
to forget himself, or to be identified with the character. The extreme elaboration of the parts injures the
broad and massy effect; the general impulse of the
machine is retarded by the variety and intricacy of the
movements. But why do we try this actor by an ideal
theory? Who is there that will stand the same test?
It is, in fact, the last forlorn hope of criticism, for it
shows that we have nothing else to compare him
with. "Take him for all in all," it will be long, very
long, before we "look upon his like again," if we are
to wait as long as we *have* waited.

We wish the introduction of the ghosts through the
trap-doors of the stage were altogether omitted. The
speeches, which they address to Richard, might be

delivered just as well from behind the scenes. These sort of exhibitions are only proper for a superstitious age; and in an age not superstitious, excite ridicule instead of terror.

Mr. Kean's acting in Richard, as we before remarked in his Shylock, presents a perpetual succession of striking pictures. He bids fair to supply us with the best Shakespeare Gallery we have had!

MR. KEAN'S HAMLET

Morning Chronicle, March 14, 1814

THAT which distinguishes the dramatic productions of Shakespeare from all others is the wonderful variety and perfect individuality of his characters. Each of these is as much itself, and as absolutely independent of the rest, as if they were living persons, not fictions of the mind. The poet appears for the time being to be identified with the character he wishes to represent, and to pass from one to the other, like the same soul, successively animating different bodies. By an art like that of the ventriloquist, he throws his imagination out of himself, and makes every word appear to proceed from the very mouth of the person whose name it bears. His plays alone are properly expressions of the passions, not descriptions of them. His characters are real beings of flesh and blood; they speak like men, not like authors. One might suppose that he had stood by at the time, and had overheard what passed. Each object and circumstance seems to exist in his mind as it existed in nature; each several train of thought and feeling goes on of itself without effort or confusion; in the world of his imagination, everything has a life, a place and being of its own.

These remarks are, we think, as applicable to *Hamlet*, as to any of Shakespeare's tragedies. It is, if not the finest, perhaps the most inimitable of all his produc-

tions. *Lear* is first, for the profound intensity of the
passion: *Macbeth*, for the wildness of the imagination,
and the glowing rapidity of the action: *Othello*, for
the progressive interest and rapid alternations of feeling: *Hamlet*, for perfect dramatic truth, and the unlooked-for development of sentiment and character.
Shakespeare has in this play shown more of the mag-
nanimity of genius than in any other. There is no attempt to force an interest, but everything is left to
time and circumstances. The interest is excited without premeditation or effort, the events succeed each
other as matters of course, the characters think, and
speak, and act, just as they would do if they were left
to themselves. The whole play is an exact transcript
of what might have taken place at the Court of Den-
mark five hundred years ago, before the modern re-
finements in morality and manners.

The character of Hamlet is itself a pure effusion of
genius. It is not a character marked by strength of
passion or will, but by refinement of thought and feeling. Hamlet is as little of the hero as a man can well
be; but he is "a young and princely novice," full of
high enthusiasm and quick sensibility—the sport of
circumstances, questioning with fortune, and refining
on his own feelings, and forced from the natural bias
of his character by the strangeness of his situation. He
seems incapable of deliberate action, and is only hurried into extremities on the spur of the occasion, when
he has no time to reflect, as in the scene where he kills
Polonius, and where he alters the letters which Rosencrantz and Guildenstern take with them. At other
times, he remained puzzled, undecided, and sceptical,
dallies with his purposes till the occasion is lost, and
always finds some reason to relapse into indolence and
thoughtfulness again. For this reason he refuses to kill
the King when he is at his prayers, and by a refinement in malice, which is only an excuse for his own
want of resolution, defers his revenge to some more

fatal opportunity, when he shall be engaged in some act "that has no relish of salvation in it." So he scruples to trust the suggestions of the Ghost, contrives the scene of the play to have surer proof of his uncle's guilt, and then rests satisfied with this confirmation of his suspicions, and the success of his experiment, instead of acting upon it. The moral perfection of this character has been called in question. It is more natural than conformable to rules; and if not more amiable, is certainly more dramatic on that account. Hamlet is not, to be sure, a Sir Charles Grandison. In general, there is little of the drab-coloured quakerism of morality in the ethical delineations of "that noble and liberal casuist," as Shakespeare has been well called. He does not set his heroes in the stock of virtue, to make mouths at their own situation. His plays are not transcribed from the "Whole Duty of Man"! We confess we are a little shocked at the want of refinement in those who are shocked at the want of refinement in Hamlet. The want of punctilious exactness of behaviour either partakes of the "licence of the time," or belongs to the very excess of intellectual refinement in the character, which makes the common rules of life, as well as his own purposes, sit loose upon him. He may be said to be amenable only to the tribunal of his own thoughts, and is too much occupied with the airy world of contemplation, to lay as much stress as he ought on the practical consequences of things. His habitual principles of action are unhinged, and "out of joint" with the time.

This character is probably of all others the most difficult to personate on the stage. It is like the attempt to embody a shadow.

> Come, then, the colours and the ground prepare,
> Dip in the rainbow, trick her off in air,
> Choose a firm cloud before it fall, and in it
> Catch, 'ere she change, the Cynthia of a minute.[1]

[1] Pope, *Moral Essays*, *Epistle II*.

Such nearly is the task which the actor imposes on himself in the part of Hamlet. It is quite remote from hardness and dry precision. The character is spun to the finest thread, yet never loses its continuity. It has the yielding flexibility of "a wave of the sea." It is made up of undulating lines, without a single sharp angle. There is no set purpose, no straining at a point. The observations are suggested by the passing scene— the gusts of passion come and go, like the sounds of music borne on the wind. The interest depends not on the action, but on the thoughts—on "that within which passeth show." Yet, in spite of these difficulties, Mr. Kean's representation of the character had the most brilliant success. It did not, indeed, come home to our feelings as Hamlet (that very Hamlet whom we read of in our youth, and seem almost to remember in our after-years), but it was a most striking and animated rehearsal of the part.

High as Mr. Kean stood in our opinion before, we have no hesitation in saying that he stands higher in it (and, we think, will in that of the public), from the powers displayed in this last effort. If it was less perfect as a whole, there were parts in it of a higher cast of excellence than any part of his Richard. We will say at once in what we think his general delineation of the character wrong. It was too strong and pointed. There was often a severity, approaching to virulence, in the common observations and answers. There is nothing of this in Hamlet. He is, as it were, wrapped up in the cloud of his reflections, and only *thinks aloud*. There should, therefore, be no attempt to impress what he says upon others by any exaggeration of emphasis or manner, no talking *at* his hearers. There should be as much of the gentleman and scholar as possible infused into the part, and as little of the actor. A pensive air of sadness should sit unwillingly upon his brow, but no appearance of fixed and sullen gloom. He is full of "weakness and melancholy," but there is no harshness in his nature. Hamlet should be the most amiable of misanthropes. There is no one line in this play which should be spoken like any one line in Richard, yet Mr. Kean did not appear to us to keep the two characters always distinct. He was least happy in the last scene with Guildenstern and Rosencrantz. In some of these more familiar scenes, he displayed more energy than was requisite, and in others, where it would have been appropriate, did not rise equal to the exigency of the occasion. In particular, the scene with Laertes, where he leaps into the grave, and utters the exclamation, " 'Tis I, Hamlet the Dane," had not the tumultuous and overpowering effect we expected from it. To point out the defects of Mr. Kean's performance of the part, is a less grateful but a much shorter task than to enumerate the many striking beauties which he gave to it, both by the power of his action and by the true feeling of nature. His surprise when he first sees the Ghost, his eagerness and filial confidence in following it, the impressive pathos of his action and voice in addressing it, "I'll call thee Hamlet, *Father*, Royal Dane," were admirable.

Mr. Kean has introduced in this part a *new reading*, as it is called, which we think perfectly correct. In the scene where he breaks from his friends to obey the command of his father, he keeps his sword pointed behind him, to prevent them from following him, instead of holding it before him to protect him from the Ghost. The manner of his taking Guildenstern and Rosencrantz under each arm, under pretence of communicating his secret to them, when he only means to trifle with them, had the finest effect, and was, we conceive, exactly in the spirit of the character. So was the suppressed tone of irony in which he ridicules those who gave ducats for his uncle's picture, though they would "make mouths at him" while his father lived. Whether the way in which Mr. Kean hesitates in repeating the first line of the speech in the inter-

view with the player, and then, after several ineffectual
attempts to recollect it, suddenly hurries on with it,
"The rugged Pyrrhus," &c., is in perfect keeping, we
have some doubts; but there was great ingenuity in
the thought, and the spirit and life of the execution
was beyond everything. Hamlet's speech in describing
his own melancholy, his instructions to the players,
and the soliloquy on death, were all delivered by Mr.
Kean in a tone of fine, clear, and natural recitation.
His pronunciation of the word "contumely" in the last
of these is, we apprehend, not authorised by custom,
or by the metre.

Both the closet scene with his mother, and his re-
monstrances to Ophelia, were highly impressive. If
there had been less vehemence of effort in the latter, it
would not have lost any of its effect. But whatever
nice faults might be found in this scene, they were
amply redeemed by the manner of his coming back
after he has gone to the extremity of the stage, from
a pang of parting tenderness to press his lips to
Ophelia's hand. It had an electrical effect on the house.
It was the finest commentary that was ever made on
Shakespeare. It explained the character at once (as he
meant it), as one of disappointed hope, of bitter regret,
of affection suspended, not obliterated, by the dis-
tractions of the scene around him! The manner in
which Mr. Kean acted in the scene of the Play before
the King and Queen was the most daring of any, and
the force and animation which he gave to it cannot
be too highly applauded. Its extreme boldness "bordered on the verge of all we hate," and the effect it
produced was a test of the extraordinary powers of
this extraordinary actor.

MR. KEAN'S OTHELLO

Morning Chronicle, May 6, 1814

"OTHELLO" was acted at Drury Lane last night, the

part of Othello by Mr. Kean.[1] His success was fully
equal to the arduousness of the undertaking. In general, we might observe that he displayed the same excellences and the same defects as in his former characters. His voice and person were not altogether in
consonance with the character, nor was there throughout that noble tide of deep and sustained passion, impetuous, but majestic, that "flows on to the Propontic,
and knows no ebb," which raises our admiration and
pity of the lofty-minded Moor. There were, however,
repeated bursts of feeling and energy which we have
never seen surpassed. The whole of the latter part of
the third act was a masterpiece of profound pathos and
exquisite conception, and its effect on the house was
electrical. The tone of voice in which he delivered the
beautiful apostrophe, "Then, oh farewell!" struck on
the heart and the imagination like the swelling notes of
some divine music. The look, the action, the expression
of voice, with which he accompanied the exclamation,
"Not a jot, not a jot;" the reflection, "I felt not *Cassio's
kisses* on her lips;" and his vow of revenge against
Cassio, and abandonment of his love for Desdemona,
laid open the very tumult and agony of the soul. In
other parts, where we expected an equal interest to be
excited, we were disappointed; and in the common
scenes we think Mr. Kean's manner, as we have remarked on other occasions, had more point and emphasis than the sense or character required.[2]

MR. KEAN'S IAGO

Morning Chronicle, May 9, 1814

THE part of Iago was played at Drury Lane on Saturday by Mr. Kean,[3] and played with admirable facility

[1] Iago by Pope, whom Leigh Hunt criticised so vigorously.
[2] For a fuller account of Kean's Othello see p. 69.
[3] Othello by Sowerby, a very mediocre performer.

and effect. It was the most faultless of his performances, the most consistent and entire. Perhaps the accomplished hypocrite was never so finely, so adroitly
portrayed—a gay, light-hearted monster, a careless,
cordial, comfortable villain. The preservation of character was so complete, the air and manner were so
much of a piece throughout, that the part seemed more
like a detached scene, or single *trait*, and of shorter
duration than it usually does. The ease, familiarity,
and tone of nature with which the text was delivered,
were quite equal to anything we have seen in the best
comic acting. It was the least overdone of all his parts,
though full of point, spirit, and brilliancy. The odiousness of the character was, in fact, in some measure,
glossed over by the extreme grace, alacrity, and rapidity of the execution. Whether this effect were "a
consummation of the art devoutly to be wished," is
another question, on which we entertain some doubts.
We have already stated it as our opinion, that Mr.
Kean is not a literal transcriber of his author's text; he
translates his characters with great freedom and ingenuity into a language of his own; but at the same
time we cannot help preferring his liberal and spirited
dramatic versions, to the dull, literal, commonplace
monotony of his competitors. Besides, after all, in the
conception of the part, he may be right and we may
be wrong. We have before complained that Mr.
Kean's Richard was not gay enough, and we should
now be disposed to complain that his Iago is not grave
enough.

MISS O'NEILL'S JULIET

Champion, October 16, 1814

WE OCCASIONALLY see something on the stage that reminds us a little of Shakespeare. Miss O'Neill's Juliet,

if it does not correspond exactly with our idea of the
character, does not degrade it. We never saw Garrick;
and Mrs. Siddons was the only person who ever embodied our idea of high tragedy. Her mind and person
were both fitted for it. The effect of her acting was
greater than could be conceived beforehand. It perfectly filled and overpowered the mind. The first time
of seeing this great actress was an epoch in everyone's
life, and left impressions which could never be forgotten. She appeared to belong to a superior order of
beings, to be surrounded with a personal awe, like
some prophetess of old, or Roman matron, the mother
of Coriolanus or the Gracchi. Her voice answered to
her form, and her expression to both. Yet she was a
pantomime actress. Her common recitation was faulty.
It was in bursts of indignation, or grief, in sudden ex-
clamations, in apostrophes and inarticulate sounds, that
she raised the soul of passion to its height, or sunk it in
despair.

We remember her manner in *The Gamester*, when
Stukeley (it was then played by Palmer), declares his
love to her. The look, first of incredulity and astonishment, then of anger, then passing suddenly into contempt, and ending in bitter scorn, and a convulsive
burst of laughter, all given in a moment, and laying
open every movement of the soul, produced an effect
which we shall never forget. Her manner of rubbing
her hands in the night scene in *Macbeth*, and of dis-
missing the guests at the banquet, were among her
finest things. We have, many years ago, wept outright
during the whole time of her playing Isabella,[1] and
this we take to have been a higher employment of the
critical faculties than doubling down the book in dog-
ears to make out a regular list of critical commonplaces.
To the tears formerly shed on such occasions, we may

[1] In Southerne's *Isabella, or the Fatal Marriage*, one of her
greatest characters.

apply the words of a modern dashing orator, "Sweet is the dew of their memory, and pleasant the balm of their recollection."

We have, we believe, been betrayed into this digression, because Miss O'Neill, more than any late actress, reminded us in certain passages, and in a faint degree, of Mrs. Siddons. This young lady, who will probably become a favourite with the public, is rather tall; and though not *of the first order of fine forms,* her figure is of that respectable kind which will not interfere with the characters she represents. Her deportment is not particularly graceful: there is a heaviness and want of firmness about it. Her features are regular, and the upper part of her face finely expressive of terror or sorrow. It has that mixture of beauty and passion which we admire so much in some of the antique statues. The lower part of her face is not equally good. From a want of fulness or flexibility about the mouth, her laugh is not at any time pleasing, and where it is a laugh of terror, is distorted and painful. Her voice, without being musical, is distinct, powerful, and capable of every necessary exertion. Her action is impressive and simple. She looks the part she has to perform, and fills up the pauses in the words by the varied expression of her countenance or gestures, without anything artificial, pointed, or far-fetched.

In the silent expression of feeling, we have seldom witnessed anything finer than her acting, where she is told of Romeo's death, her listening to the Friar's story of the poison, and her change of manner towards the Nurse, when she advises her to marry Paris. Her delivery of the speeches in the scenes where she laments Romeo's banishment, and anticipates her waking in the tomb, marked the fine play and undulation of natural sensibility, rising and falling with the gusts of passion, and at last worked up into an agony of despair, in which imagination approaches the brink of frenzy. Her actually screaming at the imaginary sight of Tybalt's ghost, appeared to us the only instance of extravagance or caricature. Not only is there a distinction to be kept up between physical and intellectual horror (for the latter becomes more general, internal, and absorbed, in proportion as it becomes more intense), but the scream, in the present instance, startled the audience, as it preceded the speech which explained its meaning. Perhaps the emphasis given to the exclamation, "*And Romeo banished*," and to the description of Tybalt, "*festering in his shroud*," was too much in that epigrammatic, pointed style, which we think inconsistent with the severe and simple dignity of tragedy.

In the last scene, at the tomb with Romeo, which, however, is not from Shakespeare,[2] though it tells admirably on the stage, she did not produce the effect we expected. Miss O'Neill seemed least successful in the former part of the character, in the garden scene, &c. The expression of tenderness bordered on hoydening, and affectation. The character of Juliet is a pure effusion of nature. It is as serious, and as much in earnest, as it is frank and susceptible. It has all the exquisite voluptuousness of youthful innocence. There is not the slightest appearance of coquetry in it, no sentimental languor, no meretricious assumption of fondness to take her lover by surprise. She ought not to laugh when she says, "I have forgot why I did call thee back," as if conscious of the artifice, nor hang in a fondling posture over the balcony. Shakespeare has given a fine idea of the composure of the character, where he first describes her at the window, leaning her cheek upon her arm. The whole expression of her love should be like the breath of flowers.

[2] This scene was interpolated by Garrick, who borrowed part of it from Otway's *Caius Marius*.

MR. KEAN'S RICHARD

Champion, October 9, 1814

WE do not think Mr. Kean at all improved by his Irish expedition. As this is a point in which we feel a good deal of interest, both on Mr. Kean's account and our own, we shall state briefly our objections to some alterations in his mode of acting, which appear to us for the worse. His pauses are twice as long as they were, and the rapidity with which he hurries over other parts of the dialogue is twice as great as it was. In both these points, his style of acting always bordered on the very verge of extravagance; and we suspect it has at present passed the line. There are, no doubt, passages in which the pauses can hardly be too long, or too marked; these must be, however, of rare occurrence, and it is in the finding out these exceptions to the general rule, and in daring to give them all their effect, that the genius of an actor discovers itself. But the most commonplace drawling monotony is not more mechanical or more offensive than the converting these exceptions into a general rule, and making every sentence an alternation of dead pauses and rapid transitions.[1] It is not in extremes that dramatic genius is shown, any more than skill in music consists in passing continually from the highest to the lowest note. The quickness of familiar utterance with which Mr. Kean pronounced the anticipated doom of Stanley,

[1] An old gentleman, riding over Putney Bridge, turned round to his servant, and said, "Do you like eggs, John?" "Yes, sir." Here the conversation ended. The same gentleman riding over the same bridge that day year, again turned round, and said, "How?" "Poached, sir," was the answer. This is the longest pause upon record, and has something of a dramatic effect, though it could not be transferred to the stage. Perhaps an actor might go so far, on the principle of indefinite pauses, as to begin a sentence in one act, and finish it in the next. (W. H.)

"Chop off his head," was quite ludicrous. Again, the manner in which, after his nephew said, "I fear no uncles dead," he suddenly turned round and answered, "And I hope none living, sir," was, we thought, quite out of character. The motion was performed, and the sounds uttered, in the smallest possible time in which a puppet could be made to mimic or gabble the part. For this we see not the least reason; and can only account for it, from a desire to give excessive effect by a display of the utmost dexterity of execution.

It is almost needless to observe that executive power in acting, as in all other arts, is only valuable as it is made subservient to truth and nature. Even some want of mechanical skill is better than the perpetual affectation of showing it. The absence of a quality is often less provoking than its abuse, because less voluntary.

The part which was least varied was the scene with Lady Anne. This is, indeed, nearly a perfect piece of acting. In leaning against the pillar at the commencement of the scene, Mr. Kean did not go through exactly the same regular evolution of graceful attitudes, and we regretted the omission. He frequently varied the execution of many of his most striking conceptions, and the attempt in general failed, as it naturally must do. We refer particularly to his manner of resting on the point of his sword before he retires to his tent, to his treatment of the letter sent to Norfolk, and to his dying scene with Richmond.

Mr. Kean's *bye-play* is certainly one of his greatest excellences, and it might be said that if Shakespeare had written marginal directions to the players, in the manner of the German dramatists, he would often have directed them to do what Mr. Kean does. Such additions to the text are, however, to be considered as lucky hits, and it is not to be supposed that an actor is to provide an endless variety of these running accompaniments, which he is not in strictness bound to provide at all. In general, we think it a rule that an actor

ought to vary his part as little as possible, unless he is
convinced that his former mode of playing it is er-
roneous. He should make up his mind as the best mode
of representing the part, and come as near to this
standard as he can, in every successive exhibition. It
is absurd to object to this mechanical uniformity as
studied and artificial. All acting is studied or artificial.
An actor is no more called upon to vary his gestures
or articulation at every new rehearsal of the character,
than an author can be required to furnish various
readings to every separate copy of his work. To a new
audience it is quite unnecessary; to those who have
seen him before in the same part, it is worse than useless. They may at least be presumed to have come to
a second representation, because they approved of the
first, and will be sure to be disappointed in almost every
alteration. The attempt is endless, and can only produce perplexity and indecision in the actor himself. He
must either return perpetually in the same narrow
round, or, if he is determined to be always new, he
may at last fancy that he ought to perform the part
standing on his head instead of his feet. Besides, Mr.
Kean's style of acting is not in the least of the unpre-
meditated, *improvisatori* kind: it is throughout elaborate and systematic, instead of being loose, off-hand,
and accidental. He comes upon the stage as little un-
prepared as any actor we know. We object particularly to his varying the original action in the dying
scene. He at first held out his hands in a way which
can only be conceived by those who saw him—in mo-
tionless despair—or as if there were some preternatural
power in the mere manifestation of his will: he now
actually fights with his doubled fists, after his sword
is taken from him, like some helpless infant.

We have been quite satisfied with the attempts we
have seen to ape Mr. Kean in this part, without wishing to see him ape himself in it. There is no such thing
as trick in matters of genius. All poetical licenses,

however beautiful in themselves, by being parodied, instantly become ridiculous. It is because beauties of this kind have no clue to them, and are reducible to no standard, that it is the peculiar province of genius to detect them; by making them common, and reducing them to a rule, you make them perfectly mechanical, and perfectly absurd into the bargain.

To conclude our hypercritical remarks: we really think that Mr. Kean was, in a great many instances, either too familiar, to emphatical, or too energetic. In the latter scenes, perhaps, his energy could not be too great; but he gave the energy of action alone. He merely gesticulated, or at best vociferated the part. His articulation totally failed him. We doubt if a single person in the house, not acquainted with the play, understood a single sentence that he uttered. It was "inexplicable dumb show and noise." We wish to throw the fault of most of our objections on the managers. Their conduct has been marked by one uniform character, a paltry attention to their own immediate interest, a distrust of Mr. Kean's abilities to perform more than the character he had succeeded in, and a contempt for the wishes of the public. They have spun him tediously out in every character, and have forced him to display the variety of his talents in the same instead of different characters. They kept him back in Shylock, till he nearly failed in Richard from a cold. Why not bring him out in Macbeth, which was at one time got up for him? Why not bring him out at once in a variety of characters, as the Dublin managers have done? It does not appear that either they or he suffered by it. It seems, by all we can find, that versatility is, perhaps, Mr. Kean's greatest excellence. Why, then, not give him his range? Why tantalise the public? Why extort from them their last shilling for the twentieth repetition of the same part, instead of letting them make their election for themselves, of what they like best? It is really very pitiful.

Ill as we conceive the London managers have treated
him, the London audiences have treated him well, and
we wish Mr. Kean, for some years at least, to stick to
them. They are his best friends; and he may assuredly
account us, who have made these sorry remarks upon
him, not among his worst. After he has got through
the season here well, we see no reason why he should
make himself hoarse with performing Hamlet at twelve
o'clock, and Richard at six, at Kidderminster. At his
time of life, with his prospects, the improvement of
his fortune is not the principal thing. A training under
Captain Barclay[2] would do more towards strengthening his mind and body, his fame and fortune, than
sharing bumper receipts with the Dublin managers,
or carousing with the whole Irish bar. Or, if Mr. Kean
does not approve of this rough regimen, he might de-
vote the summer vacation to the Muses. To a man of
genius, leisure is the first of benefits, as well as of
luxuries; where "with her best nurse, Contemplation,"
the mind

> Can plume her feathers, and let grow her wings,
> That in the various bustle of resort
> Were all-to ruffled, and sometimes impaired.[3]

It was our first duty to point out Mr. Kean's excellences to the public, and we did so with no sparing
hand; it is our second duty to him, to ourselves, and
the public, to distinguish between his excellences and
defects, and to prevent, if possible, his excellences from
degenerating into defects.

[2] Captain Barclay (1779-1854) was a noted pedestrian, his
most extraordinary feat being his walking one mile in each of
1000 successive hours at Newmarket in 1809.
[3] Milton's *Comus.*

MR. KEAN'S MACBETH

Champion, November 13, 1814
THE genius of Shakespeare was as much shown in the subtlety and nice discrimination as in the force and variety of his characters. The distinction is not preserved more completely in those which are the most opposite, than in those which in their general features and obvious appearance most nearly resemble each other. It has been observed, with very little exaggeration, that not one of his speeches could be put into the mouth of any other character than the one to which it is given, and that the transposition, if attempted, might be always detected from some circumstance in the passage itself. *If to invent according to Nature*, be the true definition of genius, Shakespeare had more of this quality than any other writer. He might be said to have been a joint-worker with Nature, and to have created an imaginary world of his own, which has all the appearance and the truth of reality. His mind, while it exerted an absolute control over the stronger workings of the passions, was exquisitely alive to the slightest impulses and most evanescent shades of character and feeling. The broad distinctions and governing principles of human nature are presented not in the abstract, but in their immediate and endless application to different persons and things. The local details, the particular accidents, have the fidelity of history, without losing anything of their general effect.

It is the business of poetry, and indeed of all works of imagination, to exhibit the species through the individual. Otherwise, there can be no opportunity for the exercise of the imagination, without which the descriptions of the painter or the poet are lifeless, unsubstantial, and vapid. If some modern critics are right.

with their sweeping generalities and vague abstractions, Shakespeare was quite wrong. In the French dramatists, only the class is represented, never the individual: their kings, their heroes, and their lovers are all the same, and they are all French—that is, they are nothing but the mouthpieces of certain rhetorical commonplace sentiments on the favourite topics of morality and the passions. The characters in Shakespeare do not declaim like pedantic schoolboys, but speak and act like men, placed in real circumstances, with "real hearts of flesh and blood beating in their bosoms." No two of his characters are the same, more than they would be so in nature. Those that are the most alike are distinguished by positive differences, which accompany and modify the leading principle of the character through its most obscure ramifications, embodying the habits, gestures, and almost the looks of the individual. These touches of nature are often so many, and so minute, that the poet cannot be supposed to have been distinctly aware of the operation of the springs by which his imagination was set at work: yet every one of the results is brought out with a truth and clearness, as if his whole study had been directed to that peculiar trait of character, or subordinate train of feeling.

Thus Macbeth, and Richard the Third, King Henry the Sixth, and Richard the Second—characters that, in their general description, and in common hands, would be merely repetitions of the same idea—are distinguished by traits as precise, though of course less violent, than those which separate Macbeth from Henry the Sixth, or Richard the Third from Richard the Second. Shakespeare has, with wonderful accuracy, and without the smallest appearance of effort, varied the portraits of imbecility and effeminacy in the two deposed monarchs. With still more powerful and masterly strokes, he has marked the different effects of ambition and cruelty, operating on different dispo-

sitions and in different circumstances, in his Macbeth
and Richard the Third. Both are tyrants and usurpers,
both violent and ambitious, both cruel and treacherous. But Richard is cruel from nature and constitution. Macbeth becomes so from accidental circumstances. He is urged to the commission of guilt by
golden opportunity, by the instigations of his wife,
and by prophetic warnings. "Fate and metaphysical
aid" conspire against his virtue and loyalty. Richard
needs no prompter, but wades through a series of
crimes to the height of his ambition, from ungovernable passions and the restless love of mischief. He is
never gay but in the prospect, or in the success, of his
villainies: Macbeth is full of horror at the thoughts
of the murder of Duncan, and of remorse after its
perpetration. Richard has no mixture of humanity in
his composition, no tie which binds him to the kind;
he owns no fellowship with others, but is himself
alone. Macbeth is not without feeling of sympathy, is
accessible to pity, is even the dupe of his uxoriousness,
and ranks the loss of friends and of his good name
among the causes that have made him sick of life. He
becomes more callous indeed as he plunges deeper in
guilt, "direness is thus made familiar to his slaugh-
terous thoughts," and he anticipates his wife in the
boldness and bloodiness of his enterprises, who, for
want of the same stimulus of action, is "troubled with
thick-coming fancies," walks in her sleep, goes mad,
and dies. Macbeth endeavours to escape from reflection on his crimes, by repelling their consequences,
and banishes remorse for the past, by meditating future
mischief. This is not the principle of Richard's cruelty, which resembles the cold malignity of a fiend,
rather than the frailty of human nature. Macbeth is
goaded on by necessity; to Richard, blood is a pastime.
    There are other essential differences. Richard is a
man of the world, a vulgar, plotting, hardened villain,
wholly regardless of everything but his own ends and

the means to accomplish them. Not so Macbeth. The superstitions of the time, the rude state of society, the local scenery and customs, all give a wildness and imaginary grandeur to his character. From the strangeness of the events which surround him, he is full of amazement and fear, and stands in doubt between the world of reality and the world of fancy. He sees sights not shown to mortal eye, and hears unearthly music. All is tumult and disorder within and without his mind. In thought he is absent and perplexed, desperate in act: his purposes recoil upon himself, are broken and disjointed: he is the double thrall of his passions and his evil destiny. He treads upon the brink of fate, and grows dizzy with his situation. Richard is not a character of imagination, but of pure will or passion. There is no conflict of opposite feelings in his breast. The apparitions which he sees are in his sleep, nor does he live, like Macbeth, in a waking dream.

Such at least, is our conception of the two characters, as drawn by Shakespeare. Mr. Kean does not distinguish them so completely as he might. His Richard comes nearer to the original than his Macbeth. He was deficient in the poetry of the character. He did not look like a man who had encountered the Weird Sisters. There should be nothing tight or compact in Macbeth, no tenseness of fibre, nor pointed decision of manner. He has, indeed, energy and manliness of soul, but "subject to all the skyey influences." He is sure of nothing. All is left at issue. He runs a-tilt with fortune, and is baffled with preternatural riddles. The agitation of his mind resembles the rolling of the sea in a storm; or, he is like a lion in the toils—fierce, impetuous, and ungovernable. In the fifth act in particular, which is in itself as busy and turbulent as possible, there was not that giddy whirl of the imagination—the character did not burnish out on all sides with those flashes of genius, of which Mr. Kean had given so fine an earnest in the conclusion of his

Richard. The scene stood still—the parts might be perfect in themselves, but they were not joined together; they wanted vitality. The pauses in the speeches were too long—the actor seemed to be studying the part, rather than performing it—striving to make every word more emphatic than the last, and "lost too poorly in himself" instead of being carried away by the grandeur of his subject. The text was not given accurately. Macbeth is represented in the play, arming before the castle, which adds to the interest of the scene.

In the delivery of the beautiful soliloquy, "My way of life is fallen into the sear, the yellow leaf," Mr. Kean was unsuccessful. That fine thoughtful melancholy did not seem to come over his mind, which characterises Mr. Kemble's recitation of these lines. The very tone of Mr. Kemble's voice has something retrospective in it—it is an echo of the past. Mr. Kean in his dress was occasionally too much docked and curtailed for the gravity of the character. His movements were too agile and mercurial, and he fought more like a modern fencing-master than a Scottish chieftain of the eleventh century. He fell at last finely, with his face downwards, as if to cover the shame of his defeat. We recollect that Mr. Cooke discovered the great actor both in the death-scene in *Macbeth*, and in that of *Richard*. He fell like the ruin of a state, like a king with his regalia about him.

The two finest things that Mr. Kean has ever done, are his recitation of the passage in *Othello*, "Then, oh, farewell the tranquil mind," and the scene in *Macbeth* after the murder. The former was the highest and most perfect effort of his art. To inquire whether his manner in the latter scene was that of a king who commits a murder, or of a man who commits a murder to become a king, would be "to consider too curiously." But, as a lesson of common humanity, it was heartrending. The hesitation, the bewildered look, the coming to himself when he sees his hands bloody; the manner in which his voice clung to his throat, and choked his utterance, his agony and tears, the force of nature overcome by passion—beggared description. It was a scene which no one who saw it can ever efface from his recollection.

MR. KEAN'S ROMEO

Champion, January 8, 1815

MR. KEAN appeared at Drury Lane in the character of Romeo, for the first time on Monday last. The house was crowded at an early hour, and neither those who went to admire, nor those who went to find fault, could go away disappointed. He discovered no new and unlooked-for excellences in the part, but displayed the same extraordinary energies which he never fails to do on every occasion. There is indeed, a set of ingenious persons who, having perceived on Mr. Kean's first appearance that he was a little man with an inharmonious voice, and no very great dignity or elegance of manner, go regularly to the theatre to confirm themselves in this singular piece of sagacity; and finding that the object of their contempt and wonder has not, since they last saw him, "added a cubit to his stature," that his tones have not become "as musical as is Apollo's lute," and that there is still an habitual want of grace about him, are determined, till such a metamorphosis is effected, not to allow a particle of genius to the actor, or of taste or common sense to those who are not stupidly blind to everything but his defects. That an actor with very moderate abilities, having the advantages of voice, person, and gracefulness of manner on his side, should acquire a very high reputation, is what we can understand, and have seen some instances of; but that an actor, with almost every physical disadvantage against him, should, without very extraordinary powers and capacities indeed, be able to excite the most enthusiastic and general admiration, would, we conceive, be a phenomenon in the history of public imposture, totally without example. In fact, the generality of critics who undertake to give the tone to public opinion, have neither the courage nor discernment to decide on the merits of a truly excellent and original actor, and are equally without the candour to acknowledge their error, after they find themselves in the wrong.

In going to see Mr. Kean in any new character, we do not go in the expectation of seeing either a perfect actor or perfect acting; because this is what we have not yet seen, either in him or in anyone else. But we go to see (what he never disappoints us in) great spirit, ingenuity, and originality given to the text in general, and an energy and depth of passion given to certain scenes and passages, which we should in vain look for from any other actor on the stage. In every character that he has played, in Shylock, in Richard, in Hamlet, in Othello, in Iago, in Luke,[1] and in Macbeth, there has been either a dazzling repetition of master-strokes of art and nature, or if at any time (from a want of physical adaptation, or sometimes of just conception of the character) the interest has flagged for a considerable interval, the deficiency has always been redeemed by some collected and overpowering display of energy or pathos, which electrified at the moment, and left a lasting impression on the mind afterwards. Such, for instance, were the murder-scene in *Macbeth*, the third act of his Othello, the interview with Ophelia in *Hamlet*, and, lastly, the scene with Friar Lawrence, and the death-scene in *Romeo*.

Of the characters that Mr. Kean has played, Hamlet and Romeo are the most like one another, at least, in adventitious circumstances; those to which Mr. Kean's

[1] In *Riches*, Sir J. B. Burgess's alteration of Massinger's *City Madam*.

powers are least adapted, and in which he has failed
most in general truth of conception and continued interest. There is in both characters the same strong
tincture of youthful enthusiasm, of tender melancholy,
of romantic thought and sentiment; but we confess we
did not see these qualities in Mr. Kean's performance
of either. His Romeo had nothing of the lover in it.
We never saw anything less ardent or less voluptuous.
In the Balcony scene in particular, he was cold, tame
and unimpressive. It was said of Garrick and Barry
in this scene, that the one acted it as if he would jump
up to the lady, and the other as if he would make the
lady jump down to him. Mr. Kean produced neither
of these effects. He stood like a statue of lead. Even
Mr. Conway might feel taller on the occasion, and
Mr. Coates[2] wonder at the taste of the public. The
only time in this scene when he attempted to give anything like an effect, was when he smiled on overhearing Juliet's confession of her passion. But the
smile was less like that of a fortunate lover, who un-
expectedly hears his happiness confirmed, than of a
discarded lover, who hears of the disappointment of
a rival. The whole of this part not only wanted "the
silver sound of lovers' tongues by night" to recommend it, but warmth, tenderness, everything which it
should have possessed. Mr. Kean was like a man waiting to receive a message from his mistress through her
confidante, not like one who was pouring out his rapturous vows to the idol of his soul. There was neither
glowing animation, nor melting softness in his manner;
his cheek was not flushed, no sigh breathed involuntary from his overcharged bosom; all was forced and
lifeless. His acting sometimes reminded us of the scene
with Lady Anne, and we cannot say a worse thing of
it, considering the difference of the two characters.

[2] Conway, whose gigantic height is cruelly harped on by
Hazlitt, was a passable Romeo, and Coates was the notorious
"Amateur of Fashion," who exhibited himself in the part.

Mr. Kean's imagination appears not to have the principles of joy or hope or love in it. He seems chiefly
sensible to pain, or to the passions that spring from it,
and to the terrible energies of mind or body, which
are necessary to grapple with or to avert it. Even over
the world of passion he holds but a divided sway;
he either does not feel, or seldom expresses, deep, sustained, internal sentiment,—there is no repose in his
mind; no feeling seems to take full possession of it,
that is not linked to action, and that does not goad
him on to the frenzy of despair. Or if he ever conveys the sublimer pathos of thought and feeling, it is
after the storm of passion, to which he has been
worked up, has subsided. The tide of feeling then at
time rolls deep, majestic, and awful, like the surging
sea after a tempest, now lifted to heaven, now laying
bare the bosom of the deep. Thus after the violence
and anguish of the scene with Iago, in the third act of
Othello, his voice in the farewell apostrophe to
Content, took the deep intonation of the pealing organ, and heaved from the heart sounds that came on
the ear like the funeral dirge of years of promised happiness. So in the midst of the extravagant and irresistible expression of Romeo's grief, at being banished
from the object of his love, his voice suddenly stops
and falters, and is choked with sobs of tenderness
when he comes to Juliet's name. Those persons must
be made of sterner stuff than ourselves, who are proof
against Mr. Kean's acting, both in this scene, and in
his dying convulsion at the close of the play. But in
the fine soliloquy beginning, "What said my man,
when my betossed soul," &c.—and at the tomb afterwards—

> O, here
> Will I set up my everlasting rest,
> And shake the yoke of inauspicious stars
> From this world-wearied flesh.

in these, where the sentiment is subdued and profound, and the passion is lost in calm, fixed despair, Mr. Kean's acting was comparatively ineffectual. There was nothing in his manner of delivering this last exquisitively beautiful speech, which echoed to the still sad music of humanity,[3] which recalled past hopes, or reposed on the dim shadowings of futurity.

Mr. Kean affects the audience from the force of passion instead of sentiment, or sinks into pathos from the violence of action, but seldom rises into it from the power of thought and feeling. In this respect, he presents almost a direct contrast to Miss O'Neill. Her energy always arises out of her sensibility. Distress takes possession of, and overcomes her faculties; she triumphs in her weakness, and vanquishes by yielding. Mr. Kean is greatest in the conflict of passion, and resistance to his fate, in the opposition of his will, in the keen excitement of his understanding. His Romeo is, in the best scenes, very superior to Miss O'Neill's Juliet; but it is with some difficulty, and after some reflection, that we should say that the finest parts of his acting are superior to the finest parts of hers—to her parting with Jaffier in Belvidera—to her terror and her joy in meeting with Biron, in *Isabella*—to the death-scene in the same character, and to the scene in the prison with her husband as Mrs. Beverley.[4] Her acting is undoubtedly more correct, equable, and faultless throughout than Mr. Kean's, and it is quite as affecting at the time, in the most impassioned parts. But it does not leave the same impression on the mind afterwards. It adds little to the stock of our ideas, or to our materials for reflection, but passes away with

[3] Is this quotation from *Tintern Abbey* conscious or unconscious? In the former case, it seems odd that Hazlitt should have omitted the quotation marks, for, though the poem had been published for fifteen years, the line could scarcely have been, at that time, one which every reader would recognise.

[4] In *The Gamester*.

the momentary illusion of the scene. And this difference of effect, perhaps, arises from the difference of the parts they have to sustain on the stage. In the female characters which Miss O'Neill plays, the distress is in a great measure physical and natural; that is, such as is common to every sensible woman in similar circumstances. She abandons herself to every impulse of grief or tenderness, and revels in the excess of an uncontrollable affliction. She can call to her aid, with perfect propriety and effect, all the weaknesses of her sex—tears, sighs, convulsive sobs, shrieks, death-like stupefaction, and laughter more terrible than all. But it is not the same in the parts in which Mr. Kean has to act. There must here be a manly fortitude, as well as a natural sensibility. There must be a restraint constantly put upon the feelings by the understanding and the will. He must be "as one, in suffering all, who suffers nothing." He cannot give way entirely to his situation or his feelings, but must endeavour to become master of them and of himself. This, in our conception, must make it more easy to give entire effect and interest to female characters on the stage, by rendering the expression of passion more obvious, simple, and natural; and must also make them less rememberable afterwards, by leaving less scope for the exercise of intellect, and for the distinct and complicated reaction of the character upon circumstances. At least, we can only account in some such way for the different impressions which the acting of these two admired performers makes on our mind, when we see, or when we think of them. As critics, we particularly feel this. Mr. Kean affords a never-failing source of observation and discussion; we can only *praise* Miss O'Neill. The peculiarity and the strong hold of Mrs. Siddons' acting was that she, in a wonderful manner, united both the extremes of acting here spoken of—that is, all the frailties of passion, with all the strength and resources of the intellect.

MR. KEAN'S IAGO

I

Examiner, July 24, 1814
WE regretted some time ago that we could only get a
casual glimpse of Mr. Kean in the character of Iago;
we have since been more fortunate, and we certainly
think his performance of the part one of the most extraordinary exhibitions on the stage. There is no one
within our remembrance, who has so completely
foiled the critics as this celebrated actor: one sagacious
person imagines that he must perform a part in a certain manner; another virtuoso chalks out a different
path for him; and when the time comes, he does the
whole off in a way that neither of them had the least
conception of, and which both of them are therefore
very ready to condemn as entirely wrong. It was ever
the trick of genius to be thus. We confess that Mr.
Kean has thrown us out more than once. For instance,
we are very much inclined to persist in the objection
we before made, that his Richard is not gay enough,
and that his Iago is not grave enough. This he may
perhaps conceive to be the mere caprice of captious
criticism; but we will try to give our reasons, and shall
leave them to Mr. Kean's better judgment.

It is to be remembered, then, that Richard was a
princely villain, borne along in a sort of triumphal car
of royal state, buoyed up with the hopes and privileges
of his birth, reposing even on the sanctity of religion,
trampling on his devoted victims without remorse, and
who looked out and laughed from the high watch-
tower of his confidence and his expectations, on the
desolation and misery he had caused around him. He
held on his way, unquestioned, "hedged in with the
divinity of kings," amenable to no tribunal, and abus-
ing his power *in contempt of mankind*. But as for

Iago, we conceive differently of him. He had not the same natural advantages. He was a mere adventurer in mischief, a painstaking, plodding knave, without patent or pedigree, who was obliged to work his uphill way by wit, not by will, and to be the founder of his own fortune. He was, if we may be allowed a vulgar allusion, a true prototype of modern Jacobinism, who thought that talents ought to decide the place; a man of "morbid sensibility" (in the fashionable phrase) full of distrust, of hatred, of anxious and corroding thoughts, and who, though he might assume a temporary superiority over others by superior adroitness, and pride himself in his skill, could not be supposed to assume it as a matter of course, as if he had been entitled to it from his birth.

We do not here mean to enter into the characters of the two men, but something must be allowed to the difference of their situations. There might be the same indifference in both as to the end in view, but there could not well be the same security as to the success of the means. Iago had to pass through a different ordeal; he had no appliances and means to boot; no royal road to the completion of his tragedy. His pretensions were not backed by authority; they were not baptised at the font; they were not holy-water proof. He had the whole to answer for in his own person, and could not shift the responsibility to the heads of others. Mr. Kean's Richard was therefore, we think, deficient in something of that regal jollity and reeling triumph of success which the part would bear; but this we can easily account for, because it is the traditional common-place idea of the character, that he is to "play the dog—to bite and snarl." The extreme unconcern and laboured levity of his Iago, on the contrary, is a refinement and original device of the actor's own mind, and deserves a distinct consideration. The character of Iago, in fact, belongs to a class of characters common to Shakespeare, and at the same time pecul-

iar to him, namely, that of great intellectual activity,
accompanied with a total want of moral principle, and
therefore displaying itself at the constant expense of
others, making use of reason as a pander to will—em-
ploying its ingenuity and its resources to palliate its
own crimes, and aggravate the faults of others, and
seeking to confound the practical distinctions of right
and, wrong, by referring them to some overstrained
standard of speculative refinement.

Some persons, more nice than wise, have thought
the whole of the character of Iago unnatural.
Shakespeare, who was quite as good a philosopher as
he was a poet, thought otherwise. He knew that the
love of power, which is another name for the love of
mischief, was natural to man. He would know this as
well or better than if it had been demonstrated to him
by a logical diagram, merely from seeing children
paddle in the dirt, or kill flies for sport. We might ask
those who think the character of Iago not natural,
why they go to see it performed, but from the interest it excites, the sharper edge which it sets on their
curiosity and imagination. Why do we go to see
tragedies in general? Why do we always read the accounts in the newpapers of dreadful fires and shocking
murders, but for the same reason? Why do so many
persons frequent executions and trials; or why do the
lower classes almost universally take delight in barbarous sports and cruelty to animals, but because there
is a natural tendency in the mind to strong excitement,
a desire to have its faculties roused and stimulated to
the utmost? Whenever this principle is not under the
restraint of humanity, or the sense of moral obligation,
there are no excesses to which it will not of itself give
rise, without the assistance of any other motive, either
of passion or self-interest. Iago is only an extreme instance of the kind; that is, of diseased intellectual activity, with an almost perfect indifference to moral
good or evil, or rather with the preference of the lat-

ter, because it falls more in with his favourite propensity, gives greater zest to his thoughts and scope to his actions. Be it observed, too (for the sake of those who are for squaring all human actions by the maxims of La Rochefoucauld), that he is quite or nearly as indifferent to his own fate as to that of others; that he runs all risks for a trifling and doubtful advantage; and is himself the dupe and victim of his ruling passion—an incorrigible love of mischief—an insatiable craving after action of the most difficult and dangerous kind. Our ancient is a philosopher who fancies that a lie that kills has more point in it than an alliteration or an antithesis; who thinks a fatal experiment on the peace of a family a better thing than watching the palpitations in the heart of a flea in an air-pump; who plots the ruin of his friends as an exercise for his understanding, and stabs men in the dark to prevent *ennui*. Now this, though it be sport, yet it is dreadful sport. There is no room for trifling and indifference, nor scarcely for the appearance of it; the very object of his whole plot is to keep his faculties stretched on the rack, in a state of watch and ward, in a sort of breathless suspense, without a moment's interval of repose. He has a desperate stake to play for, like a man who fences with poisoned weapons, and has business enough on his hands to call for the whole stock of his sober circumspection, his dark duplicity, and insidious gravity. He resembles a man who sits down to play at chess, for the sake of the difficulty and complication of the game, and who immediately becomes absorbed in it. His amusements, if they are amusements, are severe and saturnine—even his wit blisters. His gaiety arises from the success of his treachery; his ease from the sense of the torture he has inflicted on others. Even if other circumstances permitted it, the part he has to play with Othello requires that he should assume the most serious concern, and something of the plausibility of a confessor. "His cue is

villanous melancholy, with a sigh like Tom o'
Bedlam." He is repeatedly called "honest Iago,"
which looks as if there were something suspicious in
his appearance, which admitted a different construction. The tone which he adopts in the scenes with
Roderigo, Desdemona, and Cassio, is only a relaxation
from the more arduous business of the play. Yet there
is in all his conversation an inveterate misanthropy, a
licentious keenness of perception, which is always
sagacious of evil, and snuffs up the tainted scent of its
quarry with rancorous delight. An exuberance of
spleen is the essence of the character. The view which
we have here taken of the subject (if at all correct)
will not therefore justify the extreme alteration which
Mr. Kean has introduced into the part.

Actors in general have been struck only with the
wickedness of the character, and have exhibited an
assassin going to the place of execution. Mr. Kean has
abstracted the wit of the character, and makes Iago
appear throughout an excellent good fellow, and lively
bottle-companion. But though we do not wish him
to be represented as a monster, or a fiend, we see no
reason why he should instantly be converted into a
pattern of comic gaiety and good humour. The light
which illumines the character should rather resemble
the flashes of lightning in the mirky sky, which make
the darkness more terrible. Mr. Kean's Iago is, we
suspect, too much in the sun. His manner of acting the
part would have suited better with the character of
Edmund in *King Lear*, who, though in other respects
much the same, has a spice of gallantry in his constitution, and has the favour and countenance of the
ladies, which always gives a man the smug appearance
of a bridegroom! We shall in another article, illustrate
these remarks by a reference to some passages in the
text itself.

II

Examiner, August 7, 1814

THE general groundwork of the character of Iago, as it appears to us, is not absolute malignity, but a want of moral principle, or an indifference to the real consequences of the actions, which the meddling perversity of his disposition and love of immediate excitement lead him to commit. He is an amateur of tragedy in real life; and instead of exercising his ingenuity on imaginary characters, or forgotten incidents, he takes the bolder and more desperate course of getting up his plot at home, casts the principal parts among his nearest friends and connections, and rehearses it in downright earnest, with steady nerves and unabated resolution. The character is a complete abstraction of the intellectual from the moral being; or, in other words, consists in an absorption of every common feeling in the virulence of his understanding, the deliberate wilfulness of his purposes, and in his restless, untameable love of mischievous contrivance. We proceed to quote. some particular passages in support of this opinion.

In the general dialogue and reflections, which are an accompaniment to the progress of the catastrophe, there is a constant overflowing of gall and bitterness. The acuteness of his malice fastens upon everything alike, and pursues the most distant analogies of evil with a provoking sagacity. He by no means forms an exception to his own rule:—

> who has a breast so pure
> But some uncleanly apprehensions
> Keep leets and law days, and in sessions sit
> With meditations lawful?

His mirth is not natural and cheerful, but forced and extravagant, partaking of the intense activity of mind and cynical contempt of others in which it originates. Iago is not, like Candide, a believer in op-

timism, but seems to have a thorough hatred or distrust
of everything of the kind, and to dwell with gloating
satisfaction on whatever can interrupt the enjoyment
of others, and gratify his moody irritability. One of his
most characteristic speeches is that immediately after
the marriage of Othello:—

> *Roderigo.* What a full fortune does the thick-lips owe,
> If he can carry 't thus!
>   *Iago.*   Call up her father;
> Rouse him [*Othello*], make after him, poison his delight,
> Proclaim him in the streets, incense her kinsmen,
> And, though he in a fertile climate dwell,
> Plague him with flies; though that his joy be joy,
> Yet throw such changes of vexation on't
> As it may lose some colour.

The pertinacious logical following up of his favourite principle in this passage, is admirable. In the
next, his imagination runs riot in the mischief he is
plotting, and breaks out into the wildness and impetuosity of real enthusiasm:—

> *Roderigo.* Here is her father's house; I'll call aloud.
> *Iago.* Do; with like timorous accent and dire yell
> As when, by night and negligence, the fire
> Is spied in populous cities.

There is nothing here of the trim levity and epigrammatic conciseness of Mr. Kean's manner of acting
the part, which is no less paradoxical than Mrs.
Greville's celebrated Ode to Indifference.[1] Iago was a
man of genius, and not a *petit maître*. One of his most
frequent topics, on which he is rich indeed, and in
descanting on which his spleen serves him for a muse,
is the disproportionate match between Desdemona
and the Moor. This is brought forward in the first
scene, and is never lost sight of afterwards.

[1] An illusion to Mrs. Frances Greville's poem, *Prayer for
Indifference*, published about 1753.

Brabantio. What is the reason of this terrible summons?

. . . .

Iago. 'Zounds! sir, you're robb'd; for shame, put on your
    gown;
Your heart is burst, you have lost half your soul;
. . . . Arise, arise!
Awake the snorting citizens with the bell,
Or else the devil will make a grandsire of you.
Arise, I say.—[*And so on to the end of the passage*].

Now, all this goes on springs well oiled: Mr. Kean's
mode of giving the passage had the tightness of a
drumhead, and was muffled (perhaps purposely so)
into the bargain.

This is a clue to the character of the lady which Iago
is not at all ready to part with. He recurs to it again in
the second act, when in answer to his insinuations
against Desdemona, Roderigo says—

I cannot believe that in her; she is full of most blessed
    condition.
    Iago. Blessed fig's end! the wine she drinks is made of
        grapes; if she had been blessed she would never
        have loved the Moor;

And again, with still more effect and spirit afterwards, when he takes advantage of this very sug-
gestion arising in Othello's own breast:—

    Othello. And, yet, how nature erring from itself—
    Iago. Ay, there's the point: as, to be bold with you,
Not to affect many proposed matches
Of her own clime, complexion, and degree,
Whereto, we see, in all things nature tends;
Foh! one may smell in such, a will most rank,
Foul disproportion, thoughts unnatural.

This is probing to the quick. "Our Ancient" here
turns the character of poor Desdemona, as it were,
inside out. It is certain that nothing but the genius of
Shakespeare could have preserved the entire interest
and delicacy of the part, and have even drawn an ad-

ditional elegance and dignity from the peculiar circumstances in which she is placed. The character indeed has always had the greatest charm for minds of
the finest sensibility.

For our own part, we are a little of Iago's council in
this matter; and all circumstances considered, and
platonics out of the question, if we were to cast the
complexion of Desdemona physiognomically, we
should say that she had a very fair skin, and very
light auburn hair, inclining to yellow! We at the same
time give her infinite credit for purity and delicacy
of sentiment, but it so happens that purity and grossness sometimes

> —nearly are allied,
> And thin partitions do their bound divide.

Yet the reverse does not hold; so uncertain and undefinable a thing is moral character! It is no wonder that
Iago had some contempt for it, "who knew all quan-
tities of human dealings, with a learned spirit." [2] There
is considerable gaiety and ease in his dialogue with
Emilia and Desdemona on their landing. It is then holi-
day time with him; but yet the general satire will be
acknowledged (at least by one half of our readers) to
be biting enough, and his idea of his own character is
finely expressed in what he says to Desdemona, when
she asks him how he would praise her—

> O gentle lady, do not put me to 't,
> For I am nothing if not critical.

Mr. Kean's execution of this part we thought admirable; but he was quite as much at his ease in every
other part of the play, which was done (we know not
why) in a single key.

[2] So in original. What Othello says is—
> This fellow's of exceeding honesty,
> And knows all qualities, with a learned spirit,
> Of human dealings. . . .

The habitual licentiousness of Iago's conversation is not to be traced to the pleasure he takes in gross or lascivious images, but to a desire of finding out the worst side of everything, and of proving himself an over-match for appearances. He has none of "the milk of human kindness" in his composition. His imagination refuses everything that has not a strong infusion of the most unpalatable ingredients, and his moral constitution digests only poisons. Virtue, or goodness, or whatever has the least "relish of salvation in it," is, to his depraved appetite, sickly and insipid; and he even resents the good opinion entertained of his own integrity, as if it were an affront cast on the masculine sense and spirit of his character. Thus, at the meeting between Othello and Desdemona, he exclaims—"Oh, you are well tuned now: but I'll set down the pegs that make this music, *as honest as I am*" —deriving an indirect triumph over the want of penetration in others from the consciousness of his own villainy.

In most of the passages which we have hitherto quoted, Iago gives a loose to his passion for theoretical evil: in the scenes with Othello, where he has to put his theory in practice, with great risk to himself, and with dreadful consequences to others, he is proportionably guarded, insidious, dark and deliberate. In the very first scene with Othello, he takes a very different tone;—that tone of hypocritical virtue and affected delicacy, which always betrays the want of the reality.

Enter OTHELLO, IAGO, *and* Attendants.

Iago. Though in the trade of war I have slain men,
Yet do I hold it very stuff o' the conscience
To do no contriv'd murder: I lack iniquity
Sometimes to do me service. Nine or ten times
I had thought to have yerk'd him here under the ribs.
   Othello. 'Tis better as it is.
   Iago.   Nay, but he prated,
And spoke such scurvy and provoking terms

Against your honour
That, with the little godliness I have,
I did full hard forbear him. . . .

But the part in which, according to our conception,
Mr. Kean failed most, was in the third act with
Othello, where "comes the tug of war." The following
passage is, we think, decisive to our purpose:—

Iago. My noble lord,—
Othello. What dost thou say, Iago?
Iago. Did Michael Cassio, when you woo'd my lady,
Know of your love?
Othello. He did from first to last: why dost thou ask?
Iago. But for a satisfaction of my thought;
No further harm.
Othello. Why of thy thought, Iago?
Iago. I did not think he had been acquainted with her.
Othello. O! yes; and went between us very oft.
Iago. Indeed!
Othello. Indeed! ay, indeed; discern'st thou aught in
     that?
Is he not honest?
Iago. Honest, my lord?
Othello. Honest! ay, honest.
Iago. My lord, for aught I know.
Othello. What dost thou think?
Iago. Think, my lord!
Othello. Think, my lord! By heaven, he echoes me,
As if there were some monster in his thought
Too hideous to be shown. Thou dost mean something:
I heard thee say but now, thou lik'dst not that,
When Cassio left my wife; what did'st not like?
And when I told thee he was of my counsel
In my whole course of wooing, thou criedst, 'Indeed!'
And didst contract and purse thy brow together,
As if thou then hadst shut up in thy brain
Some horrible conceit. If thou dost love me,
Show me thy thought.
Iago. My lord, you know I love you.
Othello. I think thou dost;

And, for I know thou art full of love and honesty,
And weigh'st thy words before thou giv'st them breath,
Therefore these stops of thine fright me the more;
For such things in a false disloyal knave
Are tricks of custom, but in a man that's just
They are close delations, working from the heart
Which passion cannot rule.

Now, if there is anything of superficial gaiety or heedlessness in this, "it is not written in the bond."—the breaks and stops, the pursing and knitting of the brow together, the deep internal working of hypocrisy under the mask of love and honesty, escaped us on the stage. The same observation applies to what he says afterwards of himself:—

Though I perchance am vicious in my guess,—
As, I confess, it is my nature's plague
To spy into abuses, and oft my jealousy
Shapes faults that are not,—

The candour of this confession would hardly be extorted from him, if it did not correspond with the moody dissatisfaction, and suspicious, creeping, cat-like watchfulness of his general appearance. The anxious suspense, the deep artifice, the collected earnestness, and, if we may say so, the *passion* of hypocrisy, are decidedly marked in every line of the whole scene, and are worked up to a sort of paroxysm afterwards, in that inimitably characteristic apostrophe:—

O grace! O heaven forgive me!
Are you a man? Have you a soul or sense?
God be wi' you; take mine office. O wretched fool!
That lov'st to make thine honesty a vice.
O monstrous world! Take note, take note, O world!
To be direct and honest is not safe.
I thank you for this profit, and, from hence
I'll love no friend, sith love breeds such offence.

This burst of hypocritical indignation might well have called forth all Mr. Kean's powers, but it did not. We might multiply passages of the same kind, if we had time.

The philosophy of the character is strikingly unfolded in the part where Iago gets the handkerchief:—

>   .   .   .   .   this may do something.
> The Moor already changes with my poisons,
> Which at the first are scarce found to distaste,[3]
> But with a little act upon the blood,
> Burn like the mines of sulphur. . . .

We here find him watching the success of his experiment, with the sanguine anticipation of an alchemist at the moment of projection.

>   —I did say so:
> Look! where he comes! [*Enter* OTHELLO]. Not poppy, nor
>   mandragora,
> Nor all the drowsy syrups of the world,
> Shall ever medicine thee to that sweet sleep
> Which thou ow'dst yesterday.

Again he says:—

>   —Work on,
> My medicine, work! Thus credulous fools are caught;
> And many worthy and chaste dames even thus,
> All guiltless, meet reproach.

So that, after all, he would persuade us that his object is only to give an instructive example of the injustice that prevails in the world.

If he is bad enough when he has business on his hands, he is still worse when his purposes are suspended, and he has only to reflect on the misery he has occasioned. His indifference when Othello falls in a trance, is perfectly diabolical, but perfectly in character:—

[3] This passage should read—
> The Moor already changes with my poison:—
> Dangerous conceits are in their natures poisons,
> Which at the first &c.

Iago. How is it, general? have you not hurt your head?
Othello. Dost thou mock me?
Iago. I mock you! no, by heaven, &c.

The callous levity which Mr. Kean seems to consider as belonging to the character in general, is
proper here, because Iago has no feelings connected
with humanity; but he has other feelings and other
passions of his own, which are not to be trifled with.

We do not, however, approve of Mr. Kean's pointing to the dead bodies after the catastrophe. It is not
in the character of the part, which consists in the love
of mischief, not as an end, but as a means, and when
that end is attained, though he may feel no remorse,
he would feel no triumph. Besides, it is not the text of
Shakespeare. Iago does not point to the bed, but
Ludovico bids him look at it: "Look on the tragic
loading of this bed," &c.

We have already noticed that Edmund the Bastard
is like an episode of the same character, placed in less
difficult circumstances. Zanga⁴ is a vulgar caricature
of it.

MR. KEAN'S RICHARD II

Examiner, March 19, 1815

WE are not in the number of those who are anxious in
recommending the getting-up of Shakespeare's plays
in general, as a duty which our stage-managers owe
equally to the author and the reader of those wonderful compositions. The representing the very finest of
them on the stage, even by the best actors, is, we apprehend, an abuse of the genius of the poet, and even
in those of a second-rate class, the quantity of sentiment and imagery greatly outweighs the immediate
impression of the situation and story. Not only are
the more refined poetical beauties and minuter strokes

⁴ In Young's tragedy, *The Revenge*.

of character lost to the audience, but the most striking
and impressive passages, those which having once read
we can never forget, fail comparatively of their effect,
except in one or two rare instances indeed. It is only
the *pantomime* part of tragedy, the exhibition of immediate and physical distress, that which gives the
greatest opportunity for "inexpressible dumb-show
and noise," which is sure to tell, and tell completely,
on the stage. All the rest, all that appeals to our pro-
founder feelings, to reflection and imagination, all that
affects us most deeply in our closets, and in fact constitutes the glory of Shakespeare, is little else than an
interruption and a drag on the business of the stage.
Segnius peraures demissa, &c.[1] Those parts of the play
on which the reader dwells the longest, and with the
highest relish in the perusal, are hurried through in
the performance, while the most trifling and excep-
tionable are obtruded on his notice, and occupy as
much time as the most important. We do not mean to
say that there is less knowledge or display of mere
stage-effect in Shakespeare than in other writers, but
that there is a much greater knowledge and display of
other things, which divide the attention with it, and
to which it is not possible to give an equal force in the
representation. Hence it is, that the reader of the
plays of Shakespeare is almost always disappointed in
seeing them acted; and, for our own parts, we should
never go to see them acted, if we could help it.

Shakespeare has embodied his characters so very distinctly, that he stands in no need of the actor's
assistance to make them more distinct; and the representation of the character on the stage almost uni-

---

[1] Segnius irritant animos demissa per aurem,
Quam quæ sunt oculis subjecta fidelibus, et quæ
Ipse sibi tradit spectator.—HORACE, *Ars Poetica*.
A thing when heard, remember, strikes less keen
On the spectator's mind than 'tis seen.
                                        CONINGTON.

formly interferes with our conception of the character itself. The only exceptions we can recollect to this observation, are Mrs. Siddons and Mr. Kean—the former of whom in one or two characters, and the latter, not certainly in any one character, but in very many passages, have raised our imagination of the part they acted. It may be asked, then, why all great actors choose characters from Shakespeare to come out in; and again, why these become their favourite parts? First, it is not that they are able to exhibit their author, but that he enables them to show themselves off. The only way in which Shakespeare appears to greater advantage on the stage than common writers is, that he stimulates the faculties of the actor more. If he is a sensible man, he perceives how much he has to do, the inequalities he has to contend with, and he exerts himself accordingly; he puts himself at full speed, and lays all his resources under contribution; he attempts more, and makes a greater number of brilliant failures; he plays off all the tracks of his art to mimic the poet; he does all he can, and bad is often the best. We have before said that there are some few exceptions. If the genius of Shakespeare does not shine out undiminished in the actor, we perceive certain effects and refractions of it in him. If the oracle does not speak quite intelligibly, yet we perceive that the priest at the altar is inspired with the god, or possessed with a demon. To speak our minds at once, we believe that in acting Shakespeare there is a greater number of good things marred than in acting any other author. In fact, in going to see the plays of Shakespeare, it would be ridiculous to suppose that anyone ever went to see Hamlet or Othello represented by Kean or Kemble; we go to see Kean or Kemble in *Hamlet* or *Othello*. On the contrary, Miss O'Neill and Mrs. Beverley are, we take it, one and the same person. As to the second point, viz., that Shakespeare's characters are decidedly favourites on the stage in the same proportion as they

are in the closet, we deny it altogether. They either
do not tell so much, or very little more than many
others. Mrs. Siddons was quite as great in Mrs. Beverley
and Isabella[2] as in Lady Macbeth or Queen Katherine;
yet no one, we apprehend, will say that the poetry is
equal. It appears, therefore, not that the most intellectual characters excite most interest on the stage, but
that they are objects of greater curiosity; they are
nicer tests of the skill of the actor, and afford greater
scope for controversy, how far the sentiment is "overdone or come tardy off." There is more in this circumstance than people in general are aware of. We
have no hesitation in saying, for instance, that Miss
O'Neill has more popularity *in the house* than Mr.
Kean. It is quite as certain that he is more thought of
out of it. The reason is, that she is not "food for the
critics," whereas Mr. Kean notoriously is; there is no
end of the topics he affords for discussion—for praise
and blame.

All that we have said of acting in general applies to
his Richard II. It has been supposed that this is his
finest part: this is, however, a total misrepresentation.
There are only one or two electrical shocks given in
it; and in many of his characters he gives a much
greater number. The excellence of his acting is in proportion to the number of hits, for he has not equal
truth or purity of style. Richard II. was hardly given
correctly as to the general outline. Mr. Kean made it
a character of *passion*, that is, of feeling combined
with energy; whereas it is a character of *pathos*, that
is to say, of feeling combined with weakness. This,
we conceive, is the general fault of Mr. Kean's acting,
that it is always energetic or nothing. He is always
on full stretch—never relaxed. He expresses all the
violence, the extravagance and fierceness of the passions, but not their misgivings, their helplessness, and
sinkings into despair. He has too much of that strong

[2] Southerne's, not Shakespeare's.

nerve and fibre that is always equally elastic. We might instance to the present purpose his dashing the glass down with all his might in the scene with Hereford, instead of letting it fall out of his hands, as from an infant's; also, his manner of expostulating with Bolingbroke, "Why on thy knee, thus low," &c., which was altogether fierce and heroic, instead of being sad, thoughtful, and melancholy. If Mr. Kean would look into some passages in this play into that in particular, "Oh that I were a mockery king of snow, to melt away before the sun of Bolingbroke," he would find a clue to this character, and to human nature in general, which he seems to have missed—how far feeling is connected with the sense of weakness as well as of strength, or the power of imbecility, and the force of passiveness.

We never saw Mr. Kean look better than when we saw him in *Richard II.*, and his voice appeared to us to be stronger. We saw him near, which is always in his favour; and we think one reason why the editor of this paper[3] was disappointed in first seeing this celebrated actor, was his being at a considerable distance from the stage. We feel persuaded that on a nearer and more frequent view of him, he will agree that he is a perfectly original, and sometimes a perfectly natural actor; that if his conception is not always just or profound, his execution is masterly; that where he is not the very character he assumes, he makes a most brilliant rehearsal of it; that he never wants energy, ingenuity, and animation, though he is often deficient in dignity, grace, and tenderness; that if he frequently disappoints us in those parts where we expect him to do most, he as frequently surprises us by striking out

[3] Kean's first appearance took place while Leigh Hunt was in prison. On his release he went to see the new star, and published an article (February 26, 1815) in which he confessed himself on the whole disappointed. See *Dramatic Essays: Leigh Hunt*, Introduction, p. xxi.

unexpected beauties of his own; and that the objectionable parts of his acting arise chiefly from the physical impediments he has to overcome.

MR. KEAN'S ZANGA AND ABEL DRUGGER

Examiner, May 28, 1815

MR. KEAN played for his benefit on Wednesday the character of Zanga, in *The Revenge* (which he is to repeat), and character of Abel Drugger from *The Alchymist* (we are sorry to say for that night only). The house was crowded to excess. The play of *The Revenge* is an obvious transposition of *Othello:* the two principal characters are the same, only their colours are reversed. The giving the dark, treacherous, fierce, and remorseless character to the Moor, is an alteration which is more in conformity to our prejudices, as well as to historical truth. We have seen Mr. Kean in no part to which his general style of acting is so completely adapted as to this, or to which he has given greater spirit and effect. He had all the wild impetuosity of barbarous revenge, the glowing energy of the untamed children of the sun, whose blood drinks up the radiance of fiercer skies. He was like a man stung with rage, and bursting with stifled passions. His hurried motions had the restlessness of the panther's; his wily caution, his cruel eye, his quivering visage, his violent gestures, his hollow pauses, his abrupt transitions, were all in character. The very vices of Mr. Kean's general acting might almost be said to assist him in the part. What in our judgment he wants, is dignified repose, and deep internal sentiment. But in Zanga nothing of this kind is required. The whole character is violent; the whole expression is in action. The only passage which struck us as one of calm and philosophical grandeur, and in which Mr.

Kean failed from an excess of misplaced energy, was
the one in the conclusion, where he describes the tor-
tures he is about to undergo, and expresses his contempt for them. Certainly the predominant feeling
here is that of stern, collected, impenetrable fortitude,
and the expression given to it should not be that of a
pantomimic exaggeration of the physical horrors to
which he professes to rise superior. The mind in such
a situation recoils upon itself, summons up its own
powers and resources, and should seem to await the
blow of fate with the stillness of death. The scene in
which he discloses himself to Alonzo, and insults over
his misery, was terrific; the attitude in which he tram-
ples on the body of his prostrate victim, was not the
less dreadful from its being perfectly beautiful.
Among the finest instances of natural expression, were
the manner in which he interrupts himself in his rela-
tion to Alonzo, "I knew you could not bear it," and
his reflection when he sees that Alonzo is dead—"And
so is my revenge." The play should end here; the
soliloquy afterwards is a mere drawling piece of commonplace morality.

Mr. Kean's Abel Drugger was an exquisite piece of
ludicrous *naïveté*. The first word he utters, "*Sure,*"
drew bursts of laughter and applause. The mixture of
simplicity and cunning in the character could not be
given with a more whimsical effect. First, there was
the wonder of the poor Tobacconist, when he is told
by the Conjurer that his name is Abel, and that he was
born on a Wednesday; then the conflict between his
apprehensions and his cupidity, as he becomes more
convinced that Subtle is a person who has dealings
with the devil; and lastly, his contrivances to get all
the information he can without paying for it. His distress is at the height when the two-guinea pocket-piece
is found upon him: "He had received it from his
grandmother, and would fain save it for his grand-

children." The battle between him and Face
(Oxberry) was irresistible; and he went off after he
had got well through it, strutting and fluttering his
cloak about, much in the same manner that a game-
cock flaps his wings after a victory. We wish he would
do it again!

THE TEMPEST

Examiner, July 3, 1815
As WE returned some evenings ago from seeing the
Tempest at Covent Garden, we almost came to the
resolution of never going to another representation of
a play of Shakespeare's as long as we lived; and we
certainly did come to this determination, that we
never would go *by choice*. To call it a representation
is, indeed, an abuse of language: it is travesty,
caricature, anything you please but a representation.
Even those daubs of pictures, formerly exhibited under the title of the Shakespeare Gallery, had a less evident tendency to disturb and distort all the previous
notions we had imbibed from reading Shakespeare. In
the first place, it was thought fit and necessary, in order to gratify the sound sense, the steady, sober judgment, and natural unsophisticated feelings of English-
men a hundred years ago, to modernise the original
play, and to disfigure its simple and beautiful struc-
ture, by loading it with the commonplace, clap-trap
sentiments, artificial contrasts of situations and character, and all the heavy tinsel and affected formality
which Dryden had borrowed from the French school.
And be it observed, further, that these same anom-
alous, unmeaning, vulgar, and ridiculous additions, are
all that *take* in the present farcical representation of
the *Tempest*. The beautiful, the exquisitely beautiful
descriptions in Shakespeare, the still more refined
and more affecting sentiments, are not only not ap-

plauded as they ought to be (what fine murmur of applause should do them justice?)—they are not understood, nor are they even heard. The lips of the actors are seen to move, but the sounds they utter, exciting no corresponding emotions in the breast, are no more distinguished than the repetition of so many cabalistical words. The ears of the audience are not prepared to drink in the music of the poet; or grant that they were, the bitterness of disappointment would only succeed to the stupor of indifference.

Shakespeare has given Prospero, Ariel, and the other characters in this play, language such as wizards and spirits, "the gay creatures of the element," might want to express their thoughts and purposes, and this language is here put into the mouth of Messrs. Young, Abbott, and Emery, and of Misses Matthews, Bristow, and Booth. " 'Tis much." Mr. Young is in general what is called a respectable actor. Now, as this is a phrase which does not seem to be very clearly understood by those who most frequently use it, we shall take this opportunity to define it. A respectable actor, then, is one who seldom gratifies, and who seldom offends us; who never disappoints us, because we do not expect anything from him, and who takes care never to rouse our dormant admiration by any unlooked-for strokes of excellence. In short, an actor of this class (not to speak it profanely) is a mere machine, who walks and speaks his part; who, having a tolerable voice, face, and figure, reposes entirely and with a prepossessing self-complacency on these natural advantages; who never risks a failure because he never makes an effort; who keeps on the safe side of custom and decorum, without attempting improper liberties with his art; and who has not genius or spirit enough to do either well or ill. A respectable actor is on the stage, much what a pretty woman is in private life, who trusts to her outward attractions, and does not commit her taste or understanding by hazardous attempts to shine in conver-

sation. So we have generals, who leave everything to
be done by their men; patriots, whose reputation depends on their estates; and authors, who live on the
stock of ideas they have in common with their readers.

Such is the best account we can give of the class of
actors to which Mr. Young belongs, and of which he
forms a principal ornament. As long as he contents
himself to play indifferent characters, we shall say
nothing; but whenever he plays Shakespeare, we must
be excused if we take unequal revenge for the martyrdom which our feelings suffer. His Prospero was good
for nothing; and, consequently, was indescribably bad.
It was grave without solemnity, stately without dignity, pompous without being impressive, and totally
destitute of the wild, mysterious, preternatural character of the original. Prospero, as depicted by Mr.
Young, did not appear the potent wizard brooding
in gloomy abstraction over the secrets of his art, and
around whom spirits and airy shapes throng numberless "at his bidding"; but seemed himself an autom-
ation, stupidly prompted by others: his lips moved
up and down as if pulled by wires, not governed by
the deep and varied impulses of passion; and his
painted face, and snowy hair and beard, reminded us
of the masks for the representation of Pantaloon. In a
word, Mr. Young did not personate Prospero, but a
pedagogue teaching his scholars how to recite the
part, and not teaching them well.

Of one of the actors who assisted at this sacrifice of
poetical genius, Emery, we think as highly as anyone
can do: he is indeed, in his way, the most perfect actor
on the stage. His representations of common rustic life
have an absolute identity with the thing represented.
But the power of his mind is evidently that of imitation, not that of creation. He has nothing romantic,
grotesque, or imaginary about him. Everything in his
hands takes a local and habitual shape. Now, Caliban
is a mere creation; one of the wildest and most ab-

stracted of all Shakespeare's characters, whose deformity is only redeemed by the power and truth of the imagination displayed in it. It is the essence of grossness, but there is not the smallest vulgarity in it. Shakespeare has described the brutal mind of this man-monster in contact with the pure and original forms of nature; the character grows out of the soil where it is rooted, uncontrolled, uncouth, and wild, uncramped by any of the meannesses of custom. It is quite remote from anything provincial; from the manners or dialect of any country in England. Mr. Emery had nothing of Caliban but his gaberdine, which did not become him. (We liked Mr. Grimaldi's Orson[1] much better, which we saw afterwards in the pantomime.) Shakespeare has, by a process of imagination usual with him, drawn off from Caliban the elements of everything ethereal and refined, to compound them into the unearthly mould of Ariel. Nothing was ever more finely conceived than this contrast between the material and the spiritual, the gross and delicate. Miss Matthews played and sang Ariel. She is, to be sure, a very "tricksy spirit"; and all that we can say in her praise is, that she is a better representative of the sylphlike form of the character than the light and portable Mrs. Bland,[2] who used formerly to play it. She certainly does not sing the songs so well. We do not, however, wish to hear them sung, though never so well; no music can add anything to their magical effect. The words of Shakespeare would be sweet, even "after the songs of Apollo!"

[1] In Dibdin's melodrama of *Valentine and Orson*. Grimaldi first played the part at Covent Garden in October, 1806, and made a great success in it.

[2] Mrs. Bland (retired 1824) was rather corpulent, and must have been a very substantial Ariel. But she was a magnificent singer.

THE SCHOOL FOR SCANDAL

Examiner, October 15, 1815
WHY can we not always be young, and seeing *The
School for Scandal?* This play used to be one of our
great theatrical treats in our early play-going days.
What would we not give to see it once more, as it
was then acted, and with the same feelings with which
we saw it then? Not one of our favourites is left,
except little Simmons, who only served to put us in
mind more strongly of what we have lost! Genteel
comedy cannot be acted at present. Little Moses, the
money-lender, was within a hair's-breadth of being
the only person in the piece who had the appearance
or manners of a gentleman. There was a *retenu* in the
conduct of his cane and hat, precision of dress and
costume, an idiomatic peculiarity of tone, an exact
propriety both in his gestures and sentiments, which
reminded us of the good old times when everyone
belonged to a marked class in society, and maintained
himself in his characteristic absurdities by a *chevaux-
de-frise* of prejudices, forms, and ceremonies. Why do
our patriots and politicians rave for ever about the
restoration of the good old times? Till they can persuade the beaux in Bond Street to resume their swords
and bag-wigs, they will never succeed.

When we go to see a comedy of the past age acted
on the modern stage, we, too, almost begin to "cast
some longing, lingering looks behind," at the departed
sword-knots and toupees of the age of Louis XIV. We
never saw a play more completely vulgarised in the
acting than this. What shall we say of Fawcett, who
played Sir Peter Teazle with such formidable breadth
of shoulders and strength of lungs? Or to Mrs. Dobbs,
who made such a pretty, insipid little rustic of Lady
Teazle, showing her teeth like the painted dolls in a
peruke-maker's window? Or to Mrs. Gibbs, who con-

verted the delicacy of Mrs. Candour into the coarseness of a barmaid? Or to Mr. Blanchard, whose face looked so red, and his eyes so fierce, in Old Crabtree, and who seemed to have mistaken one of his stableboys for his nephew, Sir Benjamin? [1] Or (not to speak it profanely) to Mr. Young's Joseph Surface? Never was there a less prepossessing hypocrite. Mr. Young, indeed, puts on a long, disagreeable, whining face, but he does not hide the accomplished, plausible villain beneath it. Jack Palmer[2] was the man. No one ever came to near the idea of what the women call "a fine man." With what an air he trod the stage! With what pomp he handed Lady Teazle to a chair! With what elaborate duplicity he knelt to Maria! Mr. Young ought never to condescend to play comedy, nor aspire to play tragedy. Sentimental pantomime is his forte. Charles Kemble made the best Charles Surface we have seen. He acted this difficult character (difficult because it requires a union of so many requisites, a good face and figure, easy manners, evident good nature, animation and sensibility) in such a way as to make it truly interesting and delightful. The only fault we can find with him is, that he was not well dressed. Mrs. Faucit was respectable in Lady Sneerwell. Mr. Terry, as Sir Oliver Surface, wore a great coat with yellow buttons. Mr. Farley, in Trip, had a large bouquet; and why should we refuse to do justice to Mr. Claremont, who was dressed in black? *The School for Scandal* is one of the best comedies in our language (a language abounding in good comedies), and it deserves either to be well acted, or not acted at all. The wit is inferior to Congreve's, and the allusions much coarser. Its great excellence is in the invention of comic situations,[3] and

[1] Played by Tokely.
[2] The original Joseph Surface, whose personal character was exactly suited to the part.
[3] The scene where the screen falls and discovers Lady Teazle, is without a rival. Perhaps the discovery is delayed rather too long. (W. H.)

the lucky contrast of different characters. The satirical conversation at Lady Sneerwell's is an indifferent imitation of *The Way of the World*, and Sir Benjamin Backbite a foolish superfluity from the older comedy. He did not need the aid of Mr. Tokely to make him ridiculous. We have already spoken well of his actor's talents for low humour, but if he wishes to remain on the establishment, we are afraid he must keep in the kitchen.

MRS. ALSOP'S ROSALIND

Examiner, October 22, 1815

A LADY of the name of Alsop, a daughter of Mrs. Jordan (by a former husband),[1] has appeared at Covent Garden Theatre, in the character of Rosalind. Not only the circumstance of her relationship to that excellent actress, but the accounts in the papers, raised our curiosity and expectations very high. We were unwillingly disappointed. The truth is, Mrs. Alsop is a very nice little woman, who acts her part very sensibly and cleverly, and with a certain degree of arch humour, but "no more like her mother than we to Hercules." When we say this, we mean no disparagement to this lady's talents, who is a real acquisition to the stage in correct and chaste acting, but simply to prevent comparisons, which can only end in disappointment. Mrs. Alsop would make a better Celia than Rosalind. Mrs. Jordan's excellences were all natural to her. It was not as an actress, but as herself, that she charmed everyone. Nature had formed her in her most prodigal humour; and when nature is in the humour to make a woman all that is delightful, she does it most effectually. Mrs. Jordan was the same in all her characters, and inimitable in all of them, because there was no one else like her. Her face, her tones, her man-

[1] This is a very charitable way of putting it.

ner, were irresistible. Her smile had the effect of sunshine, and her laugh did one good to hear it. Her voice was eloquence itself: it seemed as if her heart was always at her mouth. She was all gaiety, openness, and good-nature. She rioted in her fine animal spirits, and gave more pleasure than any other actress, because she had the greatest spirit of enjoyment in herself. Her Nell—but we will not tantalise ourselves or our readers. Mrs. Alsop has nothing luxurious about her, and Mrs. Jordan was nothing else. Her voice is clear and articulate, but not rich or flowing. In person she is small, and her face is not prepossessing. Her delivery of the speeches was correct and excellent as far as it went, but without much richness or power. Lively good sense is what she really possesses. She also sang the Cuckoo Song very pleasingly.

Charles Kemble made an interesting Orlando. Mr. Young spoke the "Seven Ages" with propriety, and some effect. Mr. Fawcett's Touchstone was decent; and Mrs. Gibbs in Audrey, the very thing itself.

MISS O'NEILL'S ELWINA

Examiner, November 19, 1815

DURING the last week, Miss O'Neill has condescended to play the character of Elwina, in Miss Hannah More's tragedy of *Percy*. "Although this production," says a critic in the *Times*, "like every other of the excellent and enlightened author, affords equal pleasure and instruction in the perusal, we are not sure that it was ever calculated to obtain very eminent success upon the stage. The language is undoubtedly classical and flowing; the sentiment characteristically natural and pure; the fable uninterrupted; the catastrophe mournful; and the moral of unquestionable utility and truth. With all these requisites to dramatic fortune, the tragedy of *Percy* does not so strongly rivet the at-

tention as some other plays less free from striking
faults, and composed by writers of far less distinguished talent. Though the versification be sufficiently
musical, and in many passages conspicuous for nerve
as well as cadence, there is no splendid burst of imagery, nor lofty strain of poetical inspiration. Taste
and intelligence have decked their lines in every grace
of sculptured beauty: we miss but the presence of that
Promethean fire which could bid the statue 'speak.' It
may be objected, moreover, to this drama, that its incidents are too few, and too little diversified. The
grand interest which belongs to the unlooked-for preservation of Percy's life is, perhaps, too soon elicited
and expended; and if we mistake not, there is room for
doubting whether, at length, he fairly met his death,
or was ensnared once more by some unworthy treachery of Douglas. Neither do we think the passions
which are called into play by the solemn events of a
history so calamitous, have been very minutely traced,
intensely coloured, or powerfully illustrated. We have
a general impression that Douglas is racked by jealousy, Elwina by grief, and Percy by disappointment.
But we fain would have the home touches of Shakespeare."

Thus far the *Times* critic: from all which it appears
that Miss Hannah More is not like Shakespeare. The
writer afterwards tries his hand at a comparison between Miss More and Virgil; and the result, after due
deliberation, is that Virgil was the wiser man. The
part, however, to which the learned commentator has
the most decided objection, is that "where Elwina
steps out of her way to preach rather a lengthy sermon to her father, against war in general, as offensive
to the Prince of Peace." Now if this writer had
thought proper, he might have discovered that the
whole play is "a lengthy sermon," without poetry or
interest, and equally deficient in "sculptured grace,
and Promethean fire." We should not have made these

remarks, but that the writers in the above paper have a greater knack than any others, of putting a parcel of tall opaque words before them, to blind the eyes of their readers, and hoodwink their own understandings. There is one short word which might be aptly inscribed on its swelling columns—it is the word which Burchell applies to the conversation of some high-flown female critics in the "Vicar of Wakefield."

But to have done with this subject. We shall not readily forgive Miss Hannah More's heroine Elwina for having made us perceive, what we had not felt before, that there is a considerable degree of manner and monotony in Miss O'Neill's acting. The peculiar excellence which has been ascribed to Miss O'Neill (indeed over every other actress) is that of *faultless nature*. Mrs. Siddons's acting is said to have greater grandeur, to have possessed loftier flights of passion and imagination; but then it is objected that it was not a pure imitation of nature. Miss O'Neill's recitation is indeed nearer the common standard of level speaking, as her person is nearer the common size, but we will venture to say that there is as much a tone, a certain stage sing-song, in her delivery, as in Mrs. Siddons's. Through all the tedious speeches of this play, she preserved the same balanced artificial cadence, the same melancholy tone, as if her words were the continued echo of a long-drawn sigh. There is the same pitch-key, the same alternation of sad sounds, in almost every line. We do not insist upon perfection in anyone, nor do we mean to decide how far this intonation may be proper in tragedy; but we contend that Miss O'Neill does not in general speak in a natural tone of voice, nor as people speak in conversation. Her great excellence is extreme natural sensibility; that is, she perfectly conceives and expresses what would be generally felt by the female mind in the extraordinary and overpowering situations in which she is placed. In truth, in beauty, and in that irresistible pathos which goes directly to the heart, she has at present no equal, and can have no superior. There were only one or two opportunities for the display of her delightful powers in the character of Elwina, but of these she made the fullest use. The expression of mute grief, when she hears of the death of Percy, in the last act, was as fine as possible: nor could anything be more natural, more beautiful or affecting, than the manner in which she receives his scarf, and hurries out with it, tremulously clasping it to her bosom. It was one of those moments of still and breathless passion, in which the tongue is silent, while the heart breaks. We did not approve of her dying scene at all. It was a mere convulsive struggle for breath, the representation of a person in the act of suffocation—one of those agonies of human nature, which, as they do not appeal to the imagination, should not certainly be obtruded on the senses. Once or twice Miss O'Neill dropped her voice so low, and articulated so internally, that we gathered what she said rather from the motion of her lips, than from distinguishing the sound. This in Mr. Kean would be called extravagance. We were heartily glad when the play was over. From the very construction of the plot, it is impossible that any good can come of it till all the parties are dead; and when this catastrophe took place, the audience seemed perfectly satisfied.

MISS O'NEILL'S BELVIDERA AND MONIMIA

Examiner, December 10, 1815

Miss O'Neill repeated her usual characters last week. We saw her in Belvidera, and were disappointed. We do not think she plays it so well as she did last year. We thought her representation of it then as near perfection as possible; and her present acting we think chargeable, in many instances, with affectation and extravagance. She goes into the two extremes of speaking so loud as to "split the ears of the groundlings," and so low as not to be heard. She has (or we mistake) been taking a bad lesson of Mr. Kean: in our opinion, the excellences of genius are not communicable. A second-rate actor may learn of a first; but all imitation in the latter must prove a source of error: for the power with which great talent works can only be regulated by its own suggestions and the force of nature. The bodily energy which Mr. Kean exhibits cannot be transferred to female characters, without making them disgusting instead of impressive. Miss O'Neill, during the two last acts of Belvidera, is in a continual convulsion. But the intention of tragedy is to exhibit mental passion and not bodily agony, or the last only as a necessary concomitant of the former. Miss O'Neill clings so long about Jaffier, and with such hysterical violence, before she leaps upon his neck and calls for the fatal blow, that the connection of the action with the sentiment is lost in the pantomime exhibition before us. We are not fastidious; nor do we object to having the painful worked up with the catastrophe to the utmost pitch of human suffering; but we must object to a constant recurrence of such extreme agony, as a convenient commonplace or trick to bring down thunders of applause. Miss O'Neill twice, if we remember, seizes her forehead with her clenched fists, making a hissing noise through her teeth, and twice is thrown into a fit of agonised choking. Neither is her face fine enough in itself not to become unpleasant by such extreme and repeated distortion. Miss O'Neill's freedom from mannerism was her great charm, and we should be sorry to see her fall into it. Mr. C. Kemble's Jaffier had very considerable effect. Mr. Young's Pierre is his best character.

We have seen Miss O'Neill in the *Orphan*, and almost repent of what we have said above. Her Monimia is a piece of acting as beautiful as it is affecting. We never wish to see it acted otherwise or better. She is the Orphan that Otway drew.

> With pleas'd attention 'midst his scenes we find
> Each glowing thought that warms the female mind;
> Each melting sigh and every tender tear,
> The lover's wishes, and the virgin's fear,
> His every strain the Smiles and Graces own.

This idea of the character, which never leaves the mind in reading the play, was delightfully represented on the stage. Miss. O'Neill did not once overstep the limits of propriety, and was interesting in every part. Her conversation with the page was delicately familiar and playful. Her death was judiciously varied, and did not affect the imagination less, because it gave no shock to the senses. Her greatest effort, however, was in the scene with Polydore, where she asks him, "Where did you rest last night?" and where she falls senseless on the floor at his answer. The breathless expectation, the solemn injunction, the terror which the discovery strikes to her heart, as if she had been struck with lightning, had an irresistible effect. Nothing could be portrayed with greater truth and feeling. We liked Charles Kemble's Castalio not much, and Mr. Conway's Polydore not at all. It is impossible that this gentleman should become an actor, unless he could take "a cubit from his stature." Mr. Young's Chamont was quite as good as the character deserves.

MR. KEAN'S DUKE ARANZA

Examiner, December 10, 1815

MR. KEAN's appearance at Drury Lane on Tuesday, in the Duke Aranza, in the *Honey Moon*, excited considerable expectations in the public. Our own were not fulfilled. We think this the least brilliant of all his characters. It was Duke and no Duke. It had severity without dignity; and was deficient in ease, grace, and gaiety. He played the feigned character as if it were a reality. Now we believe that a spirit of raillery should be thrown over the part, so as to carry off the gravity of the imposture. There is in Mr. Kean an infinite variety of talent, with a certain monotony of genius. He has not the same ease in doing common things that he has energy on great occasions. We seldom lose sight of his Richard, and to a certain degree, in all his acting, "*he still plays the dog*." [1] His dancing was encored. George II. encored Garrick in the *Minuet de la Court:* Mr. Kean's was not like court dancing. It had more alacrity than ease.

MR. KEAN'S OTHELLO

Examiner, January 7, 1816

MR. KEAN'S Othello is his best character, and the highest effort of genius on the stage. We say this without any exception or reserve. Yet we wish it was better than it is. In parts, we think he rises as high as human genius can go: at other times, though powerful, the whole effort is thrown away in a wrong direction, and disturbs our idea of the character. There are some technical objections. Othello was tall; but that is nothing: he was black, but that is nothing. But he was not fierce, and that is everything. It is only in the last agony of human suffering that he gives way to his rage and despair, and it is in working his noble nature up to that extremity, that Shakespeare has shown his genius and his vast power over the human heart. It was in raising passion to its height, from the lowest beginnings and in spite of all obstacles, in showing the conflict of the soul, the tug and war between love and

[1] "That I should snarl and bite, and play the dog"—a line from *King Henry VI.* which Cibber transferred to his *Richard III.*

hatred, rage, tenderness, jealousy, remorse, in laying open the strength and the weaknesses of human nature, in uniting sublimity of thought with the anguish of the keenest woe, in putting in motion all the springs and impulses which make up this our mortal being, and at last blending them in that noble tide of deep and sustained passion, impetuous, but majestic, "that flows on to the Propontic and knows no ebb," that the great excellence of Shakespeare lay. Mr. Kean is in general all passion, all energy, all relentless will. He wants imagination, that faculty which contemplates events, and broods over feelings with a certain calmness and grandeur; his feelings almost always hurry on to action, and hardly ever repose upon themselves. He is too often in the highest key of passion, too uniformly on the verge of extravagance, too constantly on the rack. This does very well in certain characters, as Zanga or Bajazet, where there is merely a physical passion, a boiling of the blood, to be expressed; but it is not so in the lofty-minded and generous Moor.

We make these remarks the more freely, because there were parts of the character in which Mr. Kean showed the greatest sublimity and pathos, by laying aside all violence of action. For instance, the tone of voice in which he delivered the beautiful apostrophe, "Then, oh, farewell!" struck on the heart like the swelling notes of some divine music, like the sound of years of departed happiness. Why not all so, or all that is like it? why not speak the affecting passage—"I found not Cassio's kisses on her lips"—why not speak the last speech, in the same manner? They are both of them, we do most strenuously contend, speeches of pure pathos, of thought, and feeling, and not of passion, venting itself in violence of action or gesture. Again, the look, the action, the expression of voice, with which he accompanied the exclamation, "Not a jot, not a jot," was perfectly heart-rending. His vow of revenge against Cassio, and his abandonment of his love for Desdemona, were as fine as possible. The whole of the third act had an irresistible effect upon the house, and indeed is only to be paralleled by the murder-scene in *Macbeth*.

MR. KEAN'S SIR GILES OVERREACH

Examiner, January 14, 1816

MASSINGER'S play of *A New Way to Pay Old Debts*, which has been brought out at Drury Lane Theatre to introduce Mr. Kean in the part of Sir Giles Overreach, must have afforded a rich treat to theatrical amateurs. There is something in a good play well acted, a peculiar charm, that makes us forget ourselves and all the world.

We do not know anyone now-a-days who could write Massinger's comedy of *A New Way to Pay Old Debts*, though we do not believe that it was better acted at the time it was first brought out, than it is at present. We cannot conceive of anyone's doing Mr. Kean's part of Sir Giles Overreach so well as himself. We have seen others in the part, superior in the look and costume, in hardened, clownish, rustic insensibility; but in the soul and spirit, no one equal to him. He is a truly great actor. This is one of his very best parts. He was not at a single fault. The passages which we remarked as particularly striking and original, were those where he expresses his surprise at his nephew's answers, "His fortune swells him!—'Tis rank, he's married!" and again, where, after the exposure of his villainies, he calls to his accomplice Marall, in a half-wheedling, half-terrific tone, "Come hither, Marall, come hither." Though the speech itself is absurd and out of character, his manner of stopping when he is running at his foes, "I'm feeble, some widow's curse hangs on my sword," was exactly as if his arm had been suddenly withered, and his powers

shrivelled up on the instant. The conclusion was quite
overwhelming. Mr. Kean looked the part well, and his
voice does not fail as it used to do.

Examiner, January 21, 1816

THE admirable comedy of *A New Way to Pay Old
Debts* continues to be acted with increased effect.
Mr. Kean is received with shouts of applause in Sir
Giles Overreach. We have heard two objections to
his manner of doing this part, one of which we think
right and the other not. When he is asked, "Is he not
moved by the orphan's tears, the widow's curse?" he
answers, "Yes—as rocks by waves, or the moon by
howling wolves." Mr. Kean, in speaking the latter
sentence, dashes his voice about with the greatest violence, and howls out his indignation and rage. Now we
conceive this is wrong: for he has to express not violence, but firm, inflexible resistance to it,—not motion,
but rest. The very pause after the word *yes,* points
out the cool deliberate way in which it should be
spoken. The other objection is to his manner of pronouncing the word "Lord—Right Honourable Lord,"
which Mr. Kean uniformly does in a drawling tone,
with a mixture of fawning servility and sarcastic contempt. This has been thought inconsistent with the
part, and with the desire which Sir Giles has to en-
noble his family by alliance with a "Lord, a Right
Honourable Lord." We think Mr. Kean never showed
more genius than in pronouncing this single word,
Lord. It is a complete exposure (produced by the
violence of the character), of the elementary feelings
which make up the common respect excited by mere
rank. This is nothing but a cringing to power and
opinion, with a view to turn them to our own advantage with the world. Sir Giles is one of those
knaves who "do themselves homage." He makes use
of Lord Lovell merely as the stalking-horse of his ambition. In other respects, he has the greatest contempt

for him, and the necessity he is under of paying court to him for his own purposes, infuses a double portion of gall and bitterness into the expression of his self-conscious superiority. No; Mr. Kean was perfectly right in this, he spoke the word "Lord" *con amore.* His praise of the kiss, "It came twanging off—I like it," was one of his happiest passages. It would perhaps be as well if, in the concluding scene, he would contrive not to frighten the ladies into hysterics. But the whole together is admirable.

A MIDSUMMER NIGHT'S DREAM

Examiner, January 21, 1816

WE hope we have not been accessory to murder, in recommending a delightful poem to be converted into a dull pantomime; for such is the fate of the *Midsummer Night's Dream.* We have found to our cost, once for all, that the regions of fancy and the boards of Covent Garden are not the same thing. All that is fine in the play, was lost in the representation. The spirit was evaporated, the genius was fled; but the spectacle was fine: it was that which saved the play. Oh, ye scene-shifters, ye scene-painters, ye machinists and dressmakers, ye manufacturers of moon and stars that give no light, ye musical composers, ye men in the orchestra, fiddlers and trumpeters and players on the double drum and loud bassoon, rejoice! This is your triumph; it is not ours: and ye full-grown, well-fed, substantial, real fairies, Messieurs Treby, and Truman, and Atkins, and Misses Matthews, Carew, Burrell, and MacAlpine, we shall remember you: we shall believe no more in the existence of your fantastic tribe. Flute the bellows-mender, Snug the joiner, Starveling the tailor, farewell! you have lost the charm of your names; but thou, Nic Bottom, thou valiant Bottom, what shall we say to thee? Thou didst con-

sole us much; thou didst perform a good part well;
thou didst top the part of Bottom the weaver! He
comes out of thy hands as clean and clever a fellow as
ever. Thou art a person of exquisite whim and humour; and thou didst hector over thy companions
well, and fall down flat before the Duke, like other
Bullies, well; and thou didst sing the song of the Black
Ousel well; but chief, thou didst noddle thy ass's
head, which had been put upon thee, well; and didst
seem to say, significantly, to thy new attendants,
Peaseblossom, Cobweb, Moth, and Mustardseed, "Gentlemen, I can present you equally to my friends, and
to my enemies!" [1]

All that was good in this piece (except the scenery)
was Mr. Liston's Bottom, which was an admirable and
judicious piece of acting. Mr. Conway was Theseus.
Who would ever have taken this gentleman for the
friend and companion of Hercules? Miss Stephens
played the part of Hermia, and sang several songs very
delightfully, which, however, by no means assisted the
progress or interest of the story. Miss Foote played
Helena. She is a very sweet girl, and not at all a bad
actress; yet did anyone feel or even hear her address
to Hermia? To show how far asunder the closet and
the stage are, we give it here once more entire:

Injurious Hermia! most ungrateful maid!
Have you conspir'd, have you with these contriv'd
To bait me with this foul derision?
Is all the counsel that we two have shar'd,
The sister-vows, the hours that we have spent,
When we have chid the hasty-footed time
For parting us, O! is it all forgot?
All school-days' friendship, childhood innocence?
We, Hermia, like two artificial gods,
Created with our needles both one flower,[2]

[1] What Louis XVIII. said to his new National Guards.
(W. H.)
[2] "Have with our needles created both one flower, . . ."

Both on one sampler, sitting on one cushion,
Both warbling of one song, both in one key,
As if our hands, our sides, voices, and minds,
Had been incorporate. So we grew together,
Like to a double cherry, seeming parted,
But yet an union in partition;

.   .   .   .

And will you rent our ancient love asunder,
To join with men in scorning your poor friend?
It is not friendly, 'tis not maidenly:
Our sex, as well as I, may chide you for it,
Though I alone do feel the injury.

In turning to Shakespeare to look for this passage, the book opened at the *Midsummer Night's Dream*, the title of which half gave us back our old feeling; and in reading this one speech twice over, we have completely forgot all the noise we have heard and the sights we have seen. Poetry and the stage do not agree together. The attempt to reconcile them fails not only of effect, but of decorum. The *ideal* has no place upon the stage, which is a picture without perspective; everything there is in the foreground. That which is merely an airy shape, a dream, a passing thought, immediately becomes an unmanageable reality. Where all is left to the imagination, every circumstance has an equal chance of being kept in mind, and tells according to the mixed impression of all that has been suggested. But the imagination cannot sufficiently qualify the impressions of the senses. Any offence given to the eye is not to be got rid of by explanation. Thus Bottom's head in the play is a fantastic illusion, produced by magic spells: on the stage it is an ass's head, and nothing more; certainly a very strange costume for a gentleman to appear in. Fancy cannot be represented any more than a simile can be painted; and it is as idle to attempt it as to personate Wall or Moonshine. Fairies are not incredible, but fairies six feet high are so. Monsters are not shocking, if they are seen at a proper distance. When ghosts appear in mid-

day, when apparitions stalk along Cheapside, then may
the *Midsummer Night's Dream* be represented at
Covent Garden or at Drury Lane; for we hear that it
is to be brought out there also, and that we have to
undergo another crucifixion.

Mrs. Faucit played the part of Titania very well,
but for one circumstance—that she is a woman. The
only glimpse which we caught of the possibility of
acting the imaginary scenes properly, was from the
little girl who dances before the fairies (we do not
know her name), which seemed to show that the whole
might be carried off in the same manner—by a miracle.

LOVE FOR LOVE

Examiner, January 28, 1816

CONGREVE's comedy of *Love for Love* is, in wit and
elegance, perhaps inferior to *The Way of the World*;
but it is unquestionably the best-acting of all his plays.
It abounds in dramatic situation, in incident, in variety
of character. Still (such is the power of good writing)
we prefer reading it in the closet, to seeing it on the
stage. As it was acted the other night at Drury Lane
Theatre, many of the finest traits of character were
lost. Though *Love for Love* is much less a tissue of
epigrams than his other plays, the author has not been
able to keep his wit completely under. Jeremy is almost as witty and learned as his master. The part
which had the greatest effect in the acting was Munden's Foresight. We hardly ever saw a richer or more
powerful piece of comic acting. It was done to the
life, and indeed somewhat over; but the effect was irresistible. His look was planet-struck, his dress and
appearance like one of the signs of the Zodiac taken
down. We never saw anything more bewildered. Parsons, if we remember right, gave more imbecility,
more of the doting garrulity of age, to the part, and

blundered on with a less determined air of stupidity. Mr. Dowton did not make much of Sir Sampson Legend. He looked well, like a hale, hearty old gentleman, with a close bob-wig, and bronze complexion; but that was all. We were very much amused with Mr. Harley's Tattle. His indifference in the scene where he breaks off his engagement with Miss Prue was very entertaining. In the scene in which he teaches her how to make love, he was less successful: he delivered his lessons to his fair disciple with the air of a person giving good advice, and did not seem to have a proper sense of his good fortune. "Desire to please, and you will infallibly please," is an old maxim, and Mr. Harley is an instance of the truth of it. This actor is always in the best possible humour with himself and the audience. He is as happy as if he had jumped into the very part which he liked the best of all others. Mr. Rae, on the contrary, who played Valentine, apparently feels as little satisfaction as he communicates. He always acts with an air of injured excellence.

Mrs. Mardyn's Miss Prue was not one of her most successful characters. It was a little hard and coarse. It was not fond and yielding enough. Miss Prue is made of the most susceptible materials. She played the hoydening parts best, as where she cries out, "School's up, school's up!" and she knocked off Mr. Bartley's hat with great good-will. Mr. Bartley was Ben; and we confess we think Miss Prue's distaste to him very natural. We cannot make up our minds to like this actor; and yet we have no fault to find with him. For instance, he played the character of Ben very properly; that is, just like "a great sea-porpoise." There is an art of qualifying such a part in a manner to carry off its disagreeableness, which Mr. Bartley wants. Mrs. Harlowe's Mrs. Frail was excellent: she appeared to be the identical Mrs. Frail, with all her airs of mincing affection, and want of principle. The character was

seen quite in dishabille. The scene between her and her
sister, Mrs. Foresight, about the discovery of the pin—
"And pray, sister, where did you find that pin?"—was
managed with as much coolness as anything of this
sort that ever happened in real life. Mrs. Orger played
Mrs. Foresight with much ease and natural propriety.
She in general reposes too much on her person, and
does not display all the animation of which the character is susceptible. She is also too much, in female
parts, what the *walking fine gentleman* of the stage
used to be in male. Mr. Barnard played Jeremy with
a smart shrug in his shoulders, and the trusty air of a
valet in his situation.

MEASURE FOR MEASURE

Examiner, February 11, 1816

In the "Lectures on Dramatic Literature" by William
Schlegel, the German translator of Shakespeare, is the
following criticism on *Measure for Measure*, which
has been just acted at Covent Garden Theatre:—

"In *Measure for Measure*, Shakespeare was compelled,
by the nature of the subject, to make his poetry more
familiar with criminal justice than is usual with him. All
kinds of proceedings connected with the subject, all sorts
of active or passive persons, pass in review before us; the
hypocritical Lord Deputy, the compassionate Provost, and
the hard-hearted Hangman; a young man of quality who
is to suffer for the seduction of his mistress before marriage, loose wretches brought in by the police, nay, even a
hardened criminal whom the preparation for his execution cannot awake out of his callousness. But yet, notwithstanding this convincing truth, how tenderly and
mildly the whole is treated! The piece takes improperly
its name from the punishment: the sense of the whole is
properly the triumph of mercy over strict justice, no man
being himself so secure from errors as to be entitled to
deal it out among his equals. The most beautiful orna-

ment of the composition is the character of Isabella, who, in the intention of taking the veil, allows herself to be again prevailed on by pious love to tread the perplexing ways of the world, while the heavenly purity of her mind is not even stained with one unholy thought by the general corruption. In the humble robes of the novice of a nunnery, she is a true angel of light. When the cold and hitherto unsullied Angelo, whom the Duke has commissioned to restrain the excess of dissolute immorality by a rigid administration of the laws during his pretended absense, is even himself tempted by the virgin charms of Isabella, as she supplicates for her brother Claudio; when he first insinuates, in timid and obscure language, but at last impudently declares his readiness to grant the life of Claudio for the sacrifice of her honour; when Isabella repulses him with a noble contempt; when she relates what has happened to her brother, and the latter at first applauds her, but at length, overpowered by the dread of death, wishes to persuade her to consent to her dishonour; in these masterly scenes Shakespeare has sounded the depth of the human heart. The interest here reposes altogether on the action; curiosity constitutes no part of our delight; for the Duke, in the disguise of a monk, is always present to watch over his dangerous representatives, and to avert every evil which could possibly be apprehended: we look here with confidence to the solemn decision. The Duke acts the part of the Monk naturally, even to deception; he unites in his person the wisdom of the priest and the prince. His wisdom is merely too fond of roundabout ways; his vanity is flattered with acting invisibly like an earthly providence; he is more entertained with overhearing his subjects than governing them in the customary manner. As he at last extends pardon to all the guilty, we do not see how his original purpose of restoring the strictness of the laws by committing the execution of them to other hands, has been in any wise accomplished. The poet might have had this irony in view—that of the numberless slanders of the Duke, told him by the petulant Lucio, without knowing the person to whom he spoke, what regarded his singularities and whims was not wholly without foundation.

"It is deserving of remark, that Shakespeare, amidst the

rancour of religious parties, takes a delight in representing
the condition of a monk, and always represents his influence as beneficial. We find in him none of the black
and knavish monks, which an enthusiasm for the Protestant religion, rather than poetical inspiration, has suggested to some of our modern poets. Shakespeare merely
gives his monks an inclination to busy themselves in the
affairs of others, after renouncing the world for themselves; with respect, however, to privy frauds, he does
not represent them as very conscientious. Such are the
parts acted by the Monk in *Romeo and Juliet*, and another in *Much Ado about Nothing*, and even by the Duke,
whom, contrary to the well-known proverb, 'the cowl
seems really to make a monk' (Vol. ii. p. 169)."

This is, we confess, a very poor criticism on a very
fine play; but we are not in the humour (even if we
could) to write a better. A very obvious beauty,
which has escaped the critic, is the admirable description of life, as poetical as it is metaphysical, beginning,
"If I do lose thee, I do lose a thing," &c., to the truth
and justice of which Claudio assents, contrasted almost
immediately afterwards with his fine description of
death as the worst of ills:

> To lie in cold obstruction, and to rot;
> This sensible warm motion to become
> A kneaded clod; and the delighted spirit
> To bathe in fiery floods, or to reside
> In thrilling regions of thick-ribbed ice.
> .   .   .   'tis too horrible!
> The weariest and most loathed worldly life
> That age, ache, penury, and imprisonment
> Can lay on nature is a paradise
> To what we fear of death.

Neither has he done justice to the character of
Master Barnardine, one of the finest (and that's saying
a bold word) in all Shakespeare. He calls him a hardened criminal. He is no such thing. He is what he is
by nature, not by circumstance, "careless, reckless,
and fearless of past, present, and to come." He is

Caliban transported to the forests of Bohemia or the prisons of Vienna. He has, however, a sense of the natural fitness of things: "He has been drinking hard all night, and he will not be hanged that day," and Shakespeare has let him off at last. Emery does not play it well, for Master Barnardine is not the representative of a Yorkshireman, but of an universal class in nature. We cannot say that the Clown Pompey suffered in the hands of Mr. Liston; on the contrary, he played it inimitably well. His manner of saying "a dish of some three-pence" was worth anything. In the scene of his examination before the Justice, he delayed, and dallied, and dangled in his answers, in the true spirit of the genius of his author.

We do not understand why the philosophical critic, whom we have quoted above, should be so severe on those pleasant persons Lucio, Pompey, and Master Froth, as to call them "wretches." They seem all mighty comfortable in their occupations, and determined to pursue them, "as the flesh and fortune should serve." Shakespeare was the least moral of all writers; for morality (commonly so called) is made up of antipathies, and his talent consisted in sympathy with human nature, in all its shapes, degrees, elevations, and depressions. The object of the pedantic moralist is to make the worst of everything; *his* was to make the best, according to his own principle, "There is some soul of goodness in things evil." Even Master Barnardine is not left to the mercy of what others think of him, but when he comes in, he speaks for himself. We would recommend it to the Society for the Suppression of Vice to read Shakespeare.

Mr. Young played the Duke tolerably well. As to the cant introduced into Schlegel's account of the Duke's assumed character of a Monk, we scout it altogether. He takes advantage of the good-nature of the poet to impose on the credulity of mankind. Chaucer spoke of the Monks historically, Shakespeare poeti-

cally. It was not in the nature of Shakespeare to insult
over "the enemies of the human race" just after their
fall. We however object to them entirely in this age
of the revival of Inquisitions and Protestant massacres.
We have not that stretch of philosophical comprehension which, in German metaphysics, unites popery
and free-thinking together, loyalty and regicide, and
which binds up the Bible and Spinoza in the same
volume! Mr. Jones did not make a bad Lucio. Miss
O'Neill's Isabella, though full of merit, disappointed
us; as indeed she has frequently done of late. Her "Oh
fie, fie," was the most spirited thing in her performance. She did not seize with much force the spirit of
her author, but she seemed in complete possession of a
certain conventicle twang. She whined and sang out
her part in that querulous tone that has become unpleasant to us by ceaseless repetition. She at present
plays all her parts in the Magdalen style. We half begin
to suspect that she represents the bodies, not the souls
of women, and that her *forte* is in tears, sighs, sobs,
shrieks, and hysterics. She does not play either Juliet
or Isabella finely. She must stick to the commonplace
characters of Otway, Moore, and Miss Hannah More,
or she will ruin herself. As Sir Joshua Reynolds con-
cluded his last lecture with the name of Michael
Angelo, as Vetus wished the name of the Marquis
Wellesley to conclude his last letter, so we will conclude this article with a devout apostrophe to the
name of Mrs. Siddons.

MR. KEAN'S SIR GILES OVERREACH

Examiner, February 18, 1816

WE saw Mr. Kean's Sir Giles Overreach on Friday
night from the boxes at Drury Lane Theatre, and are
not surprised at the incredulity as to this great actor's
powers, entertained by those persons who have only

seen him from that elevated sphere. We do not hesitate to say, that those who have only seen him at that
distance, have not seen him at all. The expression of
his face is quite lost, and only the harsh and grating
tones of his voice produce their full effect on the ear.
The same recurring sounds, by dint of repetition,
fasten on the attention, while the varieties and finer
modulations are lost in their passage over the pit. All
you discover is an abstraction of his defects, both of
person, voice, and manner. He appears to be a little
man in a great passion. The accompaniment of expression is absolutely necessary to explain his tones
and gestures: and the outline which he gives of the
character, in proportion as it is bold and decided, requires to be filled up and modified by all the details of
execution. Without seeing the workings of his face,
through which you read the movements of his soul,
and anticipate their violent effects on his utterance and
action, it is impossible to understand or feel pleasure
in the part. All strong expression, deprived of its
gradations and connecting motives, unavoidably de-
generates into caricature. This was the effect uniformly produced on those about us, who kept exclaim-
ing, "How extravagant, how odd," till the last scene,
where the extreme and admirable contrasts both of
voice and gesture in which Mr. Kean's genius shows
itself, and which are in their nature more obviously
intelligible, produced a change of opinion in his
favour.

As a proof of what we have above advanced, it
was not possible to discover in the last scene, where
he is lifted from the ground by the attendants, and he
rivets his eyes in dreadful despair upon his daughter,
whether they were open or closed. The action of advancing to the middle of the stage, and his faltering ac-
cent in saying, "Marall, come hither, Marall," could
not be mistaken. The applause, however, came almost
constantly from those who were near the orchestra,

and circulated in eddies round the house. It is unpleasant to see a play from the boxes. There is no part
of the house which is so thoroughly wrapped up in
itself, and fortified against any impression from what
is passing on the stage; which seems so completely
weaned from all superstitious belief in dramatic illusion; which takes so little interest in all that is interesting. Not a cravat nor a muscle was discomposed,
except now and then by some gesticulation of Mr.
Kean, which violated the decorum of fashionable indifference, or by some expression of the author, two
hundred years old. Mr. Kean's acting is not, we understand, much relished in the upper circles. It is thought
too obtrusive and undisguised a display of nature.
Neither was Garrick's at all relished at first, by the
old Nobility, till it became the fashion to admire him.
The court-dresses, the drawing-room strut, and the
sing-song declamation, which he banished from the
stage, were thought much more dignified and im-
posir.g.

THE FAIR PENITENT

Examiner, March 10, 1816

The Fair Penitent is a tragedy which has been found
fault with both on account of its poetry and its morality. Notwithstanding these objections, it still holds
possession of the stage, where morality is not very
eagerly sought after, and poetry but imperfectly understood. We conceive that, for every purpose of
practical criticism, that is a good tragedy which draws
tears without moving laughter. Rowe's play is founded
on one of Massinger's, *The Fatal Dowry*, in which the
characters are a good deal changed, and the interest
not increased. The genius of Rowe was slow and
timid, and loved the ground: he had not "a Muse of
fire to ascend The brightest heaven of invention;" but

he had art and judgment enough to accommodate the
more daring flights of a ruder age to the polished,
well-bred mediocrity of the age he lived in. We may
say of Rowe as Voltaire said of Racine: "All his lines
are equally good." The compliment is, after all, equi-
vocal; but it is one which may be applied generally
to all poets, who in their productions are always
thinking of what they shall say, and of what others
have said, and who are never hurried into excesses of
any kind, good or bad, by trusting implicitly to the
impulse of their own genius or of the subject. The excellent author of "Tom Jones," in one of his introductory chapters, represents Rowe as an awkward
imitator of Shakespeare. He was rather an imitator
of the style and tone of sentiment of that age,—a sort
of moderniser of antiquity. The character of Calista is
quite in the *bravura* style of Massinger. She is a heroine, a virago, fair, a woman of high spirit and violent
resolutions, anything but a penitent. She dies indeed at
last, not from remorse for her vices, but because she
can no longer gratify them. She has not the slightest
regard for her virtue, and not much for her reputation; but she would brand with scorn, and blast with
the lightning of her indignation, the friend who wishes
to stop her in the career of her passions in order to
save her from destruction and infamy. She has a strong
sentiment of respect and attachment to her father, but
she will sooner consign his grey hairs to shame and
death than give up the least of her inclinations, or
sacrifice her sullen gloom to the common decencies
of behaviour. She at last pretends conversion from her
errors, in a soft, whining address to her husband, and
after having deliberately and wantonly done all the
mischief in her power, with her eyes open, wishes that
she had sooner known better, that she might have
acted differently! We do not however for ourselves
object to the morality of all this: for we apprehend that morality is little more than truth; and we

think that Rowe has given a very true and striking picture of the nature and consequences of that wilful selfishness of disposition, "which to be hated needs but to be seen." We do not think it necessary that the spectator should wait for the reluctant conversion of the character itself, to be convinced of its odiousness or folly, or that the only instruction to be derived from the drama is, not from the insight it gives us into the nature of human character and passion, but from some artificial piece of patchwork morality tacked to the end. However, Rowe has so far complied with the rules.

After what we have said of the character of Calista, Miss O'Neill will perhaps excuse us if we do not think that she was a very perfect representative of it. The character, as she gave it, was a very fine and impressive piece of acting, but it was not quite Calista. She gave the pathos, but not the spirit of the character. Her grief was sullen and sad, not impatient and ungovernable, Calista's melancholy is not a settled dejection, but a feverish state of agitation between conflicting feelings. Her eyes should look bright and sparkling through her tears. Her action should be animated and aspiring. Her present woes should not efface the traces of past raptures. There should be something in her appearance of the intoxication of pleasure, mixed with the madness of despair. The scene in which Miss O'Neill displayed most power, was that in which she is shown her letter to Lothario by Horatio, her husband's friend. The rage and shame with which her bosom seemed labouring were truly dreadful. This is the scene in which the poet has done most for the imagination, and it is the characteristic excellence of Miss O'Neill's acting, that it always rises with the expectations of the audience. She also repeated the evasive answer, "It was the day in which my father gave my hand to Altamont—as such I shall remember it for ever," in a tone of deep and suppressed emotion.

It is needless to add, that she played the part with a degree of excellence which no other actress could approach, and that she was only inferior to herself in it, because there is not the same opportunity for the display of her inimitable powers, as in some of her other characters.

MISS O'NEILL'S LADY TEAZLE

Examiner, March 24, 1816

MISS O'NEILL'S Lady Teazle at Covent Garden Theatre appears to us to be a complete failure. It was not comic; it was not elegant; it was not easy; it was not dignified; it was not playful; it was not anything that it ought to be. All that can be said of it is, that it was not tragedy. It seemed as if all the force and pathos which she displays in interesting situations had left her, but that not one spark of gaiety, one genuine expression of delight, had come in their stead. It was a piece of laboured heavy *still-life*. The only thing that had an air of fashion about her was the feather in her hat. It was not merely that she did not succeed as Miss O'Neill; it would have been a falling off in the most commonplace actress who had ever done anything tolerably. She gave to the character neither the complete finished air of fashionable indifference, which was the way in which Miss Farren played it, if we remember right, nor that mixture of artificial refinement and natural vivacity, which appears to be the true idea of the character (which however is not very well made out), but she seemed to have been thrust by some injudicious caprice of fortune, into a situation for which she was fitted neither by nature nor education. There was a perpetual affectation of the wit and the fine lady, with an evident consciousness of effort, a desire to please without any sense of pleasure. It was no better than awkward mimicry of the part, and

more like a drawling imitation of Mrs. C. Kemble's
genteel comedy than anything else we have seen. The
concluding penitential speech was an absolute sermon.
We neither liked her manner of repeating "Mim-
minee pimminee," nor of describing the lady who
rides round the ring in Hyde Park, nor of chuck-
ing Sir Peter under the chin, which was a great deal
too coarse and familiar. There was throughout an
equal want of delicacy and spirit, of ease and effect, of
nature and art. It was in general flat and insipid, and
where anything more was attempted, it was overcharged and unpleasant.

Fawcett's Sir Peter Teazle was better than when
we last saw it. He is an actor of much merit, but he
has of late got into a strange way of slurring over his
parts. Liston's Sir Benjamin Backbite was not very successful. Charles Kemble played Charles Surface very
delightfully.

MR. KEMBLE'S SIR GILES OVERREACH

Examiner, May, 5 1816

WHY they put Mr. Kemble into the part of Sir Giles
Overreach, at Covent Garden Theatre, we cannot conceive: we should suppose he would not put himself
there. Malvolio, though cross-gartered, did not set
himself in the stocks. No doubt, it is the managers'
doing, who by rope-dancing, fire-works, play-bill
puffs, and by every kind of quackery, seem determined to fill their pockets for the present, and disgust
the public in the end, if the public were an animal
capable of being disgusted by quackery. But

> Doubtless the pleasure is as great
> In being cheated as to cheat.

We do not know why we promised last week to
give some account of Mr. Kemble's Sir Giles, except

that we dreaded the task then; and certainly our re-
luctance to speak on this subject has not decreased,
the more we have thought upon it since. We have
hardly ever experienced a more painful feeling than
when, after the close of the play, the sanguine plaudits
of Mr. Kemble's friends, and the circular discharge of
hisses from the back of the pit, that came "full volley
home,"—the music struck up, the ropes were fixed,
and Madame Sachi ran up from the stage to the two-
shilling gallery, and then ran down again, as fast as
her legs could carry her, amidst the shouts of pit,
boxes, and gallery!

> So fails, so languishes, and dies away
> All that this world is proud of. So
> Perish the roses and the crowns of kings,
> Sceptres and palms of all the mighty.

We have here marred some fine lines of Mr. Words-
worth on the instability of human greatness, but it is
no matter: for he does not seem to understand the sentiment himself. Mr. Kemble, then, having been thrust
into the part, as we suppose, against his will, ran the
gauntlet of public opinion in it with a firmness and
resignation worthy of a Confessor. He did not once
shrink from his duty, nor make one effort to redeem
his reputation, by "affecting a virtue when he knew
he had it not." He seemed throughout to say to his
instigators, *You have thrust me into this part, help me
out of it, if you can; for you see I cannot help myself.*
We never saw signs of greater poverty, greater imbecility and decrepitude in Mr. Kemble, or in any
other actor: it was Sir Giles in his dotage. It was all
"Well, well," and "If you like it, have it so," an indifference and disdain of what was to happen, a nicety
about his means, a coldness as to his ends, much gentility and little nature. Was this Sir Giles Overreach?
Nothing could be more quaint and out-of-the-way.
Mr. Kemble wanted the part to come to him, for he

would not go out of his way to the part. He is, in fact, as shy of committing himself with nature, as a maid is of committing herself with a lover. All the proper forms and ceremonies must be complied with, before "they two can be made one flesh." Mr. Kemble sacrifices too much to decorum. He is chiefly afraid of being contaminated by too close an identity with the characters he represents. This is the greatest vice in an actor, who ought never to *bilk* his part. He endeavours to raise Nature to the dignity of his own person and demeanour, and declines with a graceful smile and a wave of the hand, the ordinary services she might do him. We would advise him by all means to shake hands, to hug her close, and be friends, if we did not suspect it was too late—that the lady, owing to this coyness, has eloped, and is now in the situation of Dame Hellenore among the Satyrs.[1]

The outrageousness of the conduct of Sir Giles is only to be excused by the violence of his passions, and the turbulence of his character. Mr. Kemble inverted this conception, and attempted to reconcile the character, by softening down the action. He "aggravated the part so, that he would seem like any sucking dove." For example, nothing could exceed the coolness and *sang froid* with which he raps Marall on the head with his cane, or spits at Lord Lovell: Lord Foppington himself never did any commonplace indecency more insipidly. The only passage that pleased us, or that really called forth the powers of the actor, was his reproach to Mr. Justice Greedy: "There is some fury in that *Gut*." The indignity of the word called up all the dignity of the actor to meet it, and he guaranteed the word, though "a word of naught," according to the letter and spirit of the convention between them, with a good grace, in the true old English way. Either we mistake all Mr. Kemble's excellencies, or they all disqualify him for this part. Sir Giles *hath a devil*; Mr.

[1] Spenser, *Faerie Queene*, bk. iii. canto. 10.

Kemble has none. Sir Giles is in a passion; Mr. Kemble
is not. Sir Giles has no regard to appearances; Mr.
Kemble has. It has been said of the Venus de Medicis,
"So stands the statue that enchants the world";[2] the
same might have been said of Mr. Kemble. He is the
very still-life and statuary of the stage; a perfect figure
of a man; a petrifaction of sentiment, that heaves no
sigh, and sheds no tear; an icicle upon the bust of
Tragedy. With all his faults, he has powers and faculties which no one else on the stage has; why then does
he not avail himself of them, instead of throwing himself upon the charity of criticism? Mr. Kemble has
given the public great, incalculable pleasure; and does
he know so little of the gratitude of the world as to
trust to their generosity?

EVERY MAN IN HIS HUMOUR

Examiner, June 9, 1816

MR. KEAN had for his benefit at Drury Lane Theatre,
on Wednesday, the comedy of *Every Man in His
Humour*. This play acts much better than it reads. It
has been observed of Ben Jonson, that he painted not
so much human nature as temporary manners, not the
characters of men, but their *humours*, that is to say,
peculiarities of phrase, modes of dress, gesture, &c.,
which becoming obsolete, and being in themselves altogether arbitrary and fantastical, have become unin-
telligible and uninteresting. Brainworm is a particularly dry and abstruse character. We neither know his
business nor his motives; his plots are as intricate as
they are useless, and as the ignorance of those he imposes upon is wonderful. This is the impression in
reading it. Yet from the bustle and activity of this
character on the stage, the changes of dress, the variety of affected tones and gipsy jargon, and the

___
[2] Thomson's *Seasons—Summer*.

limping, distorted gestures, it is a very amusing exhibition, as Mr. Munden plays it. Bobadil is the only actually striking character in the play, or which tells equally in the closet and the theatre. The rest, Master Matthew, Master Stephen, Cob and Cob's Wife, were living in the sixteenth century. But from the very oddity of their appearance and behaviour, they have a very droll and even picturesque effect when acted. It seems a revival of the dead. We believe in their existence when we see them. As an example of the power of the stage in giving reality and interest to what otherwise would be without it, we might mention the scene in which Brainworm praises Master Stephen's leg. The folly here is insipid, from its seeming carried to an excess,—till we see it; and then we laugh the more at it, the more incredible we thought it before.

The pathos in the principal character, Kitely, is "as dry as the remainder biscuit after a voyage." There is, however, a certain good sense, discrimination, or *logic of passion* in the part, which Mr. Kean pointed in such a way as to give considerable force to it. In the scene where he is about to confide the secret of his jealousy to his servant Thomas, he was exceedingly happy in the working himself up to the execution of his design, and in the repeated failure of his resolution. The reconciliation scene with his wife had great spirit, where he tells her, to show his confidence, that "she may sing, may go to balls, may dance," and the interruption of this sudden tide of concession with the restriction—"though I had rather you did not do all this"—was a master-stroke. It was perhaps the first time a parenthesis was ever spoken on the stage as it ought to be. Mr. Kean certainly often repeats this artifice of abrupt transition in the tones in which he expresses different passions, and still it always pleases, —we suppose, because it is natural. This gentleman is not only a good actor in himself, but he is the cause of good acting in others. The whole play was got up very effectually. Considerable praise is due to the industry and talent shown by Mr. Harley, in Captain Bobadil. He did his best in it, and that was not ill. He delivered the Captain's well-known proposal for the pacification of Europe, by killing twenty of them each his man a day, with good emphasis and discretion. Bobadil is undoubtedly the hero of the piece; his extravagant affectation carries the sympathy of the audience along with it, and his final defeat and exposure, though exceedingly humorous, is the only affecting circumstance in the play. Mr. Harley's fault, in this and other characters, is that he too frequently assumes mechanical expressions of countenance and by-tones of humour, which have not anything to do with the individual part. Mr. Hughes personified Master Matthew to the life: he appeared "like a man made after supper of a cheese-paring." Munden did Brainworm with laudible alacrity. Oxberry's Master Stephen was very happily hit off; nobody plays the traditional fool of the English stage so well; he seems not only foolish, but fond of folly. The two young gentlemen, Master Well-bred and Master Edward Knowell, were the only insipid characters.

MRS. SIDDONS

Examiner, June 16, 1816

PLAYERS should be immortal, if their own wishes or ours could make them so; but they are not. They not only die like other people, but like other people they cease to be young, and are no longer themselves, even while living. Their health, strength, beauty, voice, fails them; nor can they, without these advantages, perform the same feats, or command the same applause that they did when possessed of them. It is the common lot; players are only *not* exempt from it. Mrs. Siddons retired once from the stage: why should she

return to it again? She cannot retire from it twice
with dignity; and yet it is to be wished that she should
do all things with dignity. Any loss of reputation to
her, is a loss to the world. Has she not had enough of
glory? The homage she has received is greater than
that which is paid to queens. The enthusiasm she excited had something idolatrous about it; she was regarded less with admiration than with wonder, as if
a being of a superior order had dropped from another
sphere, to awe the world with the majesty of her appearance. She raised tragedy to the skies, or brought
it down from thence. It was something above nature.
We can conceive of nothing grander. She embodied
to our imagination the fables of mythology, of the
heroic and deified mortals of elder time. She was not
less than a goddess, or than a prophetess inspired by
the gods. Power was seated on her brow, passion
emanated from her breast as from a shrine. She was
Tragedy personified. She was the stateliest ornament
of the public mind. She was not only the idol of the
people, she not only hushed the tumultuous shouts of
the pit in breathless expectation, and quenched the
blaze of surrounding beauty in silent tears, but to the
retired and lonely student, through long years of soli-
tude, her face has shone as if an eye had appeared
from heaven; her name has been as if a voice had
opened the chambers of the human heart, or as if a
trumpet had awakened the sleeping and the dead. To
have seen Mrs. Siddons was an event in everyone's
life; and does she think we have forgot her? Or would
she remind us of herself by showing us what *she was
not?* Or is she to continue on the stage to the very last,
till all her grace and all her grandeur gone, shall leave
behind them only a melancholy blank? Or is she
merely to be played off as "the baby of a girl" for
a few nights?—"Rather than so," come, Genius of
Gil Blas, thou that didst inspire him in an evil hour to
perform his promise to the Archbishop of Grenada,

"and champion us to the utterance" of what we think on this occasion.

It is said that the Princess Charlotte has expressed a desire to see Mrs. Siddons in her best parts, and this, it is said, is a thing highly desirable. We do not know that the Princess has expressed any such wish, and we shall suppose that she has not, because we do not think it altogether a reasonable one. If the Princess Charlotte had expressed a wish to see Mr. Garrick, this would have been a thing highly desirable, but it would have been impossible; or if she had desired to see Mrs. Siddons *in her best days*, it would have been equally so; and yet, without this, we do not think it desirable that she should see her at all. It is said to be desirable that a princess should have a taste for the Fine Arts, and that this is best promoted by seeing the highest models of perfection. But it is of the first importance for princes to acquire a taste for what is reasonable: and the second thing which it is desirable they should acquire is a deference to public opinion: and we think neither of these objects likely to be promoted in the way proposed. If it was reasonable that Mrs. Siddons should retire from the stage three years ago, certainly those reasons have not diminished since, nor do we think Mrs. Siddons would consult what is due to her powers or her fame, in commencing a new career. If it is only intended that she should act a few nights in the presence of a particular person, this might be done as well in private. To all other applications she should answer, "Leave me to my repose."

Mrs. Siddons always spoke as slow as she ought: she now speaks slower than she did. "The line, too, labours, and the words move slow." [1] The machinery of the voice seems too ponderous for the power that wields it. There is too long a pause between each sentence, and between each word in each sentence. There is too much preparation. The stage waits for her. In

[1] Pope, *Essay on Criticism.*

the sleeping scene, she produced a different impression
from what we expected. It was more laboured and less
natural. In coming on formerly, her eyes were open,
but the sense was shut. She was like a person bewildered, and unconscious of what she did. She moved
her lips involuntarily; all her gestures were involuntary and mechanical. At present she acts the part
more with a view to effect. She repeats the action
when she says, "I tell you he cannot rise from his
grave," with both hands sawing the air in the style of
parliamentary oratory, the worst of all others. There
was none of this weight or energy in the way she did
the scene the first time we saw her, twenty years ago.
She glided on and off the stage almost like an apparition. In the close of the banquet scene, Mrs.
Siddons condescended to an imitation which we were
sorry for. She said, "Go, go," in the hurried familiar
tone of common life, in the manner of Mr. Kean, and
without any of that sustained and graceful spirit of
conciliation towards her guests, which used to characterise her mode of doing it. Lastly, if Mrs. Siddons has
to leave the stage again, Mr. Horace Twiss will write
another farewell address for her; if she continues on it,
we shall have to criticise her performances. We know
which of these two evils we shall think the greatest.

Too much praise cannot be given to Mr. Kemble's
performance of Macbeth. He was "himself again," and
more than himself. His action was decided, his voice
audible. His tones had occasionally indeed a learned
quaintness, like the colouring of Poussin; but the effect
of the whole was fine. His action in delivering the
speech, "To-morrow and to-morrow," was particularly striking and expressive, as if he had stumbled by
an accident on fate, and was baffled by the impenetrable obscurity of the future. In that prodigious prosing
paper, the *Times*, which seems to be written as well as
printed by a steam-engine, Mr. Kemble is compared to
the ruin of a magnificent temple, in which the divinity

still resides. This is not the case. The temple is unimpaired; but the divinity is sometimes from home.

THE MAYOR OF GARRATT

Examiner, June 30, 1816

THE acting of Dowton and Russell, in Major Sturgeon and Jerry Sneak, is well known to our readers; at least we would advise all those who have not seen it to go and see this perfect exhibition of comic talent. The strut, the bluster, the hollow swaggering, and turkey-cock swell of the Major, and Jerry's meekness, meanness, folly, good-nature, and hen-pecked air, are assuredly done to the life. The latter character is even better than the former, which is saying a bold word. Dowton's art is only an imitation of art, of an affected or assumed character; but in Russell's Jerry you see the very soul of nature, in a fellow that is "pigeon livered and lacks gall," laid open and anatomised. You can see that his heart is no bigger than a pin, and his head as soft as a pippin. His whole aspect is chilled and frightened as if he had been dipped in a pond, and yet he looks as if he would like to be snug and comfortable, if he durst. He smiles as if he would be friends with you upon any terms, and the tears come in his eyes because you will not let him. The tones of his voice are prophetic as the cuckoo's under-song. His words are made of water-gruel. The scene in which he tries to make a confidant of the Major is great; and his song of "Robinson Crusoe" as melancholy as the island itself. The reconciliation scene with his wife, and his exclamation over her, "To think that I should make my Molly *veep*," are pathetic, if the last stage of human infirmity is so. This farce appears to us to be both moral and entertaining; yet it does not take. It is considered as an unjust satire on the city and the country at large, and there is a very frequent repeti-

tion of the word "nonsense" in the house during the
performance. Mr. Dowton was even hissed, either
from the upper boxes or gallery, in his speech recount-
ing the marching of his corps "from Brentford to
Ealing, and from Ealing to Acton;" and several persons in the pit, who thought the whole *low*, were for
going out. This shows well for the progress of civilisation. We suppose the manners described in the *Mayor
of Garratt* have in the last forty years become absolete,
and the characters ideal; we have no longer either hen-
pecked or brutal husbands, or domineering wives; the
Miss Molly Jollops no longer wed Jerry Sneaks, or
admire the brave Major Sturgeons on the other
side of Temple Bar; all our soldiers have become
heroes, and our magistrates respectable, and the farce
of life is o'er!

THE DISTRESSED MOTHER

Examiner, September 22, 1816

A MR. MACREADY appeared at Covent Garden Theatre
on Monday and Friday, in the character of Orestes in
the *Distressed Mother*, a bad play for the display of
his powers, in which, however, he succeeded in
making a decidedly favourable impression upon the
audience. His voice is powerful in the highest degree,
and at the same time possesses great harmony and
modulation. His face is not equally calculated for the
stage. He declaims better than anybody we have lately
heard. He is accused of being violent, and of wanting
pathos. Neither of these objections is true. His manner of delivering the first speeches in this play was admirable, and the want of increasing interest afterwards
was the fault of the author rather than the actor. The
fine suppressed tone in which he assented to Pyrrhus's
command to convey the message to Hermione was a
test of his variety of power, and brought down re-

peated acclamations from the house. We do not lay much stress on his mad scene, though that was very good in its kind, for mad scenes do not occur very often, and, when they do, had in general better be omitted. We have not the slightest hesitation in saying that Mr. Macready is by far the best tragic actor that has come out in our remembrance, with the exception of Mr. Kean. We, however, heartily wish him well out of this character of Orestes. It is a kind of forlorn hope in tragedy. There is nothing to be made of it on the English stage beyond experiment. It is a trial, not a triumph. These French plays puzzle an English audience exceedingly. They cannot attend to the actor, for the difficulty they have in understanding the author. We think it wrong in any actor of great merit (which we hold Mr. Macready to be) to come out in an ambiguous character, to salve his reputation. An actor is like a man who throws himself from the top of a steeple by a rope. He should choose the highest steeple he can find, that, if he does not succeed in coming safe to the ground, he may break his neck at once, and so put himself and the spectators out of further pain.

Ambrose Phillips's *Distressed Mother* is a very good translation from Racine's *Andromache*. It is an alternation of topics, of *pros* and *cons*, on the casuistry of domestic and state affairs, and produced a great effect of *ennui* on the audience. When you hear one of the speeches in these rhetorical tragedies, you know as well what will be the answer to it, as when you see the tide coming up the river—you know that it will return again. The other actors filled their parts with successful mediocrity.

We highly disapprove of the dresses worn on this occasion, and supposed to be the exact Greek costume. We do not know that the Greek heroes were dressed like women, or wore their long hair straight down their backs. Or even supposing that they did, this is

not generally known or understood by the audience;
and though the preservation of the ancient costume
is a good thing, it is of more importance not to shock
our present prejudices. The managers of Covent Garden are not the Society of Antiquaries. The attention
to costume is only necessary to preserve probability;
in the present instance, it could only violate it, because
there is nothing to lead the public opinion to expect
such an exhibition. We know how the Turks are
dressed, from seeing them in the streets; we know the
costume of the Greek statues, from seeing casts in the
shop windows; we know that savages go naked, from
reading voyages and travels; but we do not know that
the Grecian chiefs at the Siege of Troy were dressed
as Mr. Charles Kemble, Mr. Abbott, and Mr.
Macready were the other evening in the *Distressed
Mother*. It is a discovery of the managers, and they
should have kept their secret to themselves. The
epithet in Homer, applied to the Grecian warriors,
κάρη κομόωντεζ, is not any proof. It signifies, not *long-
haired*, but literally *bushy-headed*, which would come
nearer to the common Brutus head than this long
dangling slip of hair. The oldest and most authentic
models we have are the Elgin Marbles, and it is certain the Theseus is a *crop*. One would think this standard might satisfy the Committee of Managers in
point of classical antiquity. But no such thing. They
are much deeper in Greek costume and the history of
the fabulous ages, than those old-fashioned fellows, the
Sculptors who lived in the time of Pericles. But we
have said quite enough on this point.

MR. MACREADY'S MENTEVOLE

Examiner, October 6, 1816

MR. MACREADY'S Mentevole, in the *Italian Lover*, is
very highly spoken of. We only saw the last act of it,

but it appeared to us to be very fine in its kind. It was natural, easy, and forcible. Indeed, we suspect some parts of it were too natural, that is, that Mr. Macready thought too much of what his feelings might dictate in such circumstances, rather than of what the circumstances must have dictated to him to do. We allude particularly to the half-significant, half-hysterical laugh, and distorted jocular leer, with his eyes towards the persons accusing him of the murder, when the evidence of his guilt comes out. Either the author did not intend him to behave in this manner, or he must have made the other parties on the stage interrupt him as a self-convicted criminal. His appeal to Manoah (the witness against him) to suppress the proofs which must be fatal to his honour and his life, was truly affecting. His resumption of a spirit of defiance was not sufficiently dignified, and was more like the self-sufficient swaggering airs of comedy, than the real grandeur of tragedy, which should always proceed from passion. Mr. Macready sometimes, to express uneasiness and agitation, composes his cravat, as he would in a drawing-room. This is, we think, neither graceful nor natural in extraordinary situations. His tones are equally powerful and flexible, varying with the greatest facility from the lowest to the highest pitch of the human voice.

MR. MACREADY'S OTHELLO

Examiner, October 13, 1816

WE have to speak this week of Mr. Macready's Othello, at Covent Garden Theatre, and, though it must be in favourable terms, it cannot be in very favourable ones. We have been rather spoiled for seeing anyone else in this character, by Mr. Kean's performance of it, and also by having read the play itself lately. Mr. Macready was more than respectable in the part; and he only failed because he attempted to excel. He did not, however, express the individual bursts of feeling, nor the deep and accumulating tide of passion, which ought to be given in Othello. It may perhaps seem an extravagant illustration, but the idea which we think any actor ought to have of this character, to play it to the height of the poetical conception, is that of a majestic serpent wounded, writhing under its pain, stung to madness, and attempting by sudden darts, or coiling up its whole force, to wreak its vengeance on those about it, and falling at last a mighty victim under the redoubled strokes of its assailants. No one can admire more than we do the force of genius and passion which Mr. Kean shows in this part, but he is not stately enough for it. He plays it like a gipsy, and not like a Moor. We miss in Mr. Kean, not the physiognomy, or the costume, so much as the *architectural* building up of the part. This character always puts us in mind of the line—

Let Afric on its hundred thrones rejoice.

It not only appears to hold commerce with meridian suns, and that its blood is made drunk with the heat of scorching skies, but it indistinctly presents to us all the symbols of Eastern magnificence. It wears a crown and turban, and stands before us like a tower. All this, it may be answered, is only saying that Mr. Kean is not so tall as a tower; but anyone, to play Othello properly, ought to look taller and grander than any tower. We shall see how Mr. Young will play it. But this is from our present purpose. Mr. Macready is tall enough for the part, and the looseness of his figure was rather in character with the flexibility of the South; but there were no sweeping outlines, no massy movements in his action.

The movements of passion in Othello (and the motions of the body should answer to those of the mind) resemble the heaving of the sea in a storm; there are no sharp, slight, angular transitions, or, if there are any, they are subject to this general swell and commotion. Mr. Kean is sometimes too wedgy and determined; but Mr. Marcready goes off like a shot, and startles our sense of hearing. One of these sudden explosions was when he is in such haste to answer the demands of the Senate on his services: "I do agnize a natural . . . hardness." &c., as if he was impatient to exculpate himself from some charge, or wanted to take them at their word lest they should retract. There is nothing of this in Othello. He is calm and collected, and the reason why he is carried along with such vehemence by his passions when they are roused, is that he is moved by their collected force. Another fault in Mr. Macready's conception was that he whined and whimpered once or twice, and tried to affect the audience by affecting a pitiful sensibility, not consistent with the dignity and masculine imagination of the character; as where he repeated, "No, not much moved," and again, "Othello's occupation's gone," in a childish treble. The only part which should approach to this effeminate tenderness of complaint is his reflection, "Yet, oh the pity of it, Iago, the pity of it!" What we liked best was his ejaculation, "Swell, bosom, with thy fraught, *for 'tis of aspicks' tongues.*" This was forcibly given, and as if his expression were choked with the bitterness of passion. We do not know how he would have spoken the speech, "Like to the Pontic sea that knows no ebb," &c., which occurs just before, for it was left out. There was also something fine in his uneasiness and inward starting at the name of Cassio, but it was too often repeated, with a view to effect. Mr. Macready got most applause in such speeches as that addressed to Iago, "Horror on horror's head accumulate!" This should be a lesson to him. He very injudiciously, we think, threw himself on a chair at the back of the stage, to deliver the farewell apostrophe to Content, and to the "pride, pomp, and circumstance of glorious war." This might be a relief to him, but it distressed the audience. On the whole, we think Mr. Macready's powers are more adapted to the declamation than to the acting of passion—that is, that he is a better orator than actor. As to Mr. Young's Iago, "we never saw a gentleman acted finer." Mrs. Faucit's Desdemona was very pretty. Mr. C. Kemble's Cassio was excellent.

MR. STEPHEN KEMBLE'S FALSTAFF

Examiner, October 13, 1816

THE town has been entertained this week by seeing Mr. Stephen Kemble in the part of Sir John Falstaff, as they were formerly with seeing Mr. Lambert in his own person. We see no more reason why Mr. Stephen Kemble should play Falstaff, than why Louis XVIIII. is qualified to fill a throne, because he is fat and belongs to a particular family. Every fat man cannot represent a great man. The knight was fat—so is the player; the Emperor was fat—so is the King who stands in his shoes. But there the comparison ends. There is no sympathy in mind—in wit, parts, or discretion. Sir John (and so we may say of the gentleman at St. Helena) "had guts in his brains." The mind was the man. His body did not weigh down his wit. His spirits shone through him. He was not a mere paunch, a bag-pudding, a lump of lethargy, a huge falling sickness, an imminent apoplexy, with water in the head.

The managers of Drury Lane, in providing a Sir John Falstaff to satisfy the taste of the town, seem to ask only, with Mr. Burke's political carcass-butchers, "How he cuts up in the cawl; how he tallows in the kidneys!" We are afraid the junto of managers of Drury Lane are not much wiser than the junto of managers of the affairs of Europe. This, according to the luminous and voluminous critic in the *Courier*, is because their affairs are not under the management of a single person. Would the same argument prove that the affairs of Europe had better have been under the direction of one man? "The gods have not made" the writer in the *Courier* logical as well as "poetical." By the rule above hinted at, every actor is qualified to play Falstaff who is physically incapacitated to play any other character. Sir John Falstaffs may be fatted up like prize oxen. Nor does the evil in this case produce its own remedy, as where an actor's success depends upon his own leanness and that of the part he plays. Sir Richard Steele tells us (in one of the *Tatlers*) of a poor actor in his time who, having nothing to do, fell away, and became such a wretched, meagre-looking object, that he was pitched upon as a proper person to represent the starved apothecary in *Romeo and Juliet*. He did this so much to the life that he was repeatedly called upon to play it; but his person improving with his circumstances, he was in a short time rendered unfit to play it with the same effect as before, and laid aside. Having no other resource, he accordingly fell away again with the loss of his part, and was again called upon to appear in it with his former reputation.[1] Anyone, on the contrary, who thrives in Falstaff, is always in an increasing capacity to overlay the part. But we have done with this unpleasant subject.

MR. KEMBLE'S CATO

Examiner, October 27, 1816
MR. KEMBLE has resumed his engagements at Covent Garden Theatre for the season—it is said in the playbills, for the last time. There is something in the word

[1] This is a very much amplified version of the story of the actor, Will Peer, as humorously told in the *Guardian*.

last that, "being mortal," we do not like on these occasions; but there is this of good in it, that it throws us
back on past recollections, and when we are about to
take leave of an old friend, we feel desirous to settle
all accounts with him, and to see that the balance is
not against us on the score of gratitude. Mr. Kemble
will, we think, find that the public are just, and his
last season, if it is to be so, will not, we hope, be the
least brilliant of his career. As his meridian was bright,
so let his sunset be golden, and without a cloud. His
reception in *Cato,* on Friday, was most flattering, and
he well deserved the cheering and cordial welcome
which he received. His voice only failed him in
strength; but his tones, his looks, his gestures, were all
that could be required in the character. He is the
most classical of actors. He is the only one of the
moderns who, both in figure and action, approaches
the beauty and grandeur of the antique. In the scene
of the soliloquy, just before his death, he was rather
inaudible, and indeed the speech itself is not worth
hearing; but his person, manner, and dress, seemed cast
in the very mould of Roman elegance and dignity.

THE IRON CHEST

Examiner, December 1, 1816

The Iron Chest is founded on the story of *Caleb
Williams,* one of the best novels in the language, and
the very best of the modern school; but the play itself
is by no means the best play that ever was written,
either in ancient or modern times, though really in
modern times we do not know of any much better.
Mr. Colman's serious style, which is in some measure
an imitation of Shakespeare's, is natural and flowing;
and there is a constant intermixture, as in our elder
drama, a *mélange* of the tragic and comic; but there
is rather a want of force and depth in the impassioned

parts of his tragedies, and what there is of this kind is impeded in its effect by the comic. The two plots (the serious and ludicrous) do not seem going on and gaining ground at the same time, but each part is intersected and crossed by the other, and has to set out again in the next scene, after being thwarted in the former one, like a person who has to begin a story over again in which he has been interrupted. In Shakespeare, the comic parts serve only as a relief to the tragic. Colman's tragic scenes are not high-wrought enough to require any such relief; and this perhaps may be a sufficient reason why modern writers, who are so sparing of their own nerves, and those of their readers, should not be allowed to depart from the effeminate simplicity of the classic style. In Shakespeare, again, the comic varieties are only an accompaniment to the loftier tragic movement; at least the only exception is in the part of Falstaff in *Henry IV.*, which is not, however, a tragedy of any deep interest. In Colman you do not know whether the comedy or tragedy is principal, whether he made the comic for the sake of the tragic, or the tragic for the sake of the comic, and you suspect he would be as likely as any of his contemporaries to parody his own most pathetic passages, just as Munden caricatures the natural touches of garrulous simplicity in old Adam Winterton, to make the galleries and boxes laugh. The great beauty of *Caleb Williams* is lost in the play. The interest of the novel arises chiefly from two things: the gradual working up of the curiosity of Caleb Williams with respect to the murder, by the incessant goading on of which he extorts the secret from Falkland, and then from the systematic persecution which he undergoes from his master, which at length urges him to reveal the secret to the world. Both these are very ingeniously left out by Mr. Colman, who jumps at a conclusion, but misses his end.

The history of the *Iron Chest* is well known to dra-

matic readers. Mr. Kemble either could not, or would
not, play the part of Sir Edward Mortimer (the Falkland of Mr. Goodwin's novel)—he made nothing of
it, or at least made short work of it, for it was only
played one night. He had a cough and a cold, and he
hemmed and hawed, and whined and drivelled through
the part in a marvellous manner. Mr. Colman was en-
raged at the ill-success of his piece, and charged it
upon Kemble's acting, who, he said, did not do his
best. Now we confess he generally tries to do his best,
and if that best is no better, it is not his fault. We
think the fault was in the part, which wants circum-
stantial dignity. Give Mr. Kemble only the *man* to
play, why, he is nothing; give him the paraphernalia
of greatness, and he is great. He "wears his heart in
compliment extern." He is the statue on the pedestal,
that cannot come down without danger of shaming its
worshippers; a figure that tells well with appropriate
scenery and dresses; but not otherwise. Mr. Kemble
contributes his own person to a tragedy—but only
that. The poet must furnish all the rest, and make the
other parts equally dignified and graceful, or Mr.
Kemble will not help him out. He will not lend dignity to the mean, spirit to the familiar; he will not
impart life and motion, passion and imagination, to
all around him, for he has neither life nor motion,
passion nor imagination in himself. He minds only the
conduct of his own person, and leaves the piece to
shift for itself. Not so Mr. Kean. "Truly he hath a
devil"; and if the fit comes over him too often, yet, as
tragedy is not the representation of *still-life*, we think
this much better than being never roused at all. We
like

> The fiery soul that working out its way,
> Fretted the pigmy body to decay,
> And o'er-inform'd the tenement of clay.[1]

[1] Dryden, *Absalom and Achitophel.*

Mr. Kean has passion and energy enough to afford to
lend it to the circumstances in which he is placed,
without leaning upon them for support. He can make
a dialogue between a master and a servant in common
life tragic, or infuse a sentiment into *The Iron Chest*.
He is not afraid of being let down by his company.
Formal dignity and studied grace are ridiculous, except in particular circumstances; passion and nature
are everywhere the same, and these Mr. Kean carries
with him into all his characters, and does not want the
others. In the last, however, which are partly things of
manner and assumption, he improves, as well as in the
recitation of set speeches; for example, in the Soliloquy on Honour in the present play. His description of
the assassination of his rival to Wilford was admirable,
and the description of his "seeing his giant form roll
before him in the dust," was terrific and grand. In the
picturesque expression of passion, by outward action,
Mr. Kean is unrivalled. The transitions in this play,
from calmness to deep despair, from concealed sus-
picion to open rage, from smooth decorous indifference to the convulsive agonies of remorse, gave Mr.
Kean frequent opportunities for the display of his
peculiar talents. The mixture of commonplace familiarity and solemn injunctions in his speeches to Wilford when in the presence of others, was what no
other actor could give with the same felicity and
force. The last scene of all—his coming to life again
after his swooning at the fatal discovery of his guilt,
and then falling back after a ghastly struggle, like a
man waked from the tomb, into despair and death in
the arms of his mistress, was one of those consumma-
tions of the art, which those who have seen and have
not felt them in this actor, may be assured that they
have never seen or felt anything in the course of their
lives, and never will to the end of them.

MR. KEMBLE'S KING JOHN

Examiner, December 8, 1816

WE wish we had never seen Mr. Kean. He has destroyed the Kemble religion; and it is the religion in
which we were brought up. Never again shall we behold Mr. Kemble with the same pleasure that we did,
nor see Mr. Kean with the same pleasure that we have
seen Mr. Kemble formerly. We used to admire Mr.
Kemble's figure and manner, and had no idea that
there was any want of art or nature. We feel the force
and nature of Mr. Kean's acting, but then we feel the
want of Mr. Kemble's person. Thus an old and delightful prejudice is destroyed, and no new enthusiasm, no second idolatry, comes to takes its place. Thus,
by degrees, knowledge robs us of pleasure, and the
cold icy hand of experience freezes up the warm current of the imagination, and crusts it over with unfeeling criticism. The knowledge we acquire of various kinds of excellence, as successive opportunities
present themselves, leads us to require a combination
of them which we never find realised in any individual,
and all the consolation for the disappointment of our
fastidious expectations is in a sort of fond and doting
retrospect of the past. It is possible, indeed, that the
force of prejudice might often kindly step in to suspend the chilling effects of experience, and we might
be able to see an old favourite, by a voluntary for-
getfulness of others things, as we saw him twenty
years ago; but his friends take care to prevent this,
and by provoking invidious comparisons, and crying
up their idol as a model of abstract perfection, force us
to be ill-natured in our own defence.

We went to see Mr. Kemble's King John, and he
became the part so well, in costume, look, and gesture,
that if left to ourselves, we could have gone to sleep

over it, and dreamt that it was fine, and "when we waked, have cried to dream again." But we were told that it was really fine, as fine as Garrick, as fine as Mrs. Siddons, as fine as Shakespeare; so we rubbed our eyes and kept a sharp look out, but we saw nothing but a deliberate intention on the part of Mr. Kemble to act the part finely. And so he did in a certain sense, but not by any means as Shakespeare wrote it, nor as it might be played. He did not harrow up the feelings, he did not electrify the sense; he did not enter into the nature of the part himself, nor consequently move others with terror or pity. The introduction to the scene with Hubert was certainly excellent: you saw instantly, and before a syllable was uttered, partly from the change of countenance, and partly from the arrangement of the scene, the purpose which had entered his mind to murder the young prince. But the remainder of this trying scene, though the execution was elaborate—painfully elaborate, and the outline well conceived, wanted the filling up, the true and master touches, the deep, piercing, heartfelt tones of nature. It was done well and skilfully, *according to the book of arithmetic*; but no more. Mr. Kemble, when he approaches Hubert to sound his disposition, puts on an insidious, insinuating, fawning aspect, and so he ought; but we think it should not be, though it was, that kind of wheedling smile, as if he was going to persuade him that the business he wished him to undertake was a mere jest, and his natural repugnance to it an idle prejudice, that might be carried off by a certain pleasant drollery of eye and manner. Mr. Kemble's look, to our apprehension, was exactly as if he had just caught the eye of some person of his acquaintance in the boxes, and was trying to suppress a rising smile at the metamorphosis he had undergone since dinner. Again, he changes his voice three times, in repeating the name of Hubert; and the changes might be fine, but they did not vibrate on our feelings; so we cannot tell. They appeared to us like a tragic *voluntary*. Through almost the whole scene, this celebrated actor did not seem to feel the part itself as it was set down for him, but to be considering how he ought to feel it, or how he should express by rule and method what he did not feel. He was sometimes slow, and sometimes hurried; sometimes familiar, and sometimes solemn; but always with an evident design and determination to be so. The varying tide of passion did not appear to burst from the source of nature in his breast, but to be drawn from a theatrical leaden cistern, and then directed through certain conduit-pipes and artificial channels, to fill the audience with well-regulated and harmless sympathy.

We are afraid, judging from the effects of this representation, that "man delights not us, nor woman neither"; for we did not like Miss O'Neill's Constance better, nor so well as Mr. Kemble's King John. This character, more than any other of Shakespeare's females, treads perhaps upon the verge of extravagance; the impatience of grief, combined with the violence of her temper, borders on insanity—her imagination grows light-headed. But still the boundary between poetry and frenzy is not passed: she is neither a virago nor mad. Miss O'Neill gave more of the vulgar than the poetical side of the character. She generally does so of late. Mr. Charles Kemble in the Bastard had the "bulk, the thews, the sinews" of Falconbridge; would that he had had "the spirit" too. There was one speech which he gave well—"Could Sir Robert make this leg?" And suiting the action to the word, as well he might, it had a great effect upon the house.

CORIOLANUS

Examiner, December 15, 1816
Coriolanus has of late been repeatedly acted at Covent

Garden Theatre. Shakespeare has in this play shown himself well versed in history and state-affairs. *Coriolanus* is a storehouse of political commonplaces. Anyone who studies it may save himself the trouble of reading Burke's "Reflections," or Paine's "Rights of Man," or the debates in both Houses of Parliament since the French Revolution or our own. The arguments for and against aristocracy, or democracy, on the privileges of the few and the claims of the many, on liberty and slavery, power and the abuse of it, peace and war, are here very ably handled, with the spirit of a poet, and the acuteness of a philosopher. Shakespeare himself seems to have had a leaning to the arbitrary side of the question, perhaps from some feeling of contempt for his own origin; and to have spared no occasion of baiting the rabble. What he says of them is very true; what he says of their betters is also very true, though he dwells less upon it. The cause of the people is indeed but ill calculated as a subject for poetry; it admits of rhetoric, which goes into argument and explanation, but it presents no immediate or distinct images to the mind, "no jutting frieze, buttress, or coigne of vantage" for poetry "to make its pendant bed and procreant cradle in." The language of poetry naturally falls in with the language of power. The imagination is an exaggerating and exclusive faculty; it takes from one thing to add to another; it accumulates circumstances together to give the greatest possible effect to a favourite object. The understanding is a dividing and measuring faculty, it judges of things, not according to their immediate impression on the mind, but according to their relations to one another. The one is a monopolising faculty, which seeks the greatest quantity of present excitement by inequality and disproportion; the other is a distributive faculty, which seeks the greatest quantity of ultimate good by justice and proportion. The one is an aristocratical, the other a republican faculty. The principle of poetry is a very anti-levelling principle. It aims at effect, is exists by contrast. It admits of no medium. It is everything by excess. It rises above the ordinary standard of sufferings and crimes. It presents an imposing appearance. It shows its head turreted, crowned, and crested. Its front is gilt and blood-stained. Before it, "it carries noise, and behind it, it leaves tears." It has its altars and its victims, sacrifices, human sacrifices. Kings, priests, nobles, are its train-bearers; tyrants and slaves its executioners— "Carnage is its daughter!" Poetry is right royal. It puts the individual for the species, the one above the infinite many, might before right. A lion hunting a flock of sheep or a herd of wild asses, is a more poetical object than they; and we even take part with the lordly beast, because our vanity, or some other feeling, makes us disposed to place ourselves in the situation of the strongest party. So we feel some concern for the poor citizens of Rome, when they meet together to compare their wants and grievances, till Coriolanus comes in, and, with blows and big words, drives this set of "poor rats," this rascal scum, to their homes and beggary, before him. There is nothing heroical in a multitude of miserable rogues not wishing to be starved, or complaining that they are like to be so; but when a single man comes forward to brave their cries, and to make them submit to the last indignities, from mere pride and self-will, our admiration of his prowess is immediately converted into contempt for their pusillanimity. The insolence of power is stronger than the plea of necessity. The tame submission to usurped authority, or even the natural resistance to it, has nothing to excite or flatter the imagination; it is the assumption of a right to insult or oppress others, that carries an imposing air of superiority with it. We had rather be the oppressor than the oppressed.

The love of power in ourselves, and the admiration

of it in others, are both natural to man; the one makes him a tyrant, the other a slave. Wrong, dressed out in pride, pomp, and circumstance, has more attraction than abstract right. Coriolanus complains of the fickleness of the people; yet the instant he cannot gratify his pride and obstinacy at their expense, he turns his arms against his country. If his country was not worth defending, why did he build his pride on its defence? He is a conqueror and a hero; he conquers other countries, and makes this a plea for enslaving his own; and when he is prevented from doing so, he leagues with its enemies to destroy his country. He rates the people "as if he were a God to punish, and not a man of their infirmity." He scoffs at one of their tribunes for maintaining their rites and franchises: "Mark you his absolute *shall?*" not marking his own absolute *will* to take everything from them; his impatience of the slightest opposition to his own pretensions being in proportion to their arrogance and absurdity. If the great and powerful had the beneficence and wisdom of gods, then all this would have been well; if with greater knowledge of what is good for the people, they had as great a care for their interest as they have for their own; if they were seated above the world, sympathising with their welfare, but not feeling the passions of men, receiving neither good nor hurt from them, but bestowing their benefits as free gifts on them, they might then rule over them like another Providence. But this is not the case. Coriolanus is unwilling that the Senate should show their "cares" for the people, lest their "cares" should be construed into "fears," to the subversion of all due authority; and he is no sooner disappointed in his schemes to deprive the people, not only of the cares of the state, but of all power to redress themselves, than Volumnia is made madly to exclaim—

> Now the red pestilence strike all trades in Rome,
> And occupations perish!

This is but natural; it is but natural for a mother to have more regard for her son than for a whole city; but then the city should be left to take some care of itself. The care of the state cannot, we here see, be safely entrusted to maternal affection, or to the domestic charities of high life. The great have private feelings of their own, to which the interests of humanity and justice must courtesy. Their interests are so far from being the same as those of the community, that they are in direct and necessary opposition to them; their power is at the expense of our weakness; their riches, of our poverty; their pride, of our degradation; their splendour, of our wretchedness; their tyranny, of our servitude. If they had the superior intelligence ascribed to them (which they have not) it would only render them so much more formidable; and from gods would convert them into devils.

The whole dramatic moral of *Coriolanus* is, that those who have little shall have less, and that those who have much shall take all that others have left. The people are poor, therefore they ought to be starved. They are slaves, therefore they ought to be beaten. They work hard, therefore they ought to be treated like beasts of burden. They are ignorant, therefore they ought not to be allowed to feel that they want food, or clothing, or rest, that they are enslaved, oppressed, and miserable. This is the logic of the imagination and the passions; which seek to aggrandise what excites admiration, and to heap contempt on misery, to raise power into tyranny, and to make tyranny absolute; to thrust down that which is low still lower, and to make wretches desperate; to exalt magistrates into kings, kings into gods; to degrade subjects to the rank of slaves, and slaves to the condition of brutes. The history of mankind is a romance, a mask, a tragedy constructed upon the principles of *poetical justice*; it is a noble or royal hunt, in which what is sport to the few is death to the many, and in which the spectators halloo and encourage the strong to set upon the weak, and cry havoc in the chase, though they do not share in the spoil. We may depend upon it, that what men delight to read in books, they will put in practice in reality.

Mr. Kemble in the part of Coriolanus was as great as ever. Miss O'Neill as Volumnia was not so great as Mrs. Siddons. There is a *fleshiness*, if we may so say, about her whole manner, voice, and person, which does not suit the character of the Roman matron. One of the most amusing things in the representation of this play is the contrast between Kemble and little Simmons. The former seems as if he would gibbet the latter on his nose, he looks so lofty. The fidgetting, uneasy, insignificant gestures of Simmons are perhaps a little caricatured; and Kemble's supercilious airs and *nonchalance* remind one of the unaccountable abstracted air, the contracted eyebrows and suspended chin, of a man who is just going to sneeze.

MR. BOOTH'S DUKE OF GLOUCESTER

Examiner, February 16, 1817

A GENTLEMAN of the name of Booth, who, we understand, has been acting with considerable applause at Worthing and Brighton, came out in Richard, Duke of Gloucester, at Covent Garden on Wednesday. We do not know well what to think of his powers, till we see him in some part in which he is more himself. His face is adapted to tragic characters, and his voice wants neither strength nor musical expression. But almost the whole of his performance was an exact copy or parody of Mr. Kean's manner of doing the same part. It was a complete, but at the same time a successful, piece of plagiarism. We do not think this kind of second-hand reputation can last upon the London boards for more than a character or two. In

the country these *doubles* of the best London performers go down very well, for they are the best they
can get, and they have not the originals to make invidious comparisons with. But it will hardly do to bring
out the same entertainment that we can have as it is
first served up at Drury Lane, in a hashed state at
Covent Garden. We do not blame Mr. Booth for bor-
rowing Mr. Kean's coat and feathers to appear in upon
a first and trying occasion, but if he wishes to gain a
permanent reputation he must come forward in his
own person. He must try to be original, and not content himself with treading in another's steps. We say
this the rather because, as far as we could judge, Mr.
Booth, in point of execution, did those passages the
best in which he now and then took leave of Mr.
Kean's decided and extreme manner, and became more
mild and tractable. Such was his recitation of the
soliloquy on his own ambitious projects, and of that
which occurs the night before the battle. In these he
seemed to yield to the impulse of his own feelings,
and to follow the natural tones and cadence of his
voice. They were the best parts of his performance.
The worst were those where he imitated, or rather
caricatured, Mr. Kean's hoarseness of delivery and
violence of action, and affected an energy without
seeming to feel it. Such were his repulse of Buckingham,
his exclamation, "What does he in the north," &c.,
his telling his attendants to set down the corse of King
Henry, &c. The scene with Lady Anne, on the contrary, which was of a softer and more insinuating
kind, he was more successful in, and, though still a
palpable imitation of Mr. Kean, it had all the originality that imitation could have, for he seemed to feel
it. His manner of saying "Good-night," and of an-
swering, when he received the anonymous paper, "A
weak invention of the enemy," we consider as mere
tricks in the art, which no one but a professed mimic
has a right to play. The dying scene was without

effect. The greatest drawback to Mr. Booth's acting is a perpetual strut, and unwieldy swagger in his ordinary gait and manner, which, though it may pass at Brighton for *grand, gracious, and magnificent*, even the lowest of the mob will laugh at in London. This is the third imitation of Mr. Kean we have seen attempted, and the only one that has not been a complete failure. The imitation of original genius is the *forlorn hope* of the candidates for fame: its faults are so easily overdone, its graces are so hard to catch. A Kemble school we can understand; a Kean school is, we suspect, a contradiction in terms. Art may be taught, because it is learnt; Nature can neither be taught nor learnt. The secrets of Art may be said to have a common or *pass* key to unlock them; the secrets of Nature have but one master-key—the heart.

MR. BOOTH'S IAGO

Examiner, February 3, 1817
THE managers of Covent Garden Theatre, after having announced in the bills that Mr. Booth's Richard the Third had met with a success unprecedented in the annals of histrionic fame (which, to do them justice, was not the case), very disinterestedly declined engaging him at more than two pounds a week, as report speaks. Now we think they were wrong, either in puffing him so unmercifully, or in haggling with him so pitifully. It was either trifling with the public or with the actor. The consequence, as it has turned out, has been that Mr. Booth, who was to start as "the fell opposite" of Mr. Kean, has been taken by the hand by that gentleman, who was an old fellow comedian of his in the country, and engaged at Drury Lane at a salary of ten pounds per week. So we hear. And it was in evident allusion to this circumstance that when Mr. Booth, as Iago, said on Thursday night, "I know

my price no less," John Bull, who has very sym-
pathetic pockets, gave a loud shout of triumph, which
resounded along all the benches of the pit. We must
say that Mr. Booth pleased us much more in Iago than
in Richard. He was, it is true, well supported by Mr.
Kean in Othello, but he also supported him better in
that character than anyone else we have seen play
with him. The two rival actors hunt very well in couple. One thing which we did not expect, and which
we think reconciled us to Mr. Booth's imitations,
was that they were here performed in the presence,
and as it were with the permission, of Mr. Kean.
There is no fear of deception in the case. The original
is there in person to answer for his identity, and "give
the world assurance of himself." The original and the
copy go together, like the substance and the shadow.
But then there neither is nor can be any idea of competition, and so far we are satisfied. In fact, Mr.
Booth's Iago was a very close and spirited repetition
of Mr. Kean's manner of doing that part. It was indeed the most spirited copy we ever saw upon the
stage, considering at the same time the scrupulous exactness with which he adhered to his model in the
most trifling *minutiæ*. We need only mention as instances of similarity in the by-play, Mr. Booth's mode
of delivering the lines, "My wit comes from my brains
like birdlime," or his significant, and we think improper, pointing to the dead bodies, as he goes out in
the last scene. The same remarks apply to his delivery,
that we made last week. He has two voices; one his
own, and the other Mr. Kean's. His delineation of
Iago is more bustling and animated; Mr. Kean's is
more close and cool. We suspect that Mr. Booth is not
only a professed and deliberate imitator of Mr. Kean,
but that he has in general the chameleon quality (we
do not mean that of living upon air, as the Covent
Garden managers supposed, but) of reflecting all objects that come in contact with him. We occasionally

caught the mellow tones of Mr. Macready rising out of the thorough bass of Mr. Kean's guttural emphasis, and the flaunting, *dégagé* robe of Mr. Young's oriental manner, flying off from the tight vest and tunic of the little "bony prizer" of the Drury Lane Company.

Of Mr. Kean's Othello we have not room to speak as it deserves, nor have we the power if we had the room; it is beyond all praise. Anyone who has not seen him in the third act of *Othello* (and seen him near) cannot have an idea of perfect tragic acting.

MRS. SIDDONS'S LADY MACBETH

Examiner, June 8, 1817

MRS. SIDDONS's appearance in Lady Macbeth at Covent Garden on Thursday drew immense crowds to every part of the house. We should suppose that more than half the number of persons were compelled to return without gaining admittance. We succeeded in gaining a seat in one of the back-boxes, and saw this wonderful performance at a distance, and consequently at a disadvantage. Though the distance of place is a disadvantage to a performance like Mrs. Siddons's Lady Macbeth, we question whether the distance of time at which we have formerly seen it is any. It is nearly twenty years since we first saw her in this character, and certainly the impression which we have still left on our minds from that first exhibition, is stronger than the one we received the other evening. The sublimity of Mrs. Siddons's acting is such, that the first impulse which it gives to the mind can never wear out, and we doubt whether this original and paramount impression is not weakened, rather than strengthened, by subsequent repetition. We do not read the tragedy of *The Robbers* twice; if we have seen Mrs. Siddons in Lady Macbeth only once, it is enough. The impression is stamped there for ever, and

any after-experiments and critical inquiries only serve
to fritter away and tamper with the sacredness of the
early recollection. We see into the details of the character, its minute excellencies or defects, but the great
masses, the gigantic proportions, are in some degree
lost upon us by custom and familiarity. It is the first
blow that staggers us; by gaining time we recover our
self-possession. Mrs. Siddons's Lady Macbeth is little
less appalling in its effects than the apparition of a preternatural being; but if we were accustomed to see a
preternatural being constantly, our astonishment
would by degrees diminish.

We do not know whether it is owing to the cause
here stated, or to a falling off in Mrs. Siddons's acting,
but we certainly thought her performance the other
night inferior to what it used to be. She speaks too
slow, and her manner has not that decided, sweeping
majesty, which used to characterise her as the Muse
of Tragedy herself. Something of apparent indecision
is perhaps attributable to the circumstance of her only
acting at present on particular occasions. An actress
who appears only once a year cannot play so well as
if she was in the habit of acting once a week. We
therefore wish Mrs. Siddons would either return to
the stage, or retire from it altogether. By her present
uncertain wavering between public and private life,
she may diminish her reputation, while she can add
nothing to it.

MR. KEMBLE'S RETIREMENT

Times, June 25, 1817

MR. KEMBLE took his leave of the stage on Monday
night, in the character of Coriolanus. On his first
coming forward to pronounce his Farewell Address,
he was received with a shout like thunder; on his retiring after it, the applause was long before it subsided

entirely away. There is something in these partings with old public favourites exceedingly affecting. They teach us the shortness of human life, and the vanity of human pleasures. Our associations of admiration and delight with theatrical performers are among our earliest recollections—among our last regrets. They are links that connect the beginning and the end of life together; *their* bright and giddy career of popularity measures the arch that spans our brief existence. It is near twenty years ago since we first saw Mr. Kemble in the same character—yet how short, the interval seems! The impression appears as distinct as if it were of yesterday. In fact, intellectual objects, in proportion as they are lasting, may be said to shorten life. Time has no effect upon them. The petty and the personal, that which appeals to our senses and our interests, is by degrees forgotten, and fades away into the distant obscurity of the past. The grand and the ideal, that which appeals to the imagination, can only perish with it, and remains with us, unimpaired in its lofty abstraction, from youth to age; as, wherever we go, we still see the same heavenly bodies shining over our heads! We forget numberless things that have happened to ourselves, one generation of follies after another; but not the first time of our seeing Mr. Kemble, nor shall we easily forget the last! Coriolanus, the character in which he took his leave of the stage, was one of the first in which we remember to have seen him; and it was one in which we were not sorry to part with him, for we wished to see him appear like himself to the last. Nor was he wanting to himself on this occasion; he played the part as well as he ever did —with as much freshness and vigour. There was no abatement of spirit and energy—none of grace and dignity; his look, his action, his expression of the character, were the same as they ever were; they could not be finer. It is mere cant to say that Mr. Kemble has quite fallen off of late— that he is not what he was. He

may have fallen off in the opinion of some jealous admirers, because he is no longer in exclusive possession
of the stage; but in himself he has not fallen off a jot.
Why, then, do we approve of his retiring? Because we
do not wish him to wait till it is *necessary* for him to
retire. On the last evening he displayed the same excellences, and gave the same prominence to the very
same passages, that he used to do. We might refer to
his manner of doing obeisance to his mother in the
triumphal procession in the second act, and to the
scene with Aufidius in the last act, as among the most
striking instances. The action with which he accompanied the proud taunt to Aufidius—

> —like an eagle in a dove-cote, I
> Flutter'd your Volscians in Corioli:
> Alone I did it—

gave double force and beauty to the image. Again,
where he waits for the coming of Aufidius in his rival's
house, he stood at the foot of the statue of Mars, himself another Mars! In the reconciliation scene with his
mother, which is the finest in the play, he was not
equally impressive. Perhaps this was not the fault of
Mr. Kemble, but of the stage itself, which can hardly
do justice to such thoughts and sentiments as here
occur:—

> —My mother bows,
> As if Olympus to a mole-hill should
> In supplication nod; . . .

Mr. Kemble's voice seemed to faint and stagger, to
be strained and cracked, under the weight of this
majestic image; but, indeed, we know of no tones deep
or full enough to bear along the swelling tide of sentiment it conveys; nor can we conceive anything in
outward form to answer to it, except when Mrs.
Siddons played the part of Volumnia.

We may on this occasion be expected to say a few

words on the general merits of Mr. Kemble as an actor, and on the principal characters he performed; in doing which, we shall

> Nothing extenuate,
> Nor set down aught in malice.

It has always appeared to us that the range of characters in which Mr. Kemble more particularly shone, and was superior to every other actor, were those which consisted in the development of some one solitary sentiment or exclusive passion. From a want of rapidity, of scope, and variety, he was often deficient in expressing the bustle and complication of different interests; nor did he possess the faculty of overpowering the mind by sudden and irresistible bursts of passions; but in giving the habitual workings of a predominant feeling, as in Penruddock, or The Stranger, in Coriolanus, Cato, and some others, where all the passions move round a central point, and are governed by one master-key, he stood unrivalled. Penruddock, in *The Wheel of Fortune*, was one of his most correct and interesting performances, and one of the most perfect on the modern stage. The deeply-rooted, mild, pensive melancholy of the character, its embittered recollections and dignified benevolence, were conveyed by Mr. Kemble with equal truth, elegance, and feeling. In The Stranger, again, which is in fact the same character, he brooded over the recollection of disappointed hope till it became a part of himself; it sunk deeper into his mind the longer he dwelt upon it; his regrets only became more profound as they became more durable. His person was moulded to the character. The weight of sentiment which oppressed him was never suspended; the spring at his heart was never lightened—it seemed as if his whole life had been a suppressed sigh! So in Coriolanus, he exhibited the ruling passion with the same unshaken firmness, he preserved the same haughty dignity of demeanour, the same energy of will, and unbending sternness of temper throughout. He was swayed by a single impulse. His tenaciousness of purpose was only irritated by opposition; he turned neither to the right nor the left; the vehemence with which he moved forward increasing every instant, till it hurried him on to the catastrophe. In Leontes, also, in *The Winter's Tale* (a character he at one time played often), the growing jealousy of the King, and the exclusive possession which this passion gradually obtains over his mind, were marked by him in the finest manner, particularly where he exclaims—

> —Is whispering nothing?
> Is leaning cheek to cheek? is meeting noses?
> Kissing with inside lip? stopping the career
> Of laughter with a sigh?—a note infallible
> Of breaking honesty,—horsing foot on foot?
> Skulking in corners? wishing clocks more swift?
> Hours, minutes? noon, midnight? and all eyes
> Blind with the pin and web but theirs, theirs only,
> That would unseen be wicked? is this nothing?
> Why, then the world and all that's in't is nothing;
> The covering sky is nothing; Bohemia nothing;
> My wife is nothing, if this be nothing! [1]

In the course of this enumeration, every proof told stronger, and followed with quicker and harder strokes; his conviction became more riveted at every step of his progress; and at the end, his mind, and "every corporal agent," appeared wound up to a frenzy of despair. In such characters, Mr. Kemble had no occasion to call to his aid either the resources of invention or the tricks of the art; his success depended on the increasing intensity with which he dwelt on a given feeling, or enforced a passion that resisted all interference or control.

[1] My wife is nothing; nor nothing have these nothings,
If this be nothing.—*Winter's Tale*, i. 2.

In Hamlet, on the contrary, Mr. Kemble in our judgment unavoidably failed from a want of flexibility, of that quick sensibility which yields to every motive, and is borne away with every breath of fancy: which is distracted in the multiplicity of its reflections, and lost in the uncertainty of its resolutions. There is a perpetual undulation of feeling in the character of Hamlet; but in Mr. Kemble's acting, "there was neither variableness nor shadow of turning." He played it like a man in armour, with a determined inveteracy of purpose, in one undeviating straight line, which is as remote from the natural grace and indolent susceptibility of the character, as the sharp angles and abrupt starts to produce an effect which Mr. Kean throws into it.

In King John, which was one of Mr. Kemble's most admired parts, the transitions of feeling, though just and powerful, were prepared too long beforehand, and were too long in executing, to produce their full effect. The actor seemed waiting for some complicated machinery to enable him to make his next movement, instead of trusting to the true impulses of passion. There was no sudden collision of opposite elements; the golden flash of genius was not there; "the fire i' th' flint was cold," for it was not struck. If an image could be constructed by magic art to play King John, it would play it in much the same manner that Mr. Kemble played it.

In Macbeth, Mr. Kemble was unequal to "the tug and war" of the passions which assail him; he stood, as it were, at bay with fortune, and maintained his ground too steadily against "fate and metaphysical aid," instead of staggering and reeling under the appalling visions of the preternatural world, and having his frame wrenched from all the holds and resting places of his will, by the stronger power of imagination. In the latter scenes, however, he displayed great

energy and spirit; and there was a fine melancholy
retrospective tone in his manner of delivering the
lines,

>   —my way of life
> Is fall'n into the sear, the yellow leaf;

which smote upon the heart, and remained there ever
after. His Richard III. wanted that tempest and whirl-
wind of the soul, that life and spirit, and dazzling
rapidity of motion, which fills the stage, and burns in
every part of it, when Mr. Kean performs this character. To Mr. Kean's acting in general, we might apply the lines of the poet where he describes

> The fiery soul that, working out its way,
> Fretted the pigmy body to decay,
> And o'er-inform'd the tenement of clay.[2]

Mr. Kemble's manner, on the contrary, had always
something dry, hard, and pedantic in it. "You shall
relish him more in the scholar than in the soldier;"
but his monotony did not fatigue, his formality did not
displease, because there was always sense and meaning in what he did. The fineness of Mr. Kemble's figure may be supposed to have led to that statue-like appearance which his acting was sometimes too apt to
assume; as the diminutiveness of Mr. Kean's person has
probably compelled him to bustle about too much, and
to attempt to make up for the want of dignity of
form, by the violence and contrast of his attitudes. If
Mr. Kemble were to remain in the same posture for
half an hour, his figure would only excite admiration;
if Mr. Kean were to stand still only for a moment, the
contrary effect would be apparent.[8] One of the hap-

[2] Dryden.
[8] Hazlitt was economical of his ideas. This passage (from "It
has always appeared to us," p. 125) is amplified from an article
which appeared in *The Champion*, November 20, 1814, the
remarks on King John and Macbeth being written in.

piest and most spirited of all Mr. Kemble's performances, and in which even his defects were blended with
his excellences to produce a perfect whole, was his
Pierre. The dissolute indifference assumed by this
character, to cover the darkness of his designs and
the fierceness of his revenge, accorded admirably with
Mr. Kemble's natural manner; and the tone of morbid, rancorous raillery, in which Pierre delights to in-
dulge, was in unison with the actor's reluctant, con-
temptuous personifications of gaiety, with the scorn-
ful spirit of his Comic Muse, which always laboured
—*invita Minerva*—against the grain. Cato was another
of those parts for which Mr. Kemble was peculiarly
fitted by his physical advantages. There was nothing
for him to do in this character, but to appear in it. It
had all the dignity of still-life. It was a studied piece of
classical costume—a conscious exhibition of elegantly
disposed drapery, that was all; yet, as a mere display
of personal and artificial grace, it was inimitable.

It has been suggested that Mr. Kemble chiefly excelled in his Roman characters, and among others in
Brutus. If it be meant that he excelled in those which
imply a certain stoicism of feeling and energy of will,
this we have already granted; but Brutus is not a character of this kind, and Mr. Kemble failed in it for that
reason. Brutus is not a stoic, but a humane enthusiast.
There is a tenderness of nature under the garb of assumed severity; an inward current of generous feelings, which burst out, in spite of circumstances, with
bleeding freshness; a secret struggle of mind, and dis-
agreement between his situation and his intentions; a
lofty inflexibility of purpose, mingled with an effeminate abstractedness of thought, which Mr. Kemble did
not give.

In short, we think the distinguishing excellence of
his acting may be summed up in one word—*intensity;*
in the seizing upon some one feeling or idea, in in-
sisting upon it, in never letting it go, and in working

it up, with a certain graceful consistency, and conscious grandeur of conception, to a very high degree of pathos or sublimity. If he had not the unexpected bursts of nature and genius he had all the regularity of art; if he did not display the tumult and conflict of opposite passions in the soul, he gave the deepest and most permanent interest to the uninterrupted progress of individual feeling; and in embodying a high idea of certain characters, which belong rather to sentiment than passion, to energy of will, than to loftiness or to originality of imagination, he was the most excellent actor of his time. This praise of him is not exaggerated; the blame we have mixed with it is not invidious. We have only to add to both, the expression of our grateful remembrances and best wishes—Hail, and farewell!

The English Stage

"For I am nothing if not critical."

⋙ The English Stage

ON ACTORS AND ACTING

Examiner, January 5, 1817 ("Round Table")
PLAYERS are "the abstracts and brief chronicles of the
time;" the motley representatives of human nature.
They are the only honest hypocrites. Their life is a
voluntary dream; a studied madness. The height of
their ambition is to be *beside themselves*. To-day
kings, to-morrow beggars, it is only when they are
themselves that they are nothing. Made up of mimic
laughter and tears, passing from the extremes of joy
or woe at the prompter's call, they wear the livery of
other men's fortunes; their very thoughts are not their
own. They are, as it were, train-bearers in the pageant
of life, and hold a glass up to humanity, frailer than
itself. We see ourselves at second-hand in them; they
show us all that we are, all that we wish to be, and all
that we dread to be. The stage is an epitome, a bet-
tered likeness of the world, with the dull part left out:
and, indeed, with this omission, it is nearly big enough
to hold all the rest. What brings the resemblance
nearer is that, as *they* imitate us, we, in our turn, imitate them. How many fine gentlemen do we owe to
the stage! How many romantic lovers are mere
Romeos in masquerade! How many soft bosoms have
heaved with Juliet's sighs! They teach us when to
laugh and when to weep, when to love and when to
hate, upon principle and with a good grace! Wherever
there is a play-house, the world will go on not amiss.
The stage not only refines the manners, but it is the
best teacher of morals, for it is the truest and most
intelligible picture of life. It stamps the image of vir-

tue on the mind by first softening the rude materials
of which it is composed, by a sense of pleasure. It
regulates the passions, by giving a loose to the imagination. It points out the selfish and depraved to our de-
testation; the amiable and generous to our admiration;
and if it clothes the more seductive vices with the borrowed graces of wit and fancy, even those graces
operate as a diversion to the coarser poison of experience and bad example, and often prevent or carry
off the infection by inoculating the mind with a certain taste and elegance. To show how little we agree
with the common declamations against the immoral
tendency of the stage on this score, we will hazard
a conjecture that the acting of *The Beggar's Opera* a
certain number of nights every year since it was first
brought out has done more towards putting down the
practice of highway robbery, than all the gibbets that
ever were erected. A person, after seeing this piece,
is too deeply imbued with a sense of humanity, is in
too good humour with himself and the rest of the
world, to set about cutting throats or rifling pockets.
Whatever makes a jest of vice leaves it too much a
matter of indifference for anyone in his senses to
rush desperately on his ruin for its sake. We suspect
that just the contrary effect must be produced by the
representation of *George Barnwell*, which is too much
in the style of the Ordinary's sermon to meet with any
better success. The mind, in such cases, instead of
being deterred by the alarming consequences held out
to it, revolts against the denunciation of them as an
insult offered to its free-will, and, in a spirit of defiance, returns a practical answer to them, by daring
the worst that can happen. The most striking lesson
ever read to levity and licentiousness is in the last act
of *The Inconstant*, where young Mirabel is preserved
by the fidelity of his mistress, Orinda, in the disguise
of a page, from the hands of assassins, into whose
power he had been allured by the temptations of vice

and beauty. There never was a rake who did not become in imagination a reformed man, during the representation of the last trying scenes of this admirable comedy.

If the stage is useful as a school of instruction, it is no less so as a source of amusement. It is a source of the greatest enjoyment at the time, and a never-failing fund of agreeable reflection afterwards. The merits of a new play, or of a new actor, are always among the first topics of polite conversation. One way in which public exhibitions contribute to refine and humanise mankind, is by supplying them with ideas and subjects of conversation and interest in common. The progress of civilisation is in proportion to the number of common-places current in society. For instance, if we meet with a stranger at an inn or in a stage-coach, who knows nothing but his own affairs—his shop, his customers, his farm, his pigs, his poultry—we can carry on no conversation with him on these local and personal matters: the only way is to let him have all the talk to himself. But if he has fortunately ever seen Mr. Liston act, this is an immediate topic of mutual conversation, and we agree together the rest of the evening in discussing the merits of that inimitable actor, with the same satisfaction as in talking over the affairs of the most intimate friend.

If the stage thus introduces us familiarly to our contemporaries, it also brings us acquainted with former times. It is an interesting revival of past ages, manners, opinions, dresses, persons, and actions—whether it carries us back to the wars of York and Lancaster, or half-way back to the heroic times of Greece and Rome, in some translation from the French, or quite back to the age of Charles II. in the scenes of Congreve and of Etherege (the gay Sir George!)— happy age, when kings and nobles led purely ornamental lives; when the utmost stretch of a morning's study went no further than the choice of a sword-

knot, or the adjustment of a side curl; when the soul
spoke out in all the pleasing elegance of dress; and
beaux and belles, enamoured of themselves in one another's follies, fluttered like gilded butterflies in giddy
mazes through the walks of St. James's Park!

A good company of comedians, a Theatre-Royal
judiciously managed, is your true Herald's College;
the only Antiquarian Society that is worth a rush. It
is for this reason that there is such an air of romance
about players, and that it is pleasanter to see them,
even in their own persons, than any of the three
learned professions. We feel more respect for John
Kemble in a plain coat than for Lord Chancellor on
the woolsack. He is surrounded, to our eyes, with a
greater number of imposing recollections: he is a
more reverend piece of formality; a more complicated
tissue of costume. We do not know whether to look
upon this accomplished actor as Pierre, or King John,
or Coriolanus, or Cato, or Leontes, or the Stranger.
But we see in him a stately hieroglyphic of humanity;
a living monument of departed greatness; a sombre
comment on the rise and fall of kings. We look after
him till he is out of sight, as we listen to a story of one
of Ossian's heroes, to "a tale of other times!"

The most pleasant feature in the profession of a
player, and which, indeed, is peculiar to it, is that we
not only admire the talents of those who adorn it, but
we contract a personal intimacy with them. There is
no class of society whom so many persons regard with
affection as actors. We greet them on the stage; we
like to meet them in the streets; they almost always
recall to us pleasant associations; and we feel our
gratitude excited, without the uneasiness of a sense of
obligation. The very gaiety and popularity, however,
which surround the life of a favourite performer,
make the retiring from it a very serious business. It
glances a mortifying reflection on the shortness of
human life, and the vanity of human pleasures. Some-

thing reminds us that "all the world's a stage, and all the men and women merely players." [1]

It has been considered as the misfortune of first-rate talents for the stage, that they leave no record behind them except that of vague rumour, and that the genius of a great actor perishes with him, "leaving the world no copy." This is a misfortune, or at least a mortifying reflection, to actors; but it is, perhaps, an advantage to the stage. It leaves an opening to originality. The *semper varium et mutabile* of the poet may be transferred to the stage, "the inconstant stage," without losing the original felicity of the application:—it has its necessary ebbs and flows, from its subjection to the influence of popular feeling, and the frailty of the materials of which it is composed, its own fleeting and shadowy essence, and cannot be expected to remain for any great length of time stationary at the same point, either of perfection or debasement. Acting, in particular, which is the chief organ by which it addresses itself to the mind—the eye, tongue, hand by which it dazzles, charms, and seizes on the public attention—is an art that seems to contain in itself the seeds of perpetual renovation and decay, following in this respect the order of nature rather than the analogy of the productions of human intellect;—for whereas in the other arts of painting and poetry, the standard works of genius, being permanent and accumulating, for awhile provoke emulation, but, in the end, overlay future efforts, and transmit only their defects to those that come after; the exertions of the greatest actor die with him, leaving to his successors only the admiration of his name, and the aspiration after imaginary excellence; so that, in effect, no one generation of actors binds another; the art is always

[1] This passage, down to "of Reynolds and of Johnson" is a slightly amplified reproduction of a paragraph in Hazlitt's criticism of Kean's Sir Giles Overreach, *Examiner*, January 14, 1816.

setting out afresh on the stock of genius and nature, and the success depends (generally speaking) on accident, opportunity, and encouragement. The harvest of excellence (whatever it may be) is removed from the ground, every twenty or thirty years, by Death's sickle; and there is room left for another to sprout up and tower to any equal height, and spread into equal luxuriance—to "dally with the wind, and court the sun"—according to the health and vigour of the stem, and the favourableness of the season. But books, pictures, remain like fixtures in the public mind, beyond a certain point encumber the soil of living truth and nature, distort or stunt the growth of original genius. When an author dies, it is no matter, for his works remain. When a great actor dies, there is a void produced in society, a gap which requires to be filled up. The literary amateur may find employment for his time in reading old authors only, and exhaust his entire spleen in scouting new ones: but the lover of the stage cannot amuse himself, in his solitary fastidiousness, by sitting to witness a play got up by the departed ghosts of first-rate actors; or be contented with the perusal of a collection of old play-bills:—he may extol Garrick, but he must go to see Kean; and, in his own defence, must admire, or at least tolerate, what he sees, or stay away against his will. If, indeed, by any spell or power of necromancy, all the celebrated actors, for the last hundred years, could be made to appear again on the boards of Covent Garden and Drury Lane, for the last time, in their most brilliant parts, what a rich treat to the town, what a feast for the critics, to go and see Betterton, and Booth, and Wilks, and Sandford, and Nokes, and Leigh, and Penkethman, and Bullock, and Estcourt, and Dogget, and Mrs. Barry, and Mrs. Montfort, and Mrs. Oldfield, and Mrs. Bracegirdle, and Mrs. Cibber, and Cibber himself, the prince of coxcombs, and Macklin, and Quin, and Rich, and Mrs. Clive, and Mrs. Pritchard,

and Mrs. Abington, and Weston, and Shuter, and
Garrick, and all the rest of those who "gladdened
life," and whose death "eclipsed the gaiety of nations!"
We should certainly be there. We should buy a ticket
for the season. We should enjoy *our hundred days*
again. We should not miss a single night. We would
not, for a great deal, be absent from Betterton's
Hamlet or his Brutus, or from Booth's Cato, as it was
first acted to the contending applause of Whigs and
Tories. We should be in the first row when Mrs.
Barry (who was kept by Lord Rochester, and with
whom Otway was in love) played Monimia or
Belvidera; and we suppose we should go to see Mrs.
Bracegirdle (with whom all the world was in love) in
all her parts. We should then know exactly whether
Penkethman's manner of picking a chicken, and
Bullock's mode of devouring asparagus, answered to
the ingenious account of them in the *Tatler;*[2] and
whether Dogget was equal to Dowton—whether Mrs.
Montfort or Mrs. Abington was the finest lady—
whether Wilks or Cibber was the best Sir Harry
Wildair,—whether Macklin was really "the Jew that
Shakespeare drew," and whether Garrick was, upon
the whole, so great an actor as the world would
have made him out! Many people have a strong desire
to pry into the secrets of futurity; for our own parts,
we should be satisfied if we had the power to recall
the dead, and live the past over again, as often as we
pleased!—Players, after all, have little reason to complain of their hard-earned, short-lived popularity. One
thunder of applause from pit, boxes, and gallery, is
equal to a whole immortality of posthumous fame; and
when we hear an actor (Liston), whose modesty is
equal to his merit, declare that he would like to see a
dog wag his tail in approbation, what must he feel
when he sets the whole house in a roar! Besides, Fame,
as if their reputation had been entrusted to her alone,

[2] *Tatler*, No. 188.

has been particularly careful of the renown of her
theatrical favourites: she forgets, one by one, and
year by year, those who have been great lawyers,
great statesmen, and great warriors in their day; but
the name of Garrick still survives with the works of
Reynolds and of Johnson.[3]

Actors have been accused, as a profession, of being
extravagant and dissipated. While they are said to be
so, as a piece of common cant, they are likely to continue so. But there is a sentence in Shakespeare which
should be stuck as a label in the mouths of our beadles
and whippers-in of morality: "The web of our life is
of a mingled yarn, good and ill together: our virtues
would be proud if our faults whipped them not: and
our crimes would despair if they were not cherished
by our virtues." With respect to the extravagance of
actors, as a traditional character, it is not to be wondered at. They live from hand to mouth: they plunge
from want into luxury; they have no means of making
money *breed*, and all professions that do not live by
turning money into money, or have not a certainty of
accumulating it in the end by parsimony, spend it. Uncertain of the future, they make sure of the present
moment. This is not unwise. Chilled with poverty,
steeped in contempt, they sometimes pass into the
sunshine of fortune, and are lifted to the very pinnacle
of public favour; yet even there they cannot calculate
on the continuance of success, but are, "like the giddy
sailor on the mast, ready with every blast to topple
down into the fatal bowels of the deep!" Besides, if
the young enthusiast, who is smitten with the stage,
and with the public as a mistress, were naturally a
close *hunks*, he would become or remain a city clerk,

---

[3] This paragraph is a reproduction of part of an article on
"the accident which has happened to Mr. Kean," *Examiner*,
March 31, 1816, and does not appear in the "Round Table"
article, its place being taken by an extract from Cibber's
Apology (his account of Mrs. Montfort).

instead of turning player. Again, with respect to the habit of convivial indulgence, an actor, to be a good one, must have a great spirit of enjoyment in himself—strong impulses, strong passions, and a strong sense of pleasure: for it is his business to imitate the passions, and to communicate pleasure to others. A man of genius is not a machine. The neglected actor may be excused if he drinks oblivion of his disappointments; the successful one if he quaffs the applause of the world, and enjoys the friendship of those who are the friends of the favourites of fortune, in draughts of nectar. There is no path so steep as that of fame: no labour so hard as the pursuit of excellence. The intellectual excitement, inseparable from those professions which call forth all our sensibility to pleasure and pain, requires some corresponding physical excitement to support our failure, and not a little to allay the ferment of the spirits attendant on success. If there is any tendency to dissipation beyond this in the profession of a player, it is owing to the prejudices entertained against them—to that spirit of bigotry which in a neighbouring country would deny actors Christian burial after their death, and to that cant of criticism which, in our own, slurs over their characters, while living, with a half-witted jest. Players are only not so respectable as a profession as they might be, because their profession is not respected as it ought to be.

A London engagement is generally considered by actors as the *ne plus ultra* of their ambition, as "a consummation devoutly to be wished," as the great prize in the lottery of their professional life. But this appears to us, who are not in the secret, to be rather the prose termination of their adventurous career; it is the provincial commencement that is the poetical and truly enviable part of it. After that, they have comparatively little to hope or fear. "The wine of life is drunk, and but the lees remain." In London, they become gentlemen, and the King's servants; but it is the romantic mixture of the hero and the vagabond that constitutes the essence of the player's life. It is the transition from their real to their assumed characters, from the contempt of the world to the applause of the multitude, that gives its zest to the latter, and raises them as much above common humanity at night as in the daytime they are depressed below it. "Hurried from fierce extremes, by contrast made more fierce,"—it is rags and a flock bed which give their splendour to a plume of feathers and a throne. We should suppose that if the most admired actor on the London stage were brought to confession on this point, he would acknowledge that all the applause he had received from "brilliant and overflowing audiences" was nothing to the light-headed intoxication of unlooked-for success in a barn. In town, actors are criticised: in country places, they are wondered at, or hooted at: it is of little consequence which, so that the interval is not too long between. For ourselves, we own that the description of the strolling player in *Gil Blas*, soaking his dry crusts in the well by the roadside, presents to us a perfect picture of human felicity.

ON PLAY-GOING AND ON SOME
OF OUR OLD ACTORS

London Magazine, No. I, January, 1820
THERE is less pedantry and affection (though not less party feeling and personal prejudice) in judging of the stage than of most other subjects; and we feel a sort of theoretical as well as instinctive predilection for the faces of play-going people, as among the most sociable, gossiping, good-natured, and humane members of society. In this point of view, as well as in others, the stage is a test and school of humanity. We do not much like any persons who do not like plays; and for this reason, that we imagine they cannot much like

themselves or anyone else. The really humane man (except in cases of unaccountable prejudices, which we do not think the most likely means to increase or preserve the natural amiableness of his disposition) is prone to the study of humanity. *Omnes boni et liberales* HUMANITATI *semper favemus.* He likes to see it brought home from the universality of precepts and general terms to the reality of persons, of tones, and actions; and to have it raised from the grossness and familiarity of sense, to the lofty but striking platform of the imagination. He likes to see the face of man with the veil of time torn from it, and to feel the pulse of nature beating in all times and places alike. The smile of good-humoured surprise at folly, the tear of pity at misfortune, do not misbecome the face of man or woman. It is something delightful and instructive to have seen Coriolanus or King John in the habiliments of Mr. Kemble, to have shaken hands almost with Othello in the person of Mr. Kean, to have cowered before the spirit of Lady Macbeth in the glance of Mrs. Siddons. The stage at once gives a body to our thoughts, and refinement and expansion to our sensible impressions. It has not the pride and remoteness of abstract science; it has not the petty egotism of vulgar life. It is particularly wanted in great cities (where it of course flourishes most) to take off from the dissatisfaction and *ennui* that creep over our own pursuits from the indifference or contempt thrown upon them by others; and at the same time to reconcile our numberless discordant, incommensurable feelings and interests together, by giving us an immediate and common topic to engage our attention, and to rally us round the standard of our common humanity. We never hate a face that we have seen in the pit; and Liston's laugh would be a cordial to wash down the oldest animosity of the most inveterate pit critics.

The only drawback on the felicity and triumphant self-complacency of a play-goer's life, arises from the

shortness of life itself. We miss the favourites, not of
another age, but of our own—the idols of our youthful enthusiasm; and we cannot replace them by others.
It does not show that *these* are worse, because they
are different from *those;* though they had been better,
they would not have been so good to us. It is the
penalty of our nature, from Adam downwards; so
Milton makes our first ancestor exclaim—

> Should God create another Eve, and I
> Another rib afford, yet loss of thee
> Would never from my heart.

We offer our best affections, our highest aspirations
after the good and beautiful, on the altar of youth; it
is well if, in our after-age, we can sometimes rekindle
the almost extinguished flame, and inhale its dying fra-
grance like the breath of incense, of sweet-smelling
flowers and gums, to detain the spirit of life, the ethereal guest, a little longer in its frail abode—to cheer
and soothe it with the pleasures of memory, not with
those of hope. While we can do this, life is worth
living for: when we can do it no longer, its spring
will soon go down, and we had better not be! Who
shall give us Mrs. Siddons again, but in a waking
dream, a beatific vision of past years, crowned with
other hopes and other feelings, whose pomp is also
faded, and their glory and their power gone! Who
shall in our time (or can ever to the eye of fancy)
fill the stage, like her, with the dignity of their persons, and the emanations of their minds? Or who shall
sit majestic on the throne of tragedy—a Goddess, a
prophetess, and a Muse—from which the lightning of
her eye flashed o'er the mind, startling its inmost
thoughts—and the thunder of her voice circled
through the labouring breast, rousing deep and scarce-
known feelings from their slumber? Who shall stalk
over the stage of horrors, its presiding genius, or
"play the hostess," at the banqueting-scene of murder?

Who shall walk in sleepless ecstasy of soul, and haunt the mind's eye ever after with the dread pageantry of suffering and of guilt? Who shall make tragedy once more stand with its feet upon the earth, and with its head raised above the skies, weeping tears and blood? That loss is not to be repaired. While the stage lasts, there will never be another Mrs. Siddons! Tragedy seemed to set with her; and the rest are but blazing comets or fiery exhalations. It is pride and happiness enough for us to have lived at the same time with her, and one person more! [1] But enough on this subject. Those feelings that we are most anxious to do justice to, are those to which it is impossible we ever should!

To turn to something less serious. We have not the same pomp of tragedy, nor the same gentility, variety, and correctness in comedy. There was the gay, fluttering, hare-brained Lewis;[2] he that was called "Gentleman Lewis"—all life, and fashion, and volubility, and whim; the greatest comic *mannerist* that perhaps ever lived; whose head seemed to be in his heels, and his wit at his fingers' ends; who never let the stage stand still, and made your heart light and your head giddy with his infinite vivacity, and bustle, and hey-day animal spirits. We wonder how Death ever caught him in his mad, whirling career, or ever fixed his volatile spirit in a dull *caput mortuum* of dust and ashes? Nobody could break open a door, or jump over a table, or scale a ladder, or twirl a cocked hat, or dangle a cane, or play a jockey-nobleman, or a nobleman's jockey, like him. He was at Covent Garden. With him was Quick,[3] who made an excellent, self-important,

---

[1] No doubt Hazlitt's idol, Napoleon. Haydon relates that Hazlitt gave up drinking because he was frightened by the effects of a prolonged debauch, in which he sought to drown his sorrow for Napoleon's defeat at Waterloo.

[2] See "Dramatic Essays," first series.

[3] John Quick ("little" Quick) was a clever comedian. He was born in 1748, made his first appearance in London in 1767,

busy, strutting, money-getting citizen; or crusty old
guardian, in a brown suit and a bob wig. There was
also Munden,[4] who was as good an actor then as he is
now; and Fawcett,[5] who was at that time a much better one than he is at present; for he, of late, seems to
slur over his parts, wishes to merge the actor in the
manager, and is grown serious before retiring from
the stage. But a few years back (when he ran the
race of popularity with Jack Bannister), nobody could
give the *view halloa* of a fox-hunting country squire
like him; and he sang AMO AMAS, as Lingo in the
Agreeable Surprise, in a style of pathos to melt the
heart of the young apprentices in the two-shilling
gallery. But he appears to have grown averse to his
profession, and indifferent to the applause he might
acquire for himself, and to the pleasures he used to
give to others. In turbulent and pragmatical characters,
and in all that cast of parts which may be called the
slang language of comedy, he hardly had his equal.
Perhaps he might consider this walk of his art as beneath his ambition; but, in our judgment, whatever a
man can do best, is worth his doing. At the same house
was little Simmons,[6] who remained there till lately, like
a veteran at his post, till he fell down a flight of steps
and broke his neck, without anyone's seeming to
know or care about the matter. Though one of those
"who had gladdened life," his death by no means
"eclipsed the gaiety of nations." The public are not
grateful. They make an effort of generosity, collect all
their reluctant admiration into a heap, and offer it up

---

retired from the stage in 1798, and died in 1831. He was the
original Tony Lumpkin in *She Stoops to Conquer*.

  [4] See "Dramatic Essays," first series.

  [5] John Fawcett (1769-1837) was for a long time stage-man-
ager at Covent Garden.

  [6] Samuel Simmons died on September 11, 1819, from the
effect of an accident, as Hazlitt states. He was a clever comedian.

with servile ostentation at the shrine of some great name, which they think reflects back its lustre on the worshippers. Or, like fashionable creditors, they pay their debts of honour for the *éclat* of the thing, and neglect the claims of humbler but sterling merit, such as was that of Simmons, one of the most correct, pointed, *naïve*, and whimsical comic actors, we have for a long time had, or are likely to have again. He was not a buffoon, but a real actor. He did not play *him-self*, nor play tricks, but played the part the author had assigned him. This was the great merit of the good old style of acting. He fitted into it like a brilliant into the setting of a ring, or as the ring fits the finger. We shall look for him often in Filch,[7] in which his appearance was a continual *double entendre*, with one eye leering at his neighbour's pockets, and the other turned to the gallows—in the spangled Beau Mordecai, in Moses, in which he had all the precision, the pragmaticalness, and impenetrable secresy of the Jew money-lender; and in my Lord Sands, where he had all the stage to himself, and seemed to fill it by the singular insignificance of his person, and the infinite airs he gave himself. We shall look for him in these and many other parts, but in vain, or for anyone equal to him.

At the other house, there was King,[8] whose acting left a taste on the palate, sharp and sweet like a quince; with an old, hard, rough, withered face, like a John-apple, puckered up into a thousand wrinkles; with shrewd hints and tart replies; "with nods and becks, and wreathed smiles;" who was the real amorous, wheedling, or hasty, choleric, peremptory old gentleman in Sir Peter Teazle and Sir Anthony Absolute; and the true, that is, the pretended, clown in Touchstone, with wit sprouting from his head like a pair of

[7] In *The Beggar's Opera.*
[8] Thomas King (1730-1805) was on the stage for over half a century. He was a comedian of the first order.

ass's ears, and folly perched on his cap like the horned
owl. There was Parsons[9] too, whom we just remember, like a worn-out "suit of office," in Elbow; and
Dodd [10] in Acres, who had the most extraordinary
way of hitching in a meaning, or subsiding into blank
folly with the best grace in nature; and whose courage
seemed literally to ooze out of his fingers in the prepa-
rations for the duel. There was Suett,[11] the delightful
old croaker, the everlasting Dicky Gossip of the stage;
and, with him, Jack Bannister,[12] whose gaiety, good
humour, cordial feeling, and natural spirits, shone
through his characters, and lighted them up like a
transparency. Bannister did not go out of himself to
take possession of his part, but put it on over his ordinary dress, like a *surtout*, snug, warm, and comfortable.
He let his personal character appear through; and it
was one great charm of his acting. In Lenitive, in *The
Prize*, when the beau is engrafted on the apothecary,
he came out of his shell like the aurelia out of the grub;
and surely never lighted on the stage, which he hardly
seemed to touch, a more delightful vision,—gilding
and cheering the motley sphere he just began to move
in—shining like a gilded pill, fluttering like a piece of
gold-leaf, gaudy as a butterfly, loud as a grasshopper,
full of life, and laughter, and joy. His Scrub, in which
he spouts a torrent of home-brewed ale against the
ceiling, in a sudden fit of laughter at the waggeries of
his brother Martin; his Son-in-law;[13] his part in *The
Grandmother*; his Autolycus; his Colonel Feignwell;
and his Walter, in *The Children in the Wood*, were all

* William Parsons (1736-1795), a comic genius, overflowing
with broad humour.
10 James Dodd (1741-1796) was a perfect actor of fops and
fatuous parts. Lamb's reference to him is well known.
11 Dicky Suett (1758-1805), of whom Lamb said that
"Shakespeare foresaw him when he framed his fools and
jesters."
12 See "Dramatic Essays," first series.
13 Signor Arionelli, in O'Keeffe's farce of *The Son-in-law*.

admirable. Most of his characters were exactly fitted for him—for his good-humoured smile, his buoyant activity, his kind heart, and his honest face; and no one else could do them so well, because no one else could play Jack Bannister. He was, some time since, seen casting a wistful eye at Drury Lane Theatre, and no doubt thinking of past times; others who also cast a wistful eye at it, do not forget him when they think of old and happy times! There were Bob and Jack Palmer,[14] the Brass and Dick of *The Confederacy;* the one the pattern of an elder, the other of a younger brother. There was Wewitzer,[15] the trustiest of Swiss valets, and the most "secret Tattle" of the stage. There was, and there still is, Irish Johnstone,[16] with his supple knees, his hat twisted round in his hand, his good-humoured laugh, his arched eyebrows, his insinuating leer, and his lubricated *brogue,* curling round the ear like a well-oiled mustachio. These were all the men. Then there was Miss Farren,[17] with her fine-lady airs and graces, with that elegant turn of her head, and motion of her fan, and tripping of her tongue; and Miss Pope,[18] the very picture of a Duenna, a maiden lady, or an antiquated dowager—the latter spring of beauty, the second childhood of vanity, more quaint, fantastic, and old-fashioned, more pert, frothy, and light-headed, than anything that can be imagined; embalmed in the follies, preserved in the spirit of affectation of the last age; and then add to these Mrs. Jordan,[19] the child of nature, whose voice was a cor-

[14] John and Robert Palmer were good comedians. Charles Lamb makes some interesting remarks on them.
[15] Ralph Wewitzer (1749-1825) was an actor of limited powers, who played valets well.
[16] John Johnstone (1750-1828) was a famous Irish comedian.
[17] Elizabeth Farren (1759-1829) was the ideal representative of fine ladies. She retired from the stage in 1797, and became Countess of Derby.
[18] See "Dramatic Essays," first series.
[19] Ibid.

dial to the heart, because it came from it, rich, full,
like the luscious juice of the rich grape; to hear whose
laugh was to drink nectar; whose smile "made a sunshine," not "in the shady place," but amidst dazzling
lights and in glad theatres; who "talked far above
singing," and whose singing was like the twang of
Cupid's bow. Her person was large, soft, and generous like her soul. It has been attempted to compare
Miss Kelly[20] to her. There is no comparison. Miss
Kelly is a shrewd, clever, arch, lively girl; tingles all
over with suppressed sensibility; licks her lips at mischief, bites her words in two, or lets a sly meaning out
of the corners of her eyes; is fidgetty with curiosity,
or unable to stand still for spite—she is always uneasy
and always interesting; but Mrs. Jordan was all exuberance and grace, "her bounty was as boundless as
the sea; her love as deep." It was her capacity for enjoyment, and the contrast she presented to everything
sharp, angular, and peevish, that communicated the
same genial heartfelt satisfaction to the spectator. Her
Nell,[21] for instance, was right royal like her liquor, and
wrapped up in measureless content with lambs' wool.
Miss Kelly is a dexterous, knowing chambermaid; Mrs.
Jordan had nothing dexterous or knowing about her.
She was Cleopatra turned into an oyster-wench, without knowing that she was Cleopatra, or caring that she
was an oyster-wench. An oyster-wench, such as she
was, would have been equal to a Cleopatra; and an
Antony would not have deserted her for the empire
of the world!

From the favourite actors of a few years back, we
turn to those of the present day: and we shall speak of
them not with grudging or stinted praise.

The first of these in tragedy is Mr. Kean. To show

[20] Frances Maria Kelly, the niece of Michael Kelly, the com-
poser and singer, was an actress of great versatility, and a
singer of more than average excellence.
[21] In *The Devil to Pay.*

that we do not conceive that tragedy regularly declines in every successive generation, we shall say, that
we do not think there has been in our remembrance
any tragic performer (with the exception of Mrs.
Siddons) equal to Mr. Kean. Nor, except in voice and
person, and the conscious ease and dignity naturally
resulting from those advantages, do we know that
even Mrs. Siddons was greater. In truth of nature and
force of passion, in discrimination and originality, we
see no inferiority to anyone on the part of Mr. Kean;
but there is an insignificance of figure, and a hoarseness of voice, that necessarily *vulgarise* or diminish
our idea of the characters he plays; and perhaps to
this may be added, a want of a certain correspondent
elevation and magnitude of thought, of which Mrs.
Siddons's noble form seemed to be only the natural
mould and receptacle. Her nature seemed always above
the circumstances with which she had to struggle; her
soul to be greater than the passion labouring in her
breast. Grandeur was the cradle in which her genius
was rocked; for her *to be* was to be sublime! She did
the greatest things with child-like ease; her powers
seemed never tasked to the utmost, and always as if
she had inexhaustible resources still in reserve. The
least word she uttered seemed to float to the end of the
stage; the least motion of her hand seemed to command
awe and obedience. Mr. Kean is all effort, all violence,
all extreme passion; he is possessed with a fury, a
demon that leaves him no repose, no time for thought,
or room for imagination. He perhaps screws himself
up to as intense a degree of feeling as Mrs. Siddons,
strikes home with as sure and as hard a blow as she
did, but he does this by straining every nerve, and
winding up every faculty to this single point alone;
and as he does it by an effort himself, the spectator
follows him by an effort also. Our sympathy in a
manner ceases with the actual impression, and does
not leave the same grand and permanent image of itself

behind. The Othello furnishes almost the only exception to these remarks. The solemn and beautiful manner in which he pronounces the farewell soliloquy is
worth all gladiatorship and pantomime in the world.
His Sir Giles is his most equal and energetic character;
but it is too equal, too energetic from the beginning to
the end. There is no reason that he should have the
same eagerness, the same *impetus*, at the commencement as at the close of his career; he should not have
the fierceness of the wild beast till he is goaded to
madness by the hunters. Sir Giles Mompesson (supposed to be the original character) we dare say, took
things more quietly, and only grew desperate with his
fortunes. Cooke played the general casting of the character better in this respect, but without the same fine
breaks and turns of passion. Cooke, indeed, compared
with Kean, had only the *slang* and *bravado* of tragedy.
Neither can we think Mr. Kemble equal to him, with
all his study, his grace, and classic dignity of form. He
was the statue of perfect tragedy, not the living soul.
Mrs. Siddons combined the advantage of form and
other organic requisites with nature and passion; Mr.
Kemble has the external requisites (at least of face
and figure) without the internal workings of the soul;
Mr. Kean has the last without the first, and, if we must
make our election between the two, we think the *vis
tragica* must take precedence of everything else. Mr.
Kean, in a word, appears to us a test, an *experimentum
crucis*, to show the triumph of genius over physical
defects, of nature over art, of passion over affectation,
and of originality over commonplace monotony. Next
to Mr. Kean, the greatest tragic performer now on the
stage is undoubtedly Miss O'Neill.[22] She cannot take
rank by the side of her great predecessor, but neither
can any other actress be at all compared with her. If

[22] "Since this article was written, the stage has lost this
lady." Note in *London Magazine*. See subsequent article, p.
200.

we had not seen Mrs. Siddons, we should not certainly
have been able to conceive anything finer than some
of her characters, such as Belvidera, Isabella in *The
Fatal Marriage*, Mrs. Beverly, and Mrs. Haller, which
(as she at first played them) in tenderness of sensibility, and the simple force of passion, could not be
surpassed. She has, however, of late carried the expression of mental agony and distress to a degree of
physical horror that is painful to behold, and which is
particularly repulsive in a person of her delicacy of
frame and truly feminine appearance. Mrs. Bunn[23] is a
beautiful and interesting actress in the sentimental
drama; and in the part of Queen Elizabeth, in Schiller's
tragedy of *Mary Stuart,* which she played lately, gave,
in the agitation of her form, the distracted thoughts
painted in her looks, and the deep but fine and mellow
tones of her voice, earnest of higher excellence than
she has yet displayed. Her voice is one of the finest on
the stage. It resembles the deep murmur of a hive of
bees in springtide, and the words drop like honey
from her lips. Mr. Macready is, in our opinion, a truly
spirited and impassioned declaimer, with a noble
voice, and a great fervour of manner; but, we apprehend, his *forte* is rather in giving a loose to the tide of
enthusiastic feeling or sentiment, than in embodying
individual character, or discriminating the diversity of
the passions. There is a gaiety and tiptoe elevation in
his personal deportment which Mr. Kean has not, but
in other more essential points there is no room for
competition. Of his Coriolanus and Richard we may
have to speak in detail hereafter.

We shall conclude this introductory sketch with a
few words on the comic actors. Emery at Covent
Garden might be said to be the best *provincial* actor
on the London boards. In his line of rustic characters

[23] Margaret Agnes Somerville (1799-1883) was famous in
the heavier parts in tragedy. She married Alfred Bunn, the
manager of Drury Lane.

he is a perfect actor. He would be a bold critic who should undertake to show that in his own walk Emery ever did anything wrong. His Hodge is an absolute reality; and his Lockitt is as sullen, as gloomy, and impenetrable as the prison walls of which he is the keeper. His Robert Tyke[24] is the sublime of tragedy in low life. Mr. Liston has more comic humour, more power of face, and a more genial and happy vein of folly, than any other actor we remember. His farce is not caricature: his drollery oozes out of his features, and trickles down his face, his voice is a pitch-pipe for laughter. He does some characters but indifferently, others respectably; but when he *puts himself whole* into a jest, it is unrivalled. Munden with all his merit, his whim, his imagination, and with his broad effects, is a caricaturist in the comparison. He distorts his features to the utmost stretch of grimace, and trolls his voice about with his tongue in the most extraordinary manner, but he does all this with an evident view to the audience; whereas Liston's style of acting is the unconscious and involuntary; he indulges his own risibility or absurd humours to please himself, and the odd noises he makes come from him as naturally as the bleating of a sheep. Elliston is an actor of great merit, and of a very agreeable class; there is a joyousness in his look, his voice, and manner; he treads the stage as if it was his "best-found and latest, as well as earliest choice;" writes himself comedian in any book, warrant, or acquaintance; hits the town between wind and water, between farce and tragedy; touches the string of a mock heroic sentiment with due pathos and vivacity; and makes the best strolling gentleman, or needy poet, on the stage. His Rover is excellent; so is his Duke in *The Honeymoon;* and in *Matrimony* he is best of all. Dowton is a genuine and excellent comedian; and, in speaking of his Major Sturgeon, we cannot pass

[24] In *The School of Reform.*

over, in disdainful silence, Russell's Jerry Sneak,[25] and Mrs. Harlowe's[26] Miss Molly Jollop. Oxberry[27] is an actor of a strong rather than of a pleasant comic vein (his Mawworm is particularly emphatical). Harley pleases others, for he seems pleased himself; and little Knight, in the simplicity and good nature of the country lad, is inimitable.

MINOR THEATRES—STROLLING PLAYERS

London Magazine, No. III, March, 1820

ONE reason that makes the Minor Theatres interesting is, that they are the connecting link that lets us down, by an easy transition, from the highest pomp and proudest display of the Thespian art, to its first rudiments and helpless infancy. With conscious happy retrospect, they lead the eye back, along the *vista* of the imagination, to the village barn, or travelling booth, or old-fashioned town-hall, or more genteel assembly-room, in which Momus first unmasked to us his fairy revels, and introduced us, for the first time in our lives, to that strange anomaly in existence, that fanciful reality, that gay waking dream, *a company of strolling players!* Sit still, draw close together, hold in your breath—not a word, not a whisper—the laugh is ready to start away, "like greyhound on the slip," the big tear of wonder and expectation is ready to steal down "the full eyes and fair cheeks of childhood,"

---

[25] Samuel Russell (1766-1845), so famous for playing this part in *The Mayor of Garratt*, that he was known as "Jerry Sneak Russell." See p. 97 of this volume for Hazlitt's criticism on this play.

[26] Mrs. Harlowe (born about 1770) was a mediocre actress.

[27] William Oxberry (1784-1824) made some reputation as a comedian, but is best known by the books of theatrical memoirs, &c., published under his name.

almost before the time. Only another moment, and
amidst blazing tapers, and the dancing sounds of
music, and light throbbing hearts, and eager looks, the
curtain rises, and the picture of the world appears before us in all its glory and in all its freshness. Life
throws its gaudy shadow across the stage; Hope shakes
his many-coloured wings, "embalmed with odours;"
Joy claps his hands, and laughs in a hundred happy
faces. Oh, childish fancy, what a mighty empire is
thine! what endless creations thou buildest out of
nothing! what "a wide O" indeed, thou choosest to
act thy thoughts and unrivalled feats upon! Thou art
better than the gilt trophy that decks the funeral pall
of kings; thou art brighter than the costly mace that
precedes them on their coronation day. Thy fear-
fullest visions are enviable happiness; thy wildest fictions are the solidest truths. Thou art the only reality.
All other possessions mock our idle grasp; but thou
performest by promising; thy smile is fruition; thy
blandishments are all that we can fairly call our own;
thou art the balm of life, the heaven of childhood, the
poet's idol, and the player's pride! The world is but
thy painting, and the stage is thine enchanted mirror.
When it first displays its shining surface to our view,
how glad, how surprised are we! We have no thought
of any deception in the scene, no wish but to realise
it ourselves with inconsiderate haste and fond impatience. We say to the air-drawn gorgeous phantom,
"Come, let me clutch thee!" A new sense comes upon
us, the scales fall off our eyes, and the scenes of life
start out in endless quick succession, crowded with
men and women actors, such as we see before us—
comparable to "those gay creatures of the element that
live in the rainbow, and play i' th' plighted clouds!" [1]

[1] I took it for a faery vision
   Of some gay creatures of the element,
   That in the colours of the rainbow live,
   And play i' the plighted clouds.—*Comus.*

Happy are we who look on and admire; and happy, we think, must they be who are so looked at and admired; and sometimes we begin to feel uneasy till we can ourselves mingle in the gay, busy, talking, fluttering, powdered, painted, perfumed, peruked, quaintly accoutred throng of coxcombs and coquettes —of tragedy heroes or heroines—in good earnest; or turn stage-players and represent them in jest, with all the impertinent and consequential airs of the originals!

It is no insignificant epoch in one's life the first time that odd-looking thing, a play-bill, is left at our door in a little market town in the country (say Wem,[2] in Shropshire). The manager, somewhat fatter and more erect, "as manager beseems," than the rest of his company, with more of the man of business, and not less of the coxcomb, in his strut and manner, knocks at the door with the end of a walking cane (his badge of office!) and a bundle of papers under his arm; presents one of them, printed in large capitals, with a respectful bow and a familiar shrug; hopes to give satisfaction in the town; hints at the liberal encouragement they received at the last place they stopped at; had every possible facility afforded by the magistrates; supped one evening with the Rev. Mr. Jenkins, a dissenting clergyman, and really a very well-informed, agreeable, sensible man, full of anecdote—no illiberal prejudices against the profession:—then talks of the strength of his company, with a careless mention of his own favourite line—his benefit fixed for an early day, but would do himself the honour to leave further particulars at a future opportunity—speaks of the stage as an elegant amusement, that most agreeably enlivens a spare evening or two in the week, and, under proper management (to which he himself paid the most assiduous attention), might be made of the greatest assistance to the cause of virtue and humanity—had seen Mr. Garrick act the last night but one before his re-

[2] Where Hazlitt was brought up.

tiring from the stage—had himself had offers from the
London boards, and, indeed, could not say he had
given up all thoughts of one day surprising them—as
it was, had no reason to repine—Mrs. F.—— tolerably
advanced in life—his eldest son a prodigious turn for
the higher walks of tragedy—had said perhaps too
much of himself—had given universal satisfaction—
hoped that the young gentleman and lady, at least,
would attend on the following evening, when *The
West Indian* would be performed at the market-hall,
with the farce of *No Song No Supper*—and so having
played his part, withdraws in the full persuasion of
having made a favourable impression, and of meeting
with every encouragement the place affords! Thus he
passes from house to house, and goes through the
routine of topic after topic, with that sort of modest
assurance which is indispensable in the manager of a
country theatre. This fellow, who floats over the
troubles of life as the froth above the idle wave, with
all his little expedients and disappointments, with
pawned paste-buckles, mortgaged scenery, empty ex-
chequer, and rebellious orchestra, is not of all men the
most miserable—he is little less happy than a king,
though not much better off than a beggar. He has
little to think of, much to do, more to say; and is accompanied, in his incessant daily round of trifling occupations, with a never-failing sense of authority and
self-importance, the one thing needful (above all
others) to the heart of man. This, however, is their
man of business in the company; he is a sort of fixture
in their little state; like Nebuchadnezzar's image, but
half of earth and half of finer metal; he is not "of
imagination all compact;" he is not, like the rest of his
aspiring crew, a feeder upon air, a drinker of applause,
tricked out in vanity and in nothing else; he is not
quite mad nor quite happy. The whining Romeo, who
goes supperless to bed, and on his pallet of straw
dreams of a crown of laurel, of waving handkerchiefs,

of bright eyes, and billets-doux breathing boundless love; the ranting Richard, whose infuriate execrations are drowned in the shouts of the all-ruling pit; he who, without a coat to his back, or a groat in his purse, snatches at Cato's robe, and binds the diadem of Cæsar on his brow; these are the men that Fancy has chosen for herself, and placed above the reach of fortune, and almost of fate. They take no thought for the morrow. What is it to them what they shall eat, or what they shall drink, or how they shall be clothed? "Their mind to them a kingdom is." It is not a poor ten shillings a week, their share in the profits of the theatre, with which they have to pay for bed, board, and lodging, that bounds their wealth. They share (and not unequally) in all the wealth, the pomp, and pleasures of the world. They wield sceptres, conquer kingdoms, court princesses, are clothed in purple, and fare sumptuously every night. They taste, in imagination, "of all earth's bliss, both living and loving:" whatever has been most the admiration or most the envy of mankind, they, for a moment, in their own eyes, and in the eyes of others, become. The poet fancies others to be this or that: the player fancies himself to be all that the poet but describes. A little rouge makes him a lover, a plume of feathers a hero, a brazen crown an emperor. Where will you buy rank, office, supreme delights, so cheap as at his shop of fancy? Is it nothing to dream whenever we please, and *seem* whatever we desire? Is real greatness, is real prosperity, more than what it seems? Where shall we find, or where shall the votary of the stage find, Fortunatus's Wishing Cap, but in the wardrobe which we laugh at; or borrow the philosopher's stone, but from the *property-man* of the theatre? He has discovered the true Elixir of Life, which is freedom from care: he quaffs the pure *aurum potabile*, which is popular applause. He who is smit with the love of this *ideal* existence, cannot be weaned from it. Hoot him from the stage, and he will stay to

sweep the lobbies or shift the scenes. Offer him twice
the salary to go into a counting-house or stand behind a counter, and he will return to poverty, steeped
in contempt, but eked out with fancy, at the end of
a week. Make a laughing-stock of an actress, lower her
salary, tell her she is too tall, awkward, stupid, and
ugly; try to get rid of her all you can—she will remain, only to hear herself courted, to listen to the
echo of her borrowed name, to live but one short
minute in the lap of vanity and tinsel show. Will you
give a man an additional ten shillings a week, and ask
him to resign the fancied wealth of the world, which
he "by his so potent art" can conjure up, and glad his
eyes, and fill his heart with it? When a little change of
dress, and the muttering a few talismanic words, make
all the difference between the vagabond and the hero,
what signifies the interval so easily passed? Would you
not yourself consent to be alternately a beggar and a
king, but that you have not the secret skill to be so?
The player has that "happy alchemy of mind:"—why
then would you reduce him to an equality with yourself? The moral of this reasoning is known and felt,
though it may be gainsaid. Wherever the players
come, they send a welcome before them, and leave
an air in the place behind them.[3] They shed a light
upon the day, that does not very soon pass off. See
how they glitter along the street, wandering, not
where business but the bent of pleasure takes them,
like mealy-coated butterflies, or insects flitting in the
sun. They seem another, happier, idler race of mortals,
prolonging the carelessness of childhood to old age,
floating down the stream of life, or wafted by the
wanton breeze to their final place of rest. We remember one (we must make the reader acquainted with

[3] So the old song joyously celebrates their arrival:—

The beggars are coming to town.
Some in rags, and some in jags, and some in velvet gown.
    (W. H.)

him) who once overtook us loitering by "Severn's
sedgy side," on a fine May morning, with a score of
play-bills streaming from his pockets, for the use of
the neighbouring villages, and a music-score in his
hand, which he sang blithe and clear, advancing with
light step and a loud voice! With a sprightly *bon jour*,
he passed on, carolling to the echo of the babbling
stream, brisk as a bird, gay as a mote, swift as an arrow
from a twanging bow, heart-whole, and with shining
face that shot back the sun's broad rays! What is become of this favourite of mirth and song? Has care
touched him? Has death tripped up his heels? Has an
indigestion imprisoned him, and all his gaiety, in a
living dungeon? Or is he himself lost and buried amidst
the rubbish of one of our larger, or of one of our
Minor Theatres?

Alas! how changed from him,
That life of pleasure, and that soul of whim!

But as this was no doubt the height of his ambition,
why should we wish to debar him of it?

This brings us back, after our intended digression,
to the subject from whence we set out—the smaller
theatres of the metropolis; which we visited lately, in
hopes to find in them a romantic contrast to the pre-
sumptuous and exclusive pretensions of the legitimate
drama, and to revive some of the associations of our
youth above described. The first attempt we made was
at the Coburg, and we were completely baulked.
Judge of our disappointment. This was not owing, we
protest, to any fault or perversity of our own; to the
crust and scales of formality which had grown over us;
to the panoply of criticism in which we go armed, and
which made us inaccessible to "pleasure's finest point;"
or to the *chevaux-de-frise* of objections, which cut us
off from all cordial participation in what was going
forward on the stage. No such thing. We went not
only willing, but determined to be pleased. We had
laid aside the pedantry of rules, the petulance of sar-

casm, and had hoped to open once more, by stealth,
the source of sacred tears, of bubbling laughter, and
concealed sighs. We were not formidable. On the contrary, we were "made of penetrable stuff." Stooping
from our pride of place, we were ready to be equally
delighted with a clown in a pantomime, or a lord-
mayor in a tragedy. We were all attention, simplicity,
and enthusiasm. But we saw neither attention, simplicity, nor enthusiasm in anybody else; and our whole
scheme of voluntary delusion and social enjoyment
was cut up by the roots. The play was indifferent, but
that was nothing. The acting was bad, but that was
nothing. The audience were low, but that was nothing.
It was the heartless indifference and hearty contempt
shown by the performers for their parts, and by the
audience for the players and the play, that disgusted
us with all of them. Instead of the rude, naked, undisguised expression of curiosity and wonder, of overflowing vanity and unbridled egotism, there was
nothing but an exhibition of the most petulant cock-
neyism and vulgar slang. All our former notions and
theories were turned topsy-turvy. The genius of St.
George's Fields prevailed, and you felt yourself in a
bridewell, or a brothel, amidst Jew-boys, pickpockets,
prostitutes, and mountebanks, instead of being in the
precincts of Mount Parnassus, or in the company of
the Muses. The object was not to admire or to excel,
but to vilify and degrade everything. The audience
did not hiss the actors (that would have implied a
serious feeling of disapprobation, and something like
a disappointed wish to be pleased), but they laughed,
hooted at, nick-named, pelted them with oranges and
witticisms, to show their unruly contempt for them
and their art; while the performers, to be even with
the audience, evidently slurred their parts, as if
ashamed to be thought to take any interest in them,
laughed in one another's faces, and in that of their
friends in the pit, and most effectually marred the

process of theatrical illusion, by turning the whole into a most unprincipled burlesque. We cannot help thinking that some part of this indecency and licentiousness is to be traced to the diminutive size of these theatres, and to the close contact into which these unmannerly censors come with the objects of their ignorant and unfeeling scorn. Familiarity breeds contempt. By too narrow an inspection, you take away that fine, hazy medium of abstraction, by which (in moderation) a play is best set off: you are, as it were, admitted behind the scenes; "see these puppets dallying;" shake hands, across the orchestra, with an actor whom you know, or take one you do not like by the beard, with equal impropriety:—you distinguish the paint, the individual features, the texture of the dresses, the patchwork and machinery by which the whole is made up; and this in some measure destroys the effect, distracts attention, suspends the interest, and makes you disposed to quarrel with the actors as impostors, and "not the men you took them for." You see Mr. Booth,[4] in Brutus, with every motion of his face *articulated*, with his under-jaws grinding out sentences, and his upper-lip twitching at words and syllables, as if a needle and thread had been passed through each corner of it, and the *gude wife* still continued sewing at her work:—you perceive the contortion and barrenness of his expression (in which there is only one form of bent brows, and close pent-up mouth for all occasions), the parsimony of his figure is exposed, and the refuse tones of his voice fall with undiminished vulgarity on the pained ear.

"Turn we to survey" where the Miss Dennetts, at the Adelphi Theatre (which should once more from them be called the *Sans Pareil*), weave the airy, the harmonious, liquid dance. Each of them it might be said, and we believe has been said—

[4] Junius Brutus Booth, whose brief rivalry with Kean is well known, was at this time playing at the Coburg Theatre.

Her, lovely Venus at a birth,
With two Sister Graces more,
To ivy-crowned Bacchus bore.

Such figures, no doubt, gave rise to the fables of
ancient mythology, and might be worshipped. They
revive the ideas of classic grace, life, and joy. They do
not seem like taught dancers, Columbines, and figu-
rantes on an artificial stage; but come bounding forward like nymphs in vales of Arcady, or, like Italian
shepherdesses, join in a lovely group of easy gracefulness, while "vernal airs attune the trembling leaves" to
their soft motions. If they were nothing in themselves, they would be complete in one another. Each
owes a double grace, youth, and beauty, to her reflection in the other two. It is the principle of proportion or harmony personified. To deny their merits
or criticise their style, is to be blind and dead to the
felicities of art and nature. Not to feel the force of
their united charm (united, yet divided, different and
yet the same), is not to see the beauty of "three red
roses on a stalk"—or of the mingled hues of the rainbow, or of the halcyon's breast, reflected in the stream
—or "the witchery of the soft, blue sky" or grace in
the waving of the branch of a tree, or tenderness in
the bending of a flower, or liveliness in the motion of
a wave of the sea. We shall not try to defend them
against the dancing-school critics, there is another
school, different from that of the *pied à plomb* and
pirouette cant, the school of taste and nature. In this
school the Miss Dennetts are (to say the least) delicious novices. Theirs is the only performance on the
stage (we include the Opera) that gives the unin-
itiated spectator an idea that dancing can be an
emanation of instinctive gaiety, or express the language of sentiment. We might show them to the
Count Stendhal, who speaks so feelingly of the beauties of a dance by Italian peasant girls, as our three
English Graces.

MR. MATHEWS AT HOME

London Magazine, No. V, May, 1820

AN actor is seldom satisfied with being extolled for
what he is, unless you admire him for being what he is
not. A great tragic actress thinks herself particularly
happy in comedy, and it is a sort of misprision of
treason not to say so. Your pen may grow wanton in
praise of the broad farcical humour of a low comedian;
but if you do not cry him up for the fine gentleman,
he threatens to leave the stage. Most of our best comic
performers came out in tragedy as their favourite line;
and Mr. Mathews does not think it enough to enliven
a whole theatre with his powers of drollery, and
whim, and personal transformation, unless, by way of
preface and apology, he first delivers an epitaph on
those talents for the legitimate drama which were so
prematurely buried at Covent Garden Theatre! If we
were to speak our minds, we should say that Mr.
Mathews shines particularly, neither as an actor, nor a
mimic of actors, but that his forte is a certain general
tact, and versatility of comic power. You would say
he is a clever performer: you would guess he is a
cleverer man. His talents are not pure, but mixed. He
is best when he is his own prompter, manager, and
performer, orchestra, and scene-shifter; and perhaps,
to make the thing complete, the audience should be
of his own providing too. If we had never known anything more of Mr. Mathews than the account we have
heard of his imitating the interior of a German family,
the wife lying a-bed grumbling at her husband's stay-
ing out, the husband's return home drunk, and the
little child's *paddling* across the room to its own bed
as soon as it hears him, we should set him down for a
man of genius. These felicitous strokes are, however,
casual and intermittent in him: they proceed from

him rather by chance than design, and are followed up
by others equally gross and superficial. Mr. Mathews
wants taste, or has been spoiled by the taste of the
town, whom "he must live to please, and please to
live." His talent, though limited, is of a lively and
vigorous fibre; capable of a succession of shifts and
disguises; he is *up* to a number of good things—single
hits here and there, but by the suddenness and abrupt-
ness of his turns, he surprises and shocks oftener than
he satisfies. His wit does not move the muscles of the
mind, but, like some practical joker, gives one a good
rap on the knuckles, or a lively box on the ear. He
serves up a *picnic* entertainment of scraps and odd
ends (some of them, we must say, old ones). He is like
a host who will not let us swallow a mouthful, but
offers us something else, and directly after brings us
the same dish again. He is in a continual hurry and
disquietude to please, and destroys half the effect by
trying to increase it. He is afraid to trust for a moment to the language of nature and character, and
wants to translate it into pantomime and grimace, like
a writing-master who, for the letter *I*, has the hieroglyphic of an eye staring you in the face. Mr.
Mathews may be said to have taken tithe of half the
talents of the stage and of the town; yet his variety is
not always charming. There is something dry and
meagre in his jokes; they do not lard the lean earth as
he walks, but seem as if they might be written upon
parchment. His humour, in short, is not like digging
into a fine Stilton cheese, but is more like the scrapings
of Shabsuger. As an actor, we think he cannot rise
higher than a waiter (certainly not a dumb one), or
than Mr. Wiggins.[1] In this last character, in particular,
by a certain panic-struck expression of countenance
at the persecution of which the hen-pecked husband is
the victim, and by the huge, unwieldly helplessness of
his person, unable to escape from it and from the

[1] A great fat character in the farce called *Mrs. Wiggins*.

rabble of boys at his heels, he excites shouts of laughter, and hits off the humour of the thing to an exact perfection. In general, his performance is of that kind which implies manual dexterity, or an assumption of bodily defect, rather than mental capacity: take from Mr. Mathews's drollest parts an odd shuffle in the gait, a restless volubility of speech and motion, a sudden suppression of features, or the continual repetition of some cant phrase with unabated vigour, and you reduce him to an almost total insignificance, and a state of still life. He is not therefore like

> A clock that wants both hands,
> As useless when it goes as when it stands:

for only keep him going, and he bustles about the stage to some purpose. As a mimic of other actors, Mr. Mathews fails as often as he succeeds (we call it a failure when it is with difficulty we can distinguish the person intended); and when he succeeds, it is more by seizing upon some peculiarity, or exaggerating some defect, than by hitting upon the true character or prominent features. He gabbles like Incledon, or croaks like Suett, or lisps like Young; but when he attempts the expressive silver-tongued cadences of John Kemble, it is the shadow of a shade. If we did not know the contrary, we should suppose he had never heard the original, but was imitating someone who had. His best imitations are taken from something characteristic or absurd that has struck his fancy, or occurred to his observation in real life—such as a chattering footman, a drunken coachman, a surly traveller, or a garrulous old Scotchwoman. This last we would fix upon as Mr. Mathews's *chef-d'œuvre*. It was a portrait of common nature, equal to Wilkie or Teniers— as faithful, as simple, as delicately humorous, and with a slight dash of pathos; but without one particle of caricature, of vulgarity, or ill-nature. We see no reason why the ingenious artist should not show his Country

Cousins[2] a gallery of such portraits, and of no others, once a year. He might exhibit it every night for a month, and we should go to see it every night! What has impressed itself on our memory as the next best thing to this exquisite piece of genuine painting, was the broad joke of the abrupt proposal of a mutton-chop to the man who is sea-sick, and the convulsive marks of abhorrence with which it is received. The representation also of the tavern-beau in the *Country Cousins* who is about to swallow a lighted candle for a glass of brandy and water, as he is going drunk to bed, is well feigned and admirably humoured; with many others, too numerous to mention. It is more to our performers' credit to suppose that the songs which he sings with such rapidity and vivacity of effect are not of his own composing; and as to his ventriloquism, it is yet in its infancy. The fault of these exhibitions— that which appears "first, midst, and last" in them—is that they turn too much upon caricaturing the most common-place and wornout topics of ridicule—the blunders of Frenchmen in speaking English,—the mis-pronunciations of the cockney dialect—the ignorance of Country Cousins, and the impertinence and foppery of relations in town. It would seem too likely, from the uniform texture of these peices, that Mr. Mathews had passed his whole time in climbing to the top of the Monument, or had never been out of a tavern or a stage-coach, a Margate-hoy, or a Dover packet-boat. We do not deny the merit of some of the cross-readings out of the two languages; but certainly we think the quantity of French and English jargon put into the mouths of French and English travellers all through these imitations must lessen their popularity instead of increasing it, as two-thirds of Mr. Mathews's auditors, we should imagine, cannot know the point on which the jest turns. We grant that John Bull is

[2] Mathews's "Entertainment" for 1820 was entitled *Country Cousins and the Sights of London.*

always very willing to laugh at Mounseer, if he knew
why or how—perhaps, even without knowing how or
why! But we thought many of the jokes of this kind,
however well contrived or intended, miscarried in
their passage through the pit, and long before they
reached the two-shilling gallery.

KNOWLES' VIRGINIUS

London Magazine, No. VII, July, 1820

Virginius is a good play: we repeat it. It is a real
tragedy; a sound historical painting. Mr. Knowles has
taken the facts as he found them, and expressed the
feelings that would naturally arise out of the occasion.
Strange to say, in this age of poetical egotism, the
author, in writing his play, has been thinking of Virginius and his daugher more than of himself! This is
the true imagination, to put yourself in the place of
others, and to feel and speak for them. Our unpre-
tending poet travels along the high road of nature and
the human heart, and does not turn aside to pluck
pastoral flowers in primrose lanes, or hunt gilded butterflies over enamelled meads, breathless and ex-
hausted; nor does he, with vain ambition, "strike his
lofty head against the stars." So far, indeed, he may
thank the gods for not having made him poetical.
Some cold, formal, affected, and interested critics have
not known what to make of this. It was not what *they*
would have done. One finds fault with the style as
poor, because it is not inflated. Another can see
nothing in it, because it is not interlarded with modern
metaphysical theories, unknown to the ancients. A
third declares that it is all borrowed from Shakespeare,
because it is true to nature. A fourth pronounces it a
superior kind of melodrama, because it pleases the
public. The two last things to which the dull and en-
vious ever think of attributing the success of any work

(and yet the only ones to which genuine success is attributable), are Genius and Nature. The one they hate, and of the other they are ignorant. The same critics who despise and slur the *Virginius* of Covent Garden, praise the *Virginius* and the *David Rizzio*[1] of Drury Lane, because (as it should appear) there is nothing in these to rouse their dormant spleen, stung equally by merit or success, and to mortify their own ridiculous, inordinate, and hopeless vanity. Their praise is of a piece with their censure; and equally from what they applaud and what they condemn, you perceive the principle of their perverse judgments. They are soothed with flatness and failure, and dote over them with parental fondness; but what is above their strength, and demands their admiration, they shrink from with loathing, and an oppressive sense of their own imbecility: and what they dare not openly condemn, they would willingly secrete from the public ear! We have described this class of critics more than once, but they breed still: all that we can do is to sweep them from our path as often as we meet with them, and to remove their dirt and cobwebs as fast as they proceed from the same noisome source. Besides the merits of *Virginius* as a literary composition, it is admirably adapted to the stage. It presents a succession of pictures. We might suppose each scene almost to be copied from a beautiful bas-relief, or to have formed a group on some antique vase. " 'Tis the taste of the ancients, 'tis classical lore." But it is a speaking and a living picture we are called upon to witness. These figures so strikingly, so simply, so harmoniously combined, start into life and action, and breathe forth words, the soul of passion—inflamed with anger, or melting with tenderness. Several passages of great

---

[1] While Macready was playing Virginius at Covent Garden, Kean was playing the same character (in another play) at Drury Lane, and Braham was acting Rizzio in a serious opera of that name.

beauty were cited in a former article on this subject;
but we might mention in addition, the fine imaginative
apostrophe of Virginius to his daughter, when the
story of her birth is questioned.

> I never saw you look so like your mother
> In all my life—

the exquisite lines end,

>   . . . The lie
> Is most unfruitful then, that makes the flower—
> The very flow'r our bed connubial grew,
> To prove its barrenness——

or the sudden and impatient answer of Virginius to
Numitorius, who asks if the slave will swear Virginia
is her child—

> To be sure she will! Is she not his slave?

or again, the dignified reply to his brother, who reminds him it is time to hasten to the Forum—

> Let the forum wait for us!

This is the true language of nature and passion; and
all that we can wish for, or require, in dramatic writing. If such language is not poetical, it is the fault of
poets, who do not write as the heart dictates! We have
seen plays that produced much more tumultuous applause; none scarcely that excited more sincere sympathy. There were no clap-traps, no sentiments that
were the understood signals for making a violent up-
roar; but we heard every one near us express heartfelt and unqualified approbation; and tears more precious supplied the place of loud huzzas. Each spectator appeared to appeal to, and to judge from, the
feelings of his own breast, not from vulgar clamour;
and we trust the success will be more lasting and
secure, as its foundations are laid in the deep and
proud humility of nature. Mr. Knowles owes everything that an author can owe to the actors; and they

owed everything to their attention to truth and to
real feeling. Mr. Macready's Virginius is his best and
most faultless performance—at once the least laboured
and the most effectual. His fine, manly voice sends
forth soothing, impassioned tones, that seem to linger
round, or burst with terrific grandeur from the home
of his heart. Mr. Kemble's[2] Icilius was heroic, spirited,
fervid, the Roman warrior and lover: and Miss Foote
was "the freeborn Roman maid," with a little bit, a
delightful little bit, of the English school-girl in her
acting. We incline to the *ideal* of our own country-
women, after all, when they are so young, so innocent,
so handsome. We are both pleased and sorry to hear
a report which threatens us with the loss of so great a
favourite; and one chief source of our regret will be,
that she will no longer play Virginia. The scenery
allotted to this tragedy encumbered the stage, and the
simplicity of the play. Temples and pictured monu-
ments adorned the scene, which were not in existence
till five hundred years after the date of the story; and
the ruins of the Capitol, of Constantine's arch, and the
temple of Jupiter Stator, frowned at once on the death
of Virginia, and the decline and fall of the Roman
Empire. As to the dresses, we leave them to our deputy
of the wardrobe; but, we believe, they were got right
at last, with some trouble. In the printed play, we observe a number of passages marked with inverted
commas, which are omitted in the representation. This
is the case almost uniformly wherever the words "Tyranny," or "Liberty," occur. Is this done by authority,[3] or is it prudence in the author, *"lest the courtiers
offended should be"*? Is the name of Liberty to be
struck out of the English language, and are we not to
hate tyrants even in an old Roman play? "Let the
galled jade wince: our withers are unwrung." We

    [2] Charles Kemble.
    [3] It was done by the authority of the Lord Chamberlain, at
the express command (it is said) of George IV.

turn to a pleasanter topic, and are glad to find an old
and early friend unaltered in sentiment as he is un-
spoiled by success: the same boy-poet, after a lapse of
years, as when we first knew him; unconscious of the
wreath he has woven round his brow, laughing and
talking of his play just as if it had been written by
anybody else, and as simple-hearted, downright, and
honest as the unblemished work he has produced! [4]

MR. FARREN—INEXPEDIENCY
OF MANY THEATRES

London Magazine, No. VIII, August, 1820

IT is our opinion that there is theatrical strength
enough in this town only to set up one good summer
or one good winter theatre. Competition may be necessary to prevent negligence and abuse, but the result
of this distribution of the *corps dramatique* into different companies is that we never, or very rarely indeed
see a play well acted in all its parts. At Drury Lane
there is only one tragic actor, Mr. Kean: all the rest
are supernumeraries. At Covent Garden they lately
had one great tragic actress, Miss O'Neill; and two or
three actors who were highly respectable, at least in
second-rate tragic characters. At present the female
throne in tragedy is vacant; and of the men "who
rant and fret their hour upon the stage," Mr.
Macready is the only one who draws houses, or who
finds admirers. He shines most, however, in the pathos
of domestic life; and we still want to see tragedy, "tur-
retted, crowned, and crested, with its front gilt and
blood-stained," stooping from the skies (not raised
from the earth) as it did in the person of John

[4] Generosity and simplicity are not the characteristic virtues
of poets. It has been disputed whether "an honest man is the
noblest work of God." But we think an honest poet is so.
—W. H.

Kemble. He is now quaffing health and burgundy in
the south of France. He perhaps finds the air that
blows from the "vine-covered hills" wholesomer than
that of a crowded house; and the lengthened murmurs
of the Mediterranean shore more soothing to the soul
than the deep thunders of the pit. Or does he sometimes recline his lofty, laurelled head upon the sea-
beat beach, and unlocking the cells of memory, listen
to the rolling Pæans, the loud never-to-be-forgotten
plaudits of enraptured multitudes, that mingle with
the music of the waves,

> And murmur as the ocean murmurs near?

Or does he still "sigh his soul towards England" and
the busy hum of Covent Garden? If we thought so
(but that we dread all returns from Elba), we would
say to him, "Come back, and once more bid Britannia
rival old Greece and Rome!"—Or where is Mr. Young
now? There is an opening for *his* pretensions too. If
the Drury Lane company are deficient in genteel
comedy, we fear that Covent Garden cannot help
them out in this respect. Mr. W. Farren is the only exception to the sweeping clause we were going to in-
sert against them. He plays the old gentleman, the
antiquated beau of the last age, very much after the
fashion that we remember to have seen in our younger
days, and that is quite a singular excellence in this. Is
it that Mr. Farren has caught glimpses of this character
in real life, hovering in the horizon of the sister kingdom, which has been long banished from this? They
had their Castle Rack-rents, their moats and ditches,
still extant in remote parts of the interior: and perhaps in famed Dublin city, the *chevaux-de-frise* of
dress, the trellis-work of lace and ruffles, the masked
battery of compliment, the portcullises of formal
speech, the whole artillery of sighs and ogling,
with all the appendages and proper costume of the
ancient *régime*, and paraphernalia of the *preux*

chevalier, may have been kept up in a state of lively decrepitude and smiling dilapidation, in a few straggling instances from the last century, which Mr. Farren had seen. The present age produces nothing of the sort; and so, according to our theory, Mr. Farren does not play the young gentleman or modern man of fashion, though he is himself a young man. For the rest, comedy is in a rich, thriving state at Covent Garden, as far as the lower kind of comic humour is concerned; but it is like an ill-baked pudding, where all the plums sink to the bottom. Emery and Liston, the two best, are of this description: Jones is a caricaturist; and Terry, in his graver parts, is not a comedian, but a moralist. Even a junction of the two companies into one would hardly furnish out one set of players competent to do justice to any of the standard productions of the English stage in tragedy or comedy; what a hopeful project it must be then to start a few more play-houses in the heart of the metropolis as nurseries of histrionic talent, still more to divide and dissipate what little concentration of genius we have, and still more to weaken and distract public patronage? As to the argument in favour of two or more theatres from the necessity of competition, we shall not dispute it, but the actual benefits are not so visible to our dim eyes as to some others. There is a competition in what is bad as well as in what is good: the race of popularity is as often gained by tripping up the heels of your antagonist, as by pressing forward yourself: there is a competition in running an indifferent piece, or a piece indifferently acted, to prevent the success of the same piece at the other house; and there is a competition in puffing, as Mr. Elliston can witness—No, there, we confess, he leaves all competition behind!

MR. ELLISTON'S GASCONADES

London Magazine, No. IX, September, 1820
THE following is a play-bill of Drury Lane Theatre,
for which we paid twopence on the spot, to verify the
fact—as some well-disposed persons, to prevent mis-
takes, purchase libellous or blasphemous publications
from their necessitous or desperate vendors.

Theatre Royal, Drury Lane.—Agreeably to the former
advertisement, this theatre is now open for the last per-
formances of Mr. Kean, before his positive departure for
America. This evening, Saturday, August 19, 1820, his
Majesty's servants will perform Shakspeare's tragedy of
Othello. Duke of Venice, Mr. Thompson; Brabantio, Mr.
Powell; Gratiano, Mr. Carr; Lodovico, Mr. Vining;
Montano, Mr. Jeffries; Othello, Mr. Kean (his last ap-
pearance in that character); Cassio, Mr. Bromley (his first
appearance in that character); Roderigo, Mr. Russell;
Iago, Junius Brutus Booth; Leonardo, Mr. Hudson;
Julio, Mr. Raymond; Manco, Mr. Moreton; Paulo, Mr.
Read; Giovanni, Mr. Starmer; Luca, Mr. Randall;
Desdemona, Mrs. W. West; Emilia, Mrs. Egerton.—This
theatre overflows every night. The patentees cannot condescend to enter into a competition of scurrility, which is
only fitted for minor theatres—what their powers really
are, will be, without any public appeal, legally decided in
November next, and any gasconade can only be supposed
to be caused by cunning or poverty.—After which, the
farce of *Modern Antiques*, &c.

A more impudent puff, and heartless piece of bravado than this, we do not remember to have witnessed.
This theatre does not overflow every night. As to the
competition of scurrility, which the manager declines,
it is he who has commenced it. The minor theatre—
that is, one of them—to wit, the Lyceum—put forth
a very proper and well-grounded remonstrance against
this portentous opening of the winter theatre in the

middle of the dog-days, to scorch up the dry, meagre, hasty harvest of the summer ones:—at which our mighty manager sets up his back, like the great cat, Rodilardus;[1] scornfully rejects their appeal to the public; says he will pounce upon them in November with the law in his hands; and that, in the meantime, all they can do to interest the public in their favour by a plain statement of facts, "can only be supposed to be caused by *cunning* or *poverty*." This is pretty well for a manager who has been so *thanked* as Mr. Elliston! His own committee may laud him for bullying other theatres, but the public will have a feeling for his weaker rivals, though the angry comedian "should threaten to swallow them up quick," and vaunt of his action of battery against them, without any public appeal, "when wind and rain beat dark November." This sorry manager, "dressed" (to use the words of the immortal bard, whom he so modestly and liberally patronises) "dressed in a little brief authority, plays such fantastic tricks before high heaven,"—not "as make the angels weep,"—but his own candle-snuffers laugh, and his own scene-shifters blush. He ought to be ashamed of himself. Why, what a beggarly account of wretched actors, what an exposure of the nakedness of the land, have we in this very play-bill, which is issued forth with such a mixture of pomp and imbecility! Mr. Kean's name, indeed, stands preeminent in lordly capitals, in defiance of Mr. Dowton's resentment,[2]—and Junius Brutus Booth, in his way, scorns to be *Mistered!* But all the rest are, we suppose—Mr. Elliston's friends. They are happy in the favour of the manager, and in the total ignorance of the town! Mr. Kean, we grant, is in himself a host; a sturdy

[1] In Rabelais.
[2] The practice of printing the names of the principal performers in large type had been laid aside for many years, but Elliston revived it this season. Kean's name alone received the distinction.

column, supporting the tottering, tragic dome of
Drury Lane! What will it be when this main, this sole
striking pillar is taken away—"You take my house,
when you do take the prop that holds my house"—
when the patentees shall have nothing to look to for
salvation but the puffing of the Great Lessee, and his
genius for law, which we grant may rival the Widow
Blackacre's—and when the cries of Othello, of Macbeth, of Richard, and Sir Giles, in the last agonies of
their despair, shall be lost, through all the long winter
months, "over a vast and unhearing ocean"? Mr. Elliston, instead of taking so much pains to announce
his own approaching dissolution, had better let Mr.
Kean pass in silence, and take his *positive departure
for America* without the pasting of placards, and the
dust and clatter of a law-suit in Westminster Hall.
It is not becoming in him, R. W. Elliston, Esq., comedian, formerly proprietor of the Surrey and the
Olympic, and author of a pamphlet on the unwar-
rantable encroachments of the Theatres-Royal, now to
insult over the plea of self-defence and self-preserva-
tion, set up by his brethren of the minor play-houses,
as the resource of "poverty and cunning!"—It is not
friendly, it is not gentlemanly. The profession, as well
as Mr. Arnold, may blame him for it; but the patentees
will no doubt thank him at their next quarterly meeting.

EXPLANATIONS—CONVERSATION ON
THE DRAMA WITH COLERIDGE

London Magazine, No. XII, December, 1820
IF theatrical criticisms were only written when there
is something worth writing about, it would be hard
upon us who live by them. Are we not to receive our
quarter's salary (like Mr. Croker in the piping time of
peace) because Mrs. Siddons has left the stage, and

"has not left her peer"? or because John Kemble will
not return to it with renewed health and vigour, to
prop a falling house, and falling art? or because Mr.
Kean has gone to America? or because Mr. Wallack
has arrived from that country? No; the duller the
stage grows, the gayer and more edifying must we become in ourselves: the less we have to say about that,
the more room we have to talk about other things.
Now would be the time for Mr. Coleridge to turn his
talents to account, and write for the stage, when there
is no topic to confine his pen, or "constrain his genius
by mastery." "With mighty wings outspread, his
imagination might brood over the void and make it
pregnant." Under the assumed head of the Drama, he
might unfold the whole mysteries of Swedenborg, or
ascend the third heaven of invention with Jacob Beh-
men: he might write a treatise on all the unknown
sciences, and finish the "Encyclopedia Metropolitana"
in a pocket form:—nay, he might bring to a satisfac-
tory close his own dissertation on the difference between the Imagination and the Fancy,[1] before, in all
probability, another great actor appears, or another
tragedy or comedy is written. He is the man of all
others to swim on empty bladders in a sea without
shore or soundings: to drive an empty stage-coach
without passengers or lading, and arrive behind his
time; to write marginal notes without a text; to look
into a millstone to foster the rising genius of the age;
to "see merit in the chaos of its elements, and discern
perfection in the great obscurity of nothing," as his
most favourite author, Sir Thomas Brown, has it on
another occasion. Alas! we have no such creative
talents: we cannot amplify, expand, raise our flimsy
discourse, as the gaseous matter fills and lifts the

[1] The Fancy is not used here in the sense of Mr. Peter
Corcoran, but in a sense peculiar to Mr. Coleridge, and
hitherto undefined by him.—W. H. [For Mr. Corcoran, see
Mr. Gosse's *Gossip in a Library*, p. 271.]

round, glittering, slow-sailing balloon, to "the up-
turned eyes of wondering mortals." Here is our bill
of fare for the month, or list of memoranda—*The
French Dancers—Farren's Deaf Lover—Macready's
Zanga—Mr. Cooper's Romeo. A new farce, not acted
a second time—Wallace, a tragedy,—and Mr. Wallack's Hamlet.* Who can make anything of such a
beggarly account as this? Not we. Yet, as poets at a
pinch invoke the Muse, so we, for once, will invoke
Mr. Coleridge's better genius, and thus we hear him
talk, diverting our attention from the players and the
play.

"The French, my dear Hazlitt," would he begin,
"are not a people of imagination. They have so little,
that you cannot persuade them to conceive it possible
that they have none. They have no poetry, no such
thing as genius, from the age of Louis XIV. It was
that, their boasted Augustan age, which stamped them
French, which put the seal upon their character, and
from that time nothing has grown up original, or lux-
uriant, or spontaneous among them; the whole has
been cast in a mould, and that a bad one. Montaigne
and Rabelais (their two greatest men, the one for
thought, and the other for imaginative humour,—for
the distinction between imagination and fancy holds
in ludicrous as well as serious composition) I consider
as Franks rather than Frenchmen, for in their time the
national literature was not *set*, was neither mounted
on stilts, nor buckramed in stays. Wit they had, too, if
I could persuade myself that Molière was a genuine
Frenchman; but I cannot help suspecting that his
mother played his reputed father false, and that an
Englishman begot him. I am sure his genius is English,
and his wit not of the Parisian cut. As a proof of this,
see how his most extravagant farces, the *Mock-doctor,
Barnaby Brittle*,[2] &c., take with us. What can be more
to the taste of our *bourgeoisie*, more adapted to our

[2] Adaptations of *Le Médecin Malgré lui* and *George Dandin.*

native tooth, than his *Country Wife*, which Wycherly did little else than translate into English? What success a translator of Racine into our vernacular tongue would meet with, I leave you to guess. His tragedies are not poetry, are not passion, are not imagination: they are a parcel of set speeches, of epigrammatic conceits, of declamatory phrases, without any of the glow, and glancing rapidity, and principle of fusion in the mind of the poet, to agglomerate them into grandeur, or blend them into harmony. The principle of the imagination resembles the emblem of the serpent, by which the ancients typified wisdom and the universe, with undulating folds, for ever varying and for ever flowing into itself,—circular, and without beginning or end. The definite, the fixed, is death: the principle of life is the indefinite, the growing, the moving, the continuous. But everything in French poetry is cut up into shreds and patches, little flowers of poetry, with tickets and labels to them, as when the daughters of Jason minced and hacked their old father into collops—we have the *disjecta membra poetæ*—not the entire and living man. The spirit of genuine poetry should inform the whole work, should breathe through, and move, and agitate the complete mass, as the soul informs and moves the limbs of a man, or as the vital principle (whatever it be) permeates the veins of the loftiest trees, building up the trunk, and extending the branches to the sun and winds of heaven, and shooting out into fruit and flowers. This is the progress of nature and of genius. This is the true poetic faculty, or that which the Greeks literally call ποίησις. But a French play (I think it is Schlegel who somewhere makes the comparison, though I had myself, before I ever read Schlegel, made the same remark) is like a child's garden set with slips of branches and flowers, stuck in the ground, not growing in it. We may weave a gaudy garland in this manner, but it withers in an hour: while the products

of genius and nature give out their odours to the gale,
and spread their tints in the sun's eye, age after age—

> Outlast a thousand storms, a thousand winters,
> Free from the Sirian star and thunder stroke,

and flourish in immortal youth and beauty. Everything French is frittered into parts: everything is
therefore dead and ineffective. French poetry is just
like chopped logic: nothing comes of it. There is
no life of the mind: neither the birth nor generation
of knowledge. It is all patch-work, all sharp points
and angles, all superficial. They receive, and give
out sensation, too readily for it ever to amount to
a sentiment. They cannot even dance, as you may
see. There is, I am sure you will agree, no expression,
no grace in their dancing. Littleness, point, is what
damns them in all they do. With all their vivacity
and animal spirits, they dance not like men and women
under the impression of certain emotions, but like
puppets; they twirl round like *tourniquets*. Not to
feel, and not to think, is all they know of this art
or of any other. You might swear that a nation that
danced in that manner would never produce a true
poet or philosopher. They have it not in them. There
is not the principle of cause and effect. They make a
sudden turn because there is no reason for it: they stop
short, or move fast, only because you expect something else. Their style of dancing is difficult: would it
were impossible." [3] (By this time several persons in the
pit had turned round to listen to this uninterrupted
discourse, and our eloquent friend went on, rather
raising his voice with a *Paulo majora canamus*.) "Look
at that Mademoiselle Milanie with 'the foot of fire,' as
she is called. You might contrive a paste-board figure,
with the help of strings or wires, to do all, and more,

---

[3] This expression is borrowed from Dr. Johnson. However,
as Dr. Johnson is not a German critic, Mr. C. need not be
supposed to acknowledge it.—W. H.

than she does—to point the toe, to raise the leg, to
jerk the body, to run like wild-fire. Antics are not
grace: to dance is not to move against time. My dear
Hazlitt, if you could have seen a dance by some Italian
peasant-girls in the Campagna of Rome, as I have, I am
sure your good taste and good sense would have approved it. They came forward slow and smiling, but
as if their limbs were steeped in luxury, and every motion seemed an echo of the music, and the heavens
looked on serener as they trod. You are right about
the Miss Dennetts,[4] though you have all the cant-
phrases against you. It is true, they break down in
some of their steps, but it is like 'the lily drooping on
its stalk green,' or like 'the flowers Proserpina let fall
from Dis's Waggon.' Those who cannot see grace in
the youth and inexperience of these charming girls,
would see no beauty in a cluster of Hyacinths, bent
with the morning dew. To show at once what is, and
is not French, there is Mademoiselle Hullin, she is
Dutch. Nay, she is just like a Dutch doll, as round-
faced, as rosy, and looks for all the world as if her
limbs were made of wax-work, and would take in
pieces, but not as if she could move them of her own
accord. Alas, poor tender thing! As to the men, I confess" (this was said to me in an audible whisper, lest
it might be construed into a breach of confidence), "I
should like, as Southey says, to have them *hamstrung!*"
—(At this moment Monsieur Hullin *père* looked as
if this charitable operation was about to be performed
on him by an extra-official warrant from the poet-
laureate.)

"Pray, Hazlitt, have you seen Macready's Zanga?"
"Yes."
"And what do you think of it?"
"I did not like it much."
"Nor I. Macready has talents and a magnificent
voice, but he is, I fear, too improving an actor to be

⁴See *ante* p. 163.

a man of genius. That little ill-looking vagabond Kean
never improved in anything. In some things he could
not, and in others he would not. The only parts of
Macready's Zanga that I liked (which of course I
only half-liked) were some things in imitation of the
extremely natural manner of Kean, and his address to
Alonzo, urging him, as the greatest triumph of his
self-denial, to sacrifice

> A wife, a bride, a mistress unenjoyed—

where his voice rose exulting on the sentiment, like
the thunder that clothes the neck of the war-horse.
The person that pleased me most in this play was Mrs.
Sterling:[5] she did justice to her part—a thing not
easy to do. I like Macready's Wallace better than his
Zanga, though the play is not a good one, and it is
difficult for the actor to find out the author's meaning.
I would not judge harshly of a first attempt, but the
faults of youthful genius are exuberance, and a continual desire of novelty; now the faults of this play are
tameness, commonplace, and claptraps. It is said to be
written by young Walker, the son of the Westminster
orator. If so, his friend, Mr. Cobbett, will probably
write a Theatrical Examiner of it in his next week's
Political Register. What, I would ask, can be worse,
more out of character and costume, than to make
Wallace drop his sword to have his throat cut by
Menteith, merely because the latter has proved himself (what he suspected) a traitor and a villain, and
then console himself for this voluntary martyrdom by
a sentimental farewell to the rocks and mountains of
his native country! This effeminate softness and
wretched cant did not belong to the age, the country,
or the hero. In this scene, however, Mr. Macready
shone much: and in the attitude in which he stood
after letting his sword fall, he displayed extreme grace

[5] An actress of no great importance, who played "Old
Women" principally.

and feeling. It was as if he had let his best friend, his trusty sword, drop like a serpent from his hand. Macready's figure is awkward, but his attitudes are graceful and well composed.—Don't you think so?"—

I answered, yes; and he then ran on in his usual manner, by inquiring into the metaphysical distinction between the grace of form and the grace that arises from motion (as, for instance, you may move a square form in a circular or waving line), and illustrated this subtle observation at great length and with much happiness. He asked me how it was that Mr. Farren, in the farce of *The Deaf Lover*, played the old gentleman so well, and failed so entirely in the young gallant? I said I could not tell. He then tried at a solution himself, in which I could not follow him so as to give the precise point of his argument. He afterwards defined to me, and those about us, the merits of Mr. Cooper and Mr. Wallack, classing the first as a respectable, and the last as a second-rate actor, with large grounds and learned definitions of his meaning on both points; and, as the lights were by this time nearly out, and the audience (except his immediate auditors) going away, he reluctantly "ended,"

But in Adam's ear so pleasing left his voice,[6]

that I quite forgot I had to write my article on the Drama the next day; nor without his aid should I have been able to wind up my accounts for the year, as Mr. Mathews gets through his AT HOME by the help of a little awkward ventriloquism.

> [6] The angel ended, and in Adam's ear
> So charming left his voice, that he awhile
> Thought him still speaking.
> *Paradise Lost*, bk. viii.

MR. KEAN AS CORIOLANUS

London Magazine, No. II, February, 1820

MR. KEAN's acting is not of the patrician order; he is one of the people, and what might be termed a *radical* performer. He can do all that may become a man "of our infirmity," "to relish all as sharply, passioned as we;" but he cannot play a god, or one who fancies himself a god, and who is sublime, not in the strength of his own feelings, but in his contempt for those of others, and in his imaginary superiority to them. That is, he cannot play Coriolanus so well as he plays some other characters, or as we have seen it played often. Wherever there was a struggle of feelings, a momentary ebullition of pity, or remorse, or anguish—wherever nature resumed her wonted rights—Mr. Kean was equal to himself, and superior to everyone else; but the prevailing characteristics of the part are inordinate self-opinion, and haughty elevation of soul, that aspire above competition or control, as the tall rock lifts its head above the skies, and is not bent or shattered by the storm, beautiful in its unconquered strength, terrible in its unaltered repose. Mr. Kean, instead of "keeping his state," instead of remaining fixed and immovable (for the most part) on his pedestal of pride, seemed impatient of this mock dignity, this *still-life* assumption of superiority; burst too often from the trammels of precedent, and the *routine* of etiquette, which should have confined him; and descended into the common arena of man, to make good his pretensions by the energy with which he contended for them, and to prove the hollowness of his supposed indifference to the opinion of others by the excessive significance and studied variations of the scorn and disgust he expressed for it. The intolerable airs and aristocratical pretensions of which he is the slave, and to which he falls a victim, did not seem *legitimate* in him, but upstart, turbulent, and vulgar. Thus his haughty answer to the mob who banish him—"I BANISH YOU"—was given with all the virulence of execration and rage of impotent despair, as if he had to strain every nerve and faculty of soul to shake off the contamination of their hated power over him, instead of being delivered with calm, majestic self-possession, as if he remained rooted to the spot, and his least motion, word, or look, must scatter them like chaff or scum from his presence. The most effective scene was that in which he stands for the consulship, and begs for "the most sweet voices" of the people whom he loathes; and the most ineffective was that in which he is reluctantly reconciled to, and overcome by, the entreaties of his mother. This decisive and affecting interview passed off as if nothing had happened, and was conducted with diplomatic gravity and skill. The casting of the other parts was a climax in bathos. Mr. Gattie was Menenius, the friend of Coriolanus, and Mr. Penley Tullus Aufidius, his mortal foe. Mr. Pope should have played the part. One would think there were processions and ovations enough in this play, as it was acted in John Kemble's time; but besides these, there were introduced others of the same sort, some of which were lengthened out as if they would reach all the way to the circus; and there was a sham fight, of melodramatic effect, in the second scene, in which Mr. Kean had like to have lost his voice. There was throughout a continual din of

Guns, drums, trumpets, blunderbuss, and thunder—

or what was very like it. In the middle of an important scene, the tinkling of the stage-bell was employed to announce a flourish of trumpets—a thing which even Mr. Glossop would not hear of, whatever the Act of

Parliament might say to enforce such a puppet-show accompaniment. There is very bad management in all this; and yet Mr. Elliston is the manager.

MR. KEAN AS HARLEQUIN—HIS IMITATIONS—HIS JAFFIER

London Magazine, No. VII, July, 1820
WE saw Mr. Kean at his benefit, at the risk of our limbs, and are sorry for the accident that happened to himself in the course of the evening. We have longed ever since we saw Mr. Kean—that is, any time these six years—to see him jump through a trap-door—hearing he could do it. "Why are these things hid? Is this a time to conceal virtues?" said we to ourselves. What was our disappointment, then, when on the point of this consummation of our wishes, and just in the moment of the projection of our hopes—when dancing with Miss Valancey, too, he broke the tendon Achilles, and down fell all our promised pleasure, our castles in the air! Good reader, it was not the jump through the trap-door that we wished literally to see, but the leap from Othello to Harlequin. What a jump! What an interval, what a gulf to pass! What an elasticity of soul and body too—what a diversity of capacity in the same diminutive person! To be Othello, a man should be all passion, abstraction, imagination; to be Harlequin, he should have his wits in his heels and in his fingers' ends! To be both is impossible or miraculous. Each doubles the wonder of the other; and in judging of the aggregate amount of merit, we must proceed, not by the rules of addition, but multiply Harlequin's lightness into Othello's gravity, and the result will give us the sum total of Mr. Kean's abilities. What a spring, what an expansive force of mind, what an untamed vigour, to rise to such a height from such a lowness; to tower like a phoenix from its ashes; to

ascend like a pyramid of fire! Why, what a complex
piece of machinery is here; what an involution of
faculties, circle within circle, that enables the same
individual to make a somersault, and that swells
the veins of his forehead with true artificial passion,
and that turns him to a marble statue with thought!
It is not being educated in the fourth form of St.
Paul's school, or cast in the antique mould of the high
Roman fashion,[1] that can do this; but it is genius alone
that can raise a man thus above his first origin, and
make him thus various from himself! It is bestriding
the microcosm of man like a Colossus; and, by uniting
the extremes of the chain of being, seemingly implies
all the intermediate links. We do not think much of
Mr. Kean's singing; we could, with a little practice
and tuition, sing nearly as well ourselves; as for his
dancing, it is but *so so*, and anybody can dance; his
fencing is good, nervous, firm, fibrous, like that of a
pocket Hercules; but for his jumping through a hole
in the wall—clean through, head over heels, like a shot
out of a culverin—"by heavens, it would have been
great!" This we fully expected at his hands, and in
this expectation we were baulked. Just as our critical
anticipations were on tip-toe, Mr. Kean suddenly
strained his ankle, as it were to spite us; we went out in
dudgeon, and were near missing his Imitations, which
would not have signified much if we had. They were
tolerable, indifferent, pretty good, but not the thing.
Mr. Mathews's or Mr. Yates's are better. They were
softened down, and fastidious. Kemble was not very
like. Incledon and Braham were the best, and Munden
was very middling. The after-piece of *The Admirable
Crichton*, in which he was to do all this, was neither
historical nor dramatic. The character, which might
have given excellent opportunities for the display of
a variety of extraordinary accomplishments in the real
progress of the story, was ill-conceived and ill-man-

[1] Evidently an allusion to Elliston and Kemble.

aged. He was made either a pedagogue or an antic. In himself he was dull and grave, instead of being high-spirited, volatile, and self-sufficient; and to show off his abilities, he was put into masquerade. We did not like it at all, though, from the prologue, we had expected more point and daring. Mr. Kean's Jaffier was fine, and in parts admirable. This, indeed, is only to say that he played it. But it was not one of his finest parts, nor indeed one in which we expected him to shine preeminently; but on that we had not depended, for we never know beforehand what he will do best or worst. He is one of those wandering fires, whose orbit is not calculable by any known rules of criticism. Mr. Elliston's Pierre was, we are happy to say, a spirited and effectual performance. We must not forget to add that Mrs. M'Gibbon's Belvidera was excellent, declaimed with impassioned propriety, and acted with dignity and grace.

MR. KEAN AS LEAR

London Magazine, No. VI, June, 1820

WE need not say how much our expectations had been previously excited to see Mr. Kean in this character, and we are sorry to be obliged to add that they were very considerably disappointed. We had hoped to witness something of the same effect produced upon an audience that Garrick is reported to have done in the part, which made Dr. Johnson resolve never to see him repeat it—the impression was so terrific and overwhelming. If we should make the same rash vow never to see Mr. Kean's Lear again, it would not be from the intensity and excess, but from the deficiency and desultoriness, of the interest excited. To give some idea of the manner in which this character might, and ought to be, made to seize upon the feelings of an audience, we have heard it mentioned that once, when

Garrick was in the middle of the mad scene, his crown
of straw came off, which circumstance, though it
would have been fatal to a common actor, did not produce the smallest interruption, or even notice in the
house. On another occasion, while he was kneeling to
repeat the curse, the first row in the pit stood up in
order to see him better; the second row, not willing
to lose the precious moments by remonstrating, stood
up too; and so, by a tacit movement, the entire pit
rose to hear the withering imprecation, while the
whole passed in such cautious silence that you might
have heard a pin drop. John Kemble (that old cam-
paigner) was also very great in the curse; so we have
heard, from very good authorities, and we put im-
plicit faith in them. What led us to look for the greatest
things from Mr. Kean in the present instance, was his
own opinion, on which we have a strong reliance. It
was always his favourite part. We have understood
he has been heard to say that "he was very much
obliged to the London audiences for the good opinion
they had hitherto expressed of him, but that when
they came to see him over the dead body of Cordelia,
they would have quite a different notion of the matter." As it happens, they have not yet had an opportunity of seeing him over the dead body of Cordelia;
for, after all, our versatile manager has acted Tate's
Lear instead of Shakespeare's; and it was suggested
that perhaps Mr. Kean played the whole ill *out of
spite*, as he could not have it his own way—a hint to
which we lent a willing ear, for we would rather think
Mr. Kean the most spiteful man, than not the best
actor, in the world! The impression, however, made
on our minds was that, instead of its being his masterpiece, he was to seek in many parts of the character;
that the general conception was often perverse or
feeble, and that there were only two or three places
where he could be said to electrify the house. It is altogether inferior to his Othello. Yet, if he had even

played it equal to that, all we could have said of Mr.
Kean would have been that he was a very wonderful
man; and such we certainly think him as it is.

Into the bursts and starts and torrent of the passion
in Othello this excellent actor appeared to have flung
himself completely; there was all the fitful fever of
the blood, the jealous madness of the brain; his heart
seemed to bleed with anguish, while his tongue
dropped broken, imperfect accents of woe; but there
is something (we don't know how) in the gigantic,
outspread sorrows of Lear, that seems to elude his
grasp, and baffle his attempts at comprehension. The
passion in Othello pours along, so to speak, like a river,
torments itself in restless eddies, or is hurled from its
dizzy height like a sounding cataract. That in Lear is
more like a sea, swelling, chafing, raging, without
bound, without hope, without beacon or anchor. Torn
from the hold of his affections and fixed purposes, he
floats a mighty wreck in the wide world of sorrows.
Othello's causes of complaint are more distinct and
pointed, and he has a desperate, a maddening remedy
for them in his revenge. But Lear's injuries are without provocation, and admit of no alleviation or atone-
ment. They are strange, bewildering, overwhelming;
they wrench asunder, and stun the whole frame; they
"accumulate horrors or horror's head," and yet leave
the mind impotent of resources, cut off, proscribed,
anathematised from the common hope of good to itself, or ill to others—amazed at its own situation, but
unable to avert it, scarce daring to look at or to weep
over it. The action of the mind, however, under this
load of disabling circumstances, is brought out in the
play in the most masterly and triumphant manner; it
staggers under them, but it does not yield. The character is cemented of human strength and human weaknesses (the firmer for the mixture); abandoned of fortune, of nature, of reason, and without any energy of
purpose or power of action left—with the grounds

of all hope and comfort failing under it—but sustained, reared to a majestic height out of the yawning abyss, by the force of the affections, the imagination, and the cords of the human heart—it stands a proud monument, in the gap of nature, over barbarous cruelty and filial ingratitude. We had thought that Mr. Kean would take possession of this time-worn, venerable figure, "that has outlasted a thousand storms, a thousand winters," and, like the gods of old, when their oracles were about to speak, shake it with present inspiration—that he would set up a living copy of it on the stage; but he failed, either from insurmountable difficulties, or from his own sense of the magnitude of the undertaking. There are pieces of ancient granite that turn the edge of any modern chisel, so perhaps the genius of no living actor can be expected to cope with Lear. Mr. Kean chipped off a bit of the character here and there, but he did not pierce the solid substance, nor move the entire mass. Indeed, he did not go the right way about it. He was too violent at first, and too tame afterwards. He sank from unmixed rage to mere dotage. Thus (to leave this general description, and come to particulars) he made the well-known curse a piece of downright rant. He "tore it to tatters, to very rags," and made it, from beginning to end, an explosion of ungovernable physical rage, without solemnity or elevation. Here it is; and let the reader judge for himself whether it should be so served.

> Hear, Nature, hear; dear goddess, hear a father
> Suspend thy purpose, if thou didst intend
> To make this creature fruitful:[1]
> Into her womb convey sterility!
> Dry up in her the organs of increase,
> And from her derogate body never spring

[1] Hear, Nature, hear! dear goddess, hear!
Suspend thy purpose, if thou didst intend
To make this creature fruitful!

> A babe to honour her! If she must teem,
> Create her child of spleen, that it may live
> And be a thwart disnatur'd torment to her!
> Let it stamp wrinkles in her brow of youth,
> With cadent tears fret channels in her cheeks,
> Turn all her mother's pains and benefits
> To laughter and contempt, that she may feel
> How sharper than a serpent's tooth it is
> To have a thankless child!—

Now this should not certainly be spoken in a fit of drunken choler, without any "compunctious visitings of nature," without any relentings of tenderness, as if it was a mere speech of hate, directed against a person to whom he had the most rooted and unalterable aversion. The very bitterness of the imprecations is prompted by, and turns upon, an allusion to the fondest recollections; it is an excess of indignation, but that indignation, from the depth of its source, conjures up the dearest images of love; it is from these that the brimming cup of anguish overflows, and the voice, in going over them, should falter, and be choked with other feelings besides anger. The curse in Lear should not be *scolded*, but recited as a Hymn to the Penates! Lear is not a Timon. From the action and attitude into which Mr. Kean put himself to repeat this passage, we had augured a different result. He threw himself on his knees, lifted up his arms like withered stumps, threw his head quite back, and in that position, as if severed from all that held him to society, breathed a heart-struck prayer, like the figure of a man obtruncated! It was the only moment worthy of himself, and of the character.

In the former part of the scene, where Lear, in answer to the cool, didactic reasoning of Goneril, asks, "Are you our daughter?" &c., Mr. Kean, we thought, failed from a contrary defect. The suppression of passion should not amount to immobility; that intensity of feeling of which the slightest intimation is supposed to convey everything, should not seem to convey nothing. There is a difference between ordinary familiarity and the *sublime* of familiarity. The mind may be staggered by a blow too great for it to bear, and may not recover itself for a moment or two; but this state of suspense of its faculties, "like a phantasma, or a hideous dream," should not assume the appearence of indifference, or *still-life*. We do not think Mr. Kean kept this distinction (though it is one in which he is often very happy) sufficiently marked in the foregoing question to his daughter, nor in the speech which follows immediately after, as a confirmation of the same sentiment of incredulity and surprise.

> Does any here know me? This is not Lear:
> Does Lear walk thus? speak thus? Where are his eyes?
> Either his notion weakens, his discernings
> Are lethargied. Ha! waking? 'tis not so.
> Who is it that can tell me who I am?
> Lear's shadow? I would learn that; for, by the marks
> Of sovereignty, knowledge, and reason,
> I should be false persuaded I had daughters.[2]
> Your name, fair gentlewoman?

These fearful interrogatories, which stand ready to start away on the brink of madness, should not certainly be asked like a common question, nor a dry sarcasm. If Mr. Kean did not speak them so, we beg his pardon. In what comes after this, in the apostrophe to Ingratitude, in the sudden call for his horses, in the defence of the character of his train as "men of choice and rarest parts," and in the recurrence to Cordelia's "most small fault," there are plenty of stops to play upon, all the varieties of agony, of anger and impatience, of asserted dignity and tender regret—Mr. Kean struck but two notes all through, the highest and the lowest.

[2] The Fool (omitted in all stage versions down to 1838) speaks the words "Lear's shadow."

This scene of Lear with Goneril, in the first act, is only to be paralleled by the doubly terrific one between him and Regan and Goneril in the second act. To call it a decided failure would be saying what we do not think; to call it a splendid success would be saying so no less. Mr. Kean did not appear to us to set his back fairly to his task, or to trust implicitly to his author, but to be trying experiments upon the audience, and waiting to see the result. We never saw this daring actor want confidence before, but he seemed to cower and hesitate before the public eye in the present instance, and to be looking out for the effect of what he did, while he was doing it. In the ironical remonstrance to Regan, for example:

> 'Dear daughter, I confess that I am old;
> Age is unnecessary,' &c.

he might be said to be waiting for the report of the house to know how low he should bend his knee in mimic reverence, how far he should sink his voice into the tones of feebleness, despondency, and mendicancy. But, if ever, it was upon *this* occasion that he ought to have raised himself above criticism, and sat enthroned (in the towering contemplations of his own mind) with Genius and Nature. They alone (and not the critic's eye, nor the tumultuous voices of the pit) are the true judges of Lear! If he had trusted only to these, his own counsellors and bosom friends, we see no limit to the effect he might have produced. But he did not give any particular effect to the exclamation—

> —Beloved Regan,
> Thy sister's naught: O Regan, she hath tied
> Sharp-tooth'd unkindness, like a vulture, here:

nor to the assurance that he will not return to her again—

> Never, Regan.
> She hath abated me of half my train;

> Look'd black upon me; struck me with her tongue,
> Most serpent-like, upon the very heart.
> All the stor'd vengeances of heaven fall
> On her ingrateful top!—

nor the description of his two daughters' looks—

> —her eyes are fierce, but thine
> Do comfort, and not burn.—

nor to that last sublime appeal to the heavens on seeing Goneril approach—

> O heavens,
> If you do love old men, if your sweet sway
> Allow obedience, if yourselves are old,
> Make it your cause; send down and take my part!
> Art not asham'd to look upon this beard?
> Oh, Regan, wilt thou take her by the hand?

One would think there are tones, and looks, and gestures, answerable to these words, to thrill and harrow up the thoughts, to "appeal the guilty, and make mad the free," or that might "create a soul under the ribs of death!" But we did not see or hear them. It was Mr. Kean's business to furnish them; it would have been ours to feel them, if he had! It is not enough that Lear's crosses and perplexities are expressed by single strokes. There should be an agglomeration of horrors, closing him in like a phalanx. His speech should be thick with the fulness of his agony. His face should, as it were, encrust and stiffen into amazement at his multiplied afflictions. A single image of ruin is nothing —there should be a growing desolation all around him. His wrongs should seem enlarged tenfold through the solid atmosphere of his despair—his thoughts should be vast and lurid, like the sun when he declines—he should be "a huge dumb heap of woe!" The most that Mr. Kean did was to make some single hits here and there; but these did not tell, because they were separated from the main body and movement of the pas-

sion. They might be compared to interlineations of
the character, rather than parts of the text. In the sudden reiteration of the epithet, "*fiery* quality of the
Duke," applied to Cornwall by Gloucester, at which
his jealousy blazes out to extravagance, we thought
Mr. Kean feeble and indecisive; but in breaking away
at the conclusion of the scene, "I will do such things,—
What they are yet I know not,—but they shall be The
terrors of the earth"—he made one of those tremen-
dous bursts of energy and grandeur, which shed a
glory round every character he plays.

Mr. Kean's performance of the remainder of the
character, when the king's intellects begin to fail him,
and are, at last, quite disordered, was curious and
quaint, rather than impressive or natural. There appeared a degree of perversity in all this—a determination to give the passages in a way in which nobody
else would give them, and in which nobody else would
expect them to be given. But singularity is not always
excellence. Why, for instance, should our actor lower
his voice in the soliloquy in the third act, "Blow
winds, and crack your cheeks," &c., in which the
tumult of Lear's thoughts, and the extravagance of his
expressions, seem almost contending with the violence
of the storm? We can conceive no reason but that it
was contrary to the practice of most actors hitherto.
Mr. Rae's manner of mouthing the passage would have
been "more germane to the matter." In asking his companion—

> How dost, my boy? Art cold?
> I am cold myself—

there was a shrinking of the frame, and a chill glance
of the eye, like the shivering of an ague-fit; but no
other feeling surmounted the physical expression. On
meeting with Edgar, as Mad Tom, Lear wildly exclaims, with infinite beauty and pathos, "Didst thou give
all to thy two daughters? And art thou come to this?"

And again, presently after, he repeats, "What, have his daughters brought him to this pass? Couldst thou save nothing? Didst thou give them all?" questions which imply a strong prepossession, the eager indulgence of a favourite idea which has just struck his heated fancy; but which Mr. Kean pronounced in a feeble, sceptical, querulous undertone, as if wanting information as to some ordinary occasion of insignificant distress. We do not admire these cross-readings of a work like *Lear*. They may be very well when the actor's ingenuity, however paradoxical, is more amusing than the author's sense; but it is not so in this case. From some such miscalculation, or desire of finding out a clue to the character other than "was set down" for him, Mr. Kean did not display his usual resources and felicitous spirit in these terrific scenes; he drivelled, and looked vacant, and moved his lips, so as not to be heard, and did nothing, and appeared, at times, as if he would quite forget himself. The pauses were too long, the indications of remote meaning were too significant to be well understood. The spectator was big with expectation of seeing some extraordinary means employed: but the general result did not correspond to the waste of preparation. In a subsequent part, Mr. Kean did not give to the reply of Lear, "Ay, every inch a king!" the same vehemence and emphasis that Mr. Booth did; and in this he was justified, for, in the text, it is an exclamation of indignant irony, not of conscious superiority; and he immediately adds, with deep disdain, to prove the nothingness of his pretensions—

When I do stare, see how the subject quakes.

Almost the only passage in which Mr. Kean obtained his usual heart-felt tribute, was in his interview with Cordelia, after he awakes from sleep, and has been restored to his senses—

Pray, do not mock me:
I am a very foolish fond old man,
Fourscore and upward, not an hour more or less;
And, to deal plainly,
I fear I am not in my perfect mind.
Methinks I should know you and know this man;
Yet I am doubtful: for I am mainly ignorant
What place this is, and all the skill I have
Remembers not these garments; nor I know not
Where I did lodge last night. *Do not laugh at me;*
For, as I am a man, I think this lady
To be my child Cordelia.
　　Cordelia. And so I am, I am.

In uttering the last words, Mr. Kean staggered faintly
into Cordelia's arms, and his sobs of tenderness, and his
ecstasy of joy commingled, drew streaming tears from
the brightest eyes—

　　Which sacred pity had engender'd there.

Mr. Rae was very effective in the part of Edgar, and
was received with very great applause. If this gentleman could rein in a certain "false gallop" in his voice
and gait, he would be a most respectable addition,
from the spirit and impressiveness of his declamation, to
the general strength of any theatre, and we heartily
congratulate him on his return to Drury Lane.

MISS O'NEILL'S RETIREMENT

London Magazine, No. II, February, 1820
THE stage has lost one of its principal ornaments and
fairest supports, in the person of Miss O'Neill. As Miss
Somerville changed her name for that of Mrs. Bunn,
and still remains on the stage, so Miss O'Neill has al-
tered hers for Mrs. Beecher, and has, we fear, quitted

us for good and all.[1] "There were two upon the house-top: one was taken, and the other was left!" Though, on our own account, we do not think this "a consummation devoutly to be wished," yet we cannot say we are sorry on hers. Hymen has, in this instance, with his flaming torch and saffron robe, borne a favourite actress from us, and held her fast, beyond the seas and sounding shores, "to our moist vows denied"; but, whatever complaints or repinings have been heard on the occasion, we think Miss O'Neill was in the right to do as she has done. *Fast bind fast find* is an old proverb, and a good one, and is in no doubt applicable to both sexes, and on both sides of the water. A husband, like death, cancels all other claims, and we think more especially any imaginary and imperfect obligations (with a clipped sixpence, and clap hands and a bargain) to the stage or to the town. Miss O'Neill (for so her name may yet linger on our tongues) made good her retreat in time from the world's "slippery turns," and we are glad that she has done so. It is better to retire from the stage when young, with fame and fortune, than to have to return to it when old (as Mrs. Crawford, Mrs. Abington, and so many others have done), in poverty, neglect, and scorn. There is no marriage for better and for worse to the public; it is but a "Mr. Limberham, or Kind Keeper," [2] at the very best; it does not tie itself to worship its favourites, or "with its worldly goods them endow, through good report or evil report, in sickness or in health, till death them do part." No such thing is even thought of; they must be always young, always beautiful and dazzling, and allowed to be so; or they are instantly discarded, and they pass from their full-blown pride, and the

[1] Miss O'Neill made her last appearance on July 13, 1819, and was married to Mr. (afterwards Sir) William Wrixon Beecher in December of the same year. She died on October 29, 1872.
[2] The title of Dryden's notorious play.

purple light that irradiates them, into "the list of weeds and worn-out faces." If a servant of the theatre dismisses himself without due warning, it makes a great deal of idle talk; but, on the other hand, does the theatre never dismiss one of its servants without formal notice, and is anything then said about it? How many old favourites of the town—that many-headed abstraction, with new opinions, whims, and follies, ever sprouting from its teeming brain—how many decayed veterans of the stage do we remember, in the last ten or twenty years, laid aside "in monumental mockery"; thrown from the pinnacle of prosperity and popularity, to pine in poverty and obscurity, their names forgotten, or staring in large capitals, asking for a benefit at some minor theatre! How many of these are to be seen, walking about with shrunk shanks and tattered hose, avoiding the eye of the stranger whom they suppose to have known them in better days, straggling through the streets with faltering steps, and on some hopeless errand—with sinking hearts, or heartbroken long ago—engaged, dismissed again, tampered with, tantalised, trifled with, pelted, hooted, scorned, unpitied; performing quarantine at a distance from the centre of all their hopes and wishes, as if their names were a stain on their former reputations;—or perhaps received once more—tolerated, endured out of charity, in the very places that they once adorned and gladdened by their presence! And all this, often without any fault in themselves, any misconduct, any change, but in the taste and humour of the audience; or from their own imprudence, in not guarding (while they had an opportunity) against the ingratitude and treachery of that very public that claims them as its property, and would make them its slaves and puppets for life—or during pleasure? We might make out a long list of superannuated pensioners on public patronage, who have had the last grudging pittance of favour withdrawn from them, but that it could do no sort of good, and that we would not expose the names themselves to the gaze and wonder of vulgar curiosity. We are only not sorry that Miss O'Neill has put it out of the power of the nobility, gentry, and her friends in general, to add her name to the splendid, tarnished list; and that she cannot, like so many of her predecessors, be chopped and changed, and hacked, and bandied about, in tragedy or in comedy, in farce or in pantomime, in dance or song, at the Surrey, or the Coburg, or the Sans Pareil theatres; or even be sent to mingle her silvery cadences with Mr. Kean's hoarse notes at Old Drury.

Miss O'Neill was in size of the middle form; her complexion was fair, and her person not inelegant. She stooped somewhat in the shoulders, but not so as to destroy grace or dignity; in moving across the stage, she dragged a little in her step, with some want of firmness and elasticity. The action of her hands and arms, however (one of the least common, and therefore, we suppose, one of the most difficult accomplishments an actor or actress has to acquire), was perfectly just, simple, and expressive. They either remained in unconscious repose by her side, or, if employed, it was to anticipate or confirm the language of the eye and tongue. There was no affectation, no unmeaning display, or awkward deficiency in her gesticulation; but her body and mind seemed to be under the guidance of the same impulse, to move in concert, and to be moulded into unity of effect by a certain natural grace, earnestness, and good sense. The contour of her face was nearly oval, and her features approached to the regularity of the Grecian outline. The expression of them was confined either to the extremity of pain and agony, or to habitual softness and placidity, with an occasional smile of great sweetness. Her voice was deep, clear, and mellow, capable of the most forcible exertion, but, in ordinary speaking, "gentle and low, an excellent thing in woman!" She, however, owed com-

paratively little to physical qualifications; there was
nothing in her face, voice, or person, sufficiently striking to have obtruded her into notice, or to have been
a factitious substitute for other requisites. Her external
advantages were merely the medium through which
her internal powers displayed their refulgence, without obstruction or refraction (with the exception hereafter to be stated); they were the passive instruments,
which her powerful and delicate sensibility wielded
with the utmost propriety, ease, and effect. Her excellence (unrivalled by any actress since Mrs. Siddons)
consisted in truth of nature and force of passion. Her
correctness did not seem the effect of art or study, but
of instinctive sympathy, of a conformity of mind and
disposition to the character she was playing, as if she
had unconsciously become the very person. There
were no catching lights, no pointed hits, no theatrical
tricks, no female arts resorted to, in her best or general
style of acting; there was a singleness, an entireness,
and harmony in it, that gave it a double charm as well
as a double power. It rested on the centre of its own
feelings. Her style of acting was smooth, round, polished, and classical, like a marble statue; self-sup-
ported and self-involved; owing its resemblance to life
to the truth of imitation, not to startling movements
and restless contortion, but returning continually
within the softened line of beauty and nature. Her
manner was, in this respect, the opposite of Mr.
Kean's, of whom no man can say (either in a good or
in a bad sense) that he is like a marble statue, but of
whom it may be said, with some appearance of truth,
that he is like a paste-board figure, the little, uncouth,
disproportioned parts of which children pull awry,
twitch, and jerk about in fifty odd and unaccountable
directions, to laugh at—or, like the mock figure of
harlequin, that is stuck against the wall, and pulled in
pieces, and fastened together again, with twenty idle,

pantomimic, eccentric absurdities! Or he seems to
have St. Anthony's fire in his veins, St. Vitus's dance in
his limbs, and a devil tugging at every part—one
shrugging his shoulders, another wagging his head,
another hobbling in his legs, another tapping his
breast; one straining his voice till it is ready to crack,
another suddenly, and surprisingly, dropping it down
into an inaudible whisper, which is made distinct and
clear by the *bravos* in the pit, and the shouts of the
gallery. There was not any of this paltry patch-work,
these vulgar snatches at applause, these stops, and
starts, and breaks, in Miss O'Neill's performance,
which was sober, sedate, and free from pretence and
mummery. We regret her loss the more, and fear we
shall have to regret it more deeply every day. In a
word, Mr. Kean's acting is like an anarchy of the passions, in which each upstart humour, or frenzy of the
moment, is struggling to get violent possession of some
bit or corner of his fiery soul and pigmy body—to
jostle out, and lord it over the rest of the rabble of
short-lived and furious purposes. Miss O'Neill seemed
perfect mistress of her own thoughts, and if she was
not indeed the rightful queen of tragedy, she had at
least all the decorum, grace, and self-possession of one
of the Maids of Honour waiting around its throne.
Miss O'Neill might have played to the greatest advantage in one of the tragedies of Sophocles, which are
the perfection of the stately, elegant, and simple drama
of the Greeks: we cannot conceive of Mr. Kean making a part of any such classical group. Perhaps, however, we may magnify his defects in this particular, as
we have been accused of over-rating his general
merits. We do not think it an easy matter "to praise
him or blame him too much." We have never heard
anything to alter the opinion we always entertained of
him! he can only do it himself—by his own acting.
While we owe it to him to speak largely of his genius

and his powers, we owe it to the public to protest against the eccentricities of the one, or the abuses of the other.

To return from this digression. With all the purity and simplicity, Miss O'Neill possessed the utmost force of tragedy. Her soul was like the sea—calm, beautiful, smiling, smooth, and yielding; but the storm of adversity lashed it into foam, laid bare its centre, or heaved its billows against the skies. She could repose on gentleness, or dissolve in tenderness, and at the same time give herself up to all the agonies of woe. She could express fond affection, pity, rage, despair, madness. She felt all these passions in their simple and undefinable elements only. She felt them as a woman —as a mistress, as a wife, a mother, or a friend. She seemed to have the most exquisite sense of the pressure of those soft ties that were woven round her heart, and that bound her to her place in society; and the rending them asunder appeared to give a proportionable revulsion to her frame, and disorder to her thoughts. There was nothing in her acting of a preternatural or *ideal* cast, that could lift the mind above mortality, or might be fancied to descend from another sphere. But she gave the full, the true, and unalloyed expression to all that is common, obvious, and heartfelt in the charities of private life, and in the conflict of female virtue and attachment with the hardest trials and intolerable griefs. She did not work herself up to the extremity of passion by questioning with her own thoughts, or raise herself above circumstances by ascending the platform of imagination, or arm herself against fate by strengthening her will to meet it; no, she yielded to calamity, she gave herself up entire, and with entire devotion, to her unconquerable despair; it was the tide of anguish swelling in her own breast that overflowed to the breasts of the audience, and filled their eyes with tears, as the loud torrent projects itself from the cliff to the abyss below, and bears everything before it in its resistless course. The source of her command over public sympathy lay, in short, in the intense conception and unrestrained expression of what she and every other woman of natural sensibility would feel in given circumstances, in which she and every other woman was liable to be placed. Her Belvidera, Isabella, Mrs. Beverley, &c., were all characters of this strictly feminine class of heroines, and she played them to the life. They were made of softness and suffering. We recollect the first time we saw her in Belvidera, when the manner in which she threw herself into the arms of Jaffier, before they part, was as if her heart would have leaped out of her bosom if she had not done so. It staggered the spectator like a blow. Again, her first meeting with Biron, in *Isabella*, was no less admirable and impressive. She looked at, she saw, she knew him; her surprise, her joy, were painted in her face, and woke every nerve to rapture. She seemed to have perfected all that her heart could do. But the sudden alteration of her look and manner, the shuddering and recoil within herself, when she recovers from her surprise and recollects her situation, married to another—at once on the verge of ecstasy and perdition—baffled description, and threw all that she had before done into the shade—"like to another morn, risen on mid noon." We could mention many other instances, but they are still too fresh in the memory of our readers to make it necessary. It must be confessed, as perhaps the only drawback on Miss O'Neill's merit, or on the pleasure derived from seeing her, that she sometimes carried the expression of grief, or agony of mind, to a degree of physical horror that could hardly be borne. Her shrieks, in the concluding scenes of some of her parts, were like those of mandrakes, and you stopped your ears against them; her looks were of "moody madness, laughing wild, amidst severest woe," and you turned your eyes from them, for they seemed to sear like the lightning. Her eye-balls rolled in her head, her words rattled in her throat. This was carrying reality too far. The sufferings of the body are no longer proper for dramatic exhibition when they become objects of painful attention in themselves, and are not merely indicative of what passes in the mind—comments and interpreters of the moral scene within. The effect was the more ungrateful, from the very contrast (as we before hinted) between this lady's form and delicate complexion, and the violent conflict into which she was thrown. She seemed like the little flower, not the knotted oak, contending with the pitiless storm. There appeared no reason why she should "mar that whiter skin of hers than snow, or monumental alabaster," or rend and dishevel, with ruthless hand, those graceful locks, fairer than the opening day. But these were faults arising from pushing truth and nature to an excess; and we should, at present, be glad to see "the best virtues" of others make even an approach to them. Her common style of speaking had a certain mild and equable intonation, not quite free from *manner*; but in the more impassioned parts she became proportionably natural, bold, and varied. In comedy, Miss O'Neill did not, in our judgment, excel; her *forte* was the serious. Had we never seen her play anything but Lady Teazle, we should not have felt the regret at parting with her which we now do, in common with every lover of genius and of the genuine drama.

INDEX

209

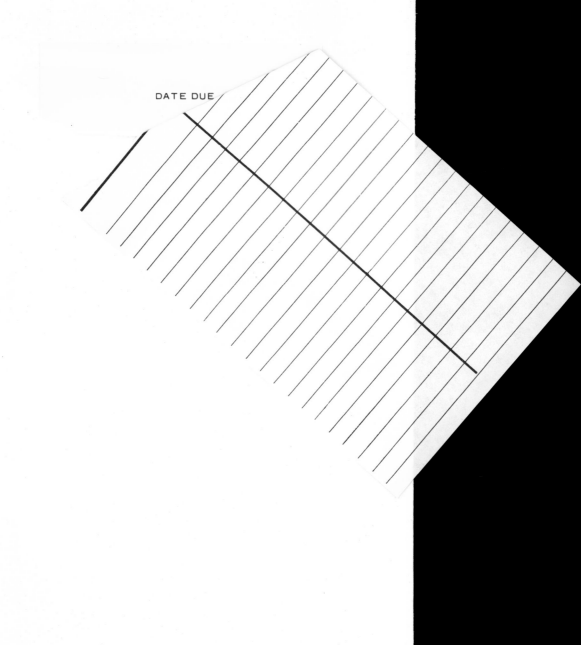

DATE DUE